The Japanese Cookbook

The Japanese Cookbook

David Scott

line drawings by Steve Hardstaff

BARRIE & JENKINS
COMMUNICA - EUROPA

First published in 1978 by
Barrie and Jenkins Ltd
24 Highbury Crescent London N5 1RX

ISBN 0 214 20576 2

Typeset by Computacomp (UK) Ltd
Fort William, Scotland

Printed and bound in Great Britain
by W & J Mackay Limited, Chatham

ACKNOWLEDGEMENTS

Many thanks to friends in Japan, particularly Yukinori, Akiko, Hirokazu and members of the Okinawan Uechi-Ryu Karate-Do Association. Special thanks to Jean for managing to decipher my handwriting, and for expertly typing the manuscript, and to Maire for her encouragement during the writing of the book. Finally, a special thanks to Nancy Duin, my editor, whose friendly and expert advice was invaluable throughout the preparation of *The Japanese Cookbook*.

CONTENTS

PREFACE

The prime aim of this book is to give a series of straightforward and, in the main, simple recipes for traditional Japanese meals. The book will be of value to anyone keen on cooking, and interested in preparing out-of-the-ordinary dishes. There are other Japanese cookery books, but I have generally found them not orientated to the Western cook. Too much emphasis has been placed on Classical Japanese cookery, and this often requires more time and special ingredients and skills than most people have. Thus there will be no recipes for elaborate festive meals, but there will be lots of authentic Japanese dishes of the sort prepared by the average Japanese housewife.

Grains, vegetables, seafood and fruit are the staple ingredients of the Japanese diet, and the emphasis in the recipes will be on these ingredients. However, meat and poultry are becoming more popular, especially in the cities, and recipes containing beef, pork and chicken are given.

The Japanese use very little oil in their cooking, and this, together with the low meat content of their diet, contributes to the very low incidence of heart disease in Japan. People on a low fat diet may find the book helpful in suggesting new ideas for their low fat meals.

Finally, a chapter in the book is devoted to Japanese-influenced macrobiotic cookery. The philosophy of Zen Buddhism, and the traditional Japanese diet have contributed more than any other source to the food ideas of the macrobiotic movement, and this chapter will illustrate the connection between the two.

INTRODUCTION

About a thousand years ago, the Chinese gave the name Nippon to the group of islands we know as Japan. They believed this was the land that marked the end of the Eastern World. Here was where the sun rose out of the sea, and the name they gave it means beginning of the sun.

In the Middle Ages the Fukien province of China, visited by Portuguese sailors on their way to Japan, was where the sailors picked up the local pronunciation of Nippon, and further corrupted it to Japao. Writing about this strange land, they described Japan as being so different from their homeland that it was the reverse of Europe.

The natives wore loose fitting smocks or kimonos. They ate lots of rice, vegetables, fish, fruit and sometimes the flesh of wild game. In contrast to the customs of the Western sailors, cleanliness was an important habit, especially at meal-times. Society was complex, and many traditions were to be adhered to, much the same as today.

Tradition has been a major influence on Japanese cooking, and changes have been slow. In the fourteenth century under Zen Buddhist influence, aristocrats, monks and later ordinary folk stopped eating meat, and only in the last century has this started to change. The other influence on Japanese cooking has been Chinese cuisine, and many Japanese dishes have been inspired by the Chinese.

Like the Chinese, the Japanese serve dishes in much smaller amounts than their Western counterparts, but they do serve a larger variety. In the preparation of the dishes, each ingredient is valued for its taste, appearance and freshness. Bowls, dishes, utensils are chosen for their harmony with the food, and this is always eaten with hashi or wooden chopsticks, since wood is thought to be the material most in harmony with the food.

You do not require special equipment or skills to serve authentic Japanese meals; all you need to do is take care over the preparation of all the various dishes, e.g. clean the vegetables extra thoroughly, cut them especially neatly, etc. Choose your favourite room, and around a low table in the middle, lay a cushion for each guest.

With good company, your favourite crockery, chopsticks and a respect for the food to be eaten, you have all you need to create the harmony and pleasure of a true Japanese dinner.

INGREDIENTS

With the exception of a few items, nearly all the ingredients required for the following recipes can be bought in ordinary grocers, whole/health food stores or Chinese provision merchants. The soya bean products, tofu and miso, and seaweeds may be difficult to obtain outside large cities, but nowadays even if you live in the country there is a good chance that the local small town will contain a wholefood shop. If that is not the case, tofu can be made (a quick simple recipe is given) and as a last resort if you really want to try it edible seaweed can be collected from our own shores! There will of course be many recipes that do not require any specialist ingredients.

RICE

Rice in the Japanese diet is now as important, if not more so, than bread is in the West. It was not always the staple diet of the Japanese, and especially in mountainous areas where rice is hard to grow, buckwheat was more popular. However, its popularity grew as extra supplies brought in from Korea became more generally available and by the fifteenth century, rice was a basic commodity. The peasants ate their rice unpolished, but the nobles would eat only the polished variety. This became the accepted practice, and today white polished rice is the norm. A short grain variety is favoured, and compared to our way of preparing rice, the Japanese version is slightly overcooked. This way the rice is easy to pick up in mouth-size amounts with chopsticks. Rice is always served at every meal, including breakfast, plain and unsalted.

TOFU, MISO AND SHOYU

Along with rice, the soya bean products tofu, miso and shoyu, or soya sauce, are basic to Japanese cookery. They are very useful ingredients and can be used in many ways and in many other recipes than given in this book.

Tofu is a fermented soya bean product introduced into the Far East by the Chinese. It is cheap to produce and provides a valuable source of protein and minerals for a people like the Japanese who eat little meat and even less dairy produce. It can be used in some of the ways we use cheese in cooking. Unlike cheese, it contains no fat, and tofu has the property of aiding the digestion of other foods. Tofu is white, and has the consistency of delicate custard. It is usually bought in squares about 3" (7.5 cm) by 3" (7.5 cm) and 1" (2.5 cm) deep. Cut into cubes and added to soups, meat, fish, vegetables or salad dishes, it is delicious. Fried and grilled tofu are also very popular.

Shops where tofu is made and sold are common all over Japan. The tofu man walking through the streets with his hand-cart and trays of freshly made tofu is a common sight. Making tofu, as with many other Japanese pursuits, has acquired the status of an art, but it can be made at home in the traditional manner. The process is quite long-winded, and I would refer you to *The Book of Tofu* by N. Shurtlerf and A. Aoyagi for further information. Later in this book there is a quick recipe for making tofu, using only soya flour and lemon juice. Otherwise, if you live in a town with a Chinese quarter, you can always locate the man who supplies tofu to the local Chinese restaurants.

Miso, the second of the soya bean trio, is a

fermented soya bean paste. It is rich in protein and vitamins and it is a basic part of the diet of many countries in the Far East. Japanese mythology places miso along with rice as a gift from the Gods, and it is recognised as an essential requirement of a healthy diet.

Naturally fermented miso will keep indefinitely, and the flavour improves with age. It is stored in wooden vats, and just as we may lay down a good wine, so the Japanese housewife may have several varieties of miso in store. Each one is savoured for its different flavour and maturity. The nutritive value of miso is most important in the Japanese diet. Combined with rice or other grains, it supplies all the essential amino acids, and it is a good source of vitamins B12, often lacking in a vegetarian diet. Carefully fermented, it contains enzymes most helpful to the digestion.

Miso is traditionally fermented for four to five days, and then aged for two years or more. The taste of the finished product depends on many factors, and no two miso taste exactly the same. Of the miso pastes available in the West, there are three main varieties. Mugi miso is the most common and popular. Made from 50 per cent barley and 50 per cent soya beans, it is an all-purpose miso, medium brown in colour. Hacho miso is aged for longer than mugi, and contains more salt. It is stronger in flavour and darker in colour. Used more often in the winter months, hacho miso wards off the cold. Kome miso is lighter and more delicately flavoured than the other two. It is used in the preparation of dishes that require more subtle flavours.

Miso, a remarkably versatile ingredient, appears in one guise or another at most Japanese meals. As a base for soups or sauces, in a marinade for fish, meat or vegetables, as a dressing with vinegar or lemon for salads or in the stock for stews. Surprisingly its most common appearance is at the breakfast table. Miso soup with rice, toasted seaweed and a fresh egg to drop into the boiling soup, sets up the Japanese worker for a day at the factory or office.

Shoyu or soy sauce, the last of our family of three, is familiar to all Chinese restaurant patrons. It is used by the Japanese as an all-purpose seasoning, much as we use salt. It does not impart the same flavour to each dish, but rather highlights the individual flavour of each ingredient. Shoyu is made from a mixture of soya beans, wheat and salt, fermented together for up to two years. The resulting mash is pressed and filtered, and the liquid extract is heated rapidly to seal in the flavour and stop the fermentation process. The product tastes completely unlike the artificially flavoured, chemical-filled liquid found in most bottles claiming to contain soy sauce. Make sure when you buy shoyu that you ask for the variety imported from Japan. Tamari is a brand name for traditional Japanese shoyu, and this is the type to buy. Be careful when using shoyu to reduce the amount of salt you usually use, since shoyu itself contains salt.

NOODLES

Noodles follow rice and soya beans as basic foodstuffs. They come in all shapes and sizes, prepared from wheat, buckwheat or rice flour. There are thousands of small cafés in Japan where all they serve are noodle dishes. They are quick-service establishments, and the customers eat their noodles fast with lots of slurping noises finally sucking the stock, in which the noodles floated, straight from the bowl. The Japanese casual diner seems to eat at a rate that defies the digestion process, perhaps in compensation for the time devoted to formal meals.

Somen and udon are two types of wheat flour noodle. The former is a very thin noodle, often eaten cold; vermicelli is a substitute. Udon are soft, large white noodles, for which egg noodles or thick spaghetti can be used as replacements. Buckwheat, or a mixture of buckwheat and wheat flour, is used to make soba noodles. They are very popular in Japan, and the soba shops or noodle cafés do a roaring trade delivering bowls of steaming hot noodles to local businesses and shopkeepers. Packages of the various dried noodles are available at wholefood stores, but if you have the time, it's much more satisfying to make your own fresh noodles. They are very useful in the kitchen, and can be used in many ways. Added to a soup they will make it into a meal, sautéed with vegetables or served with a sauce they make a main course dish, or served on their own as a side dish, noodles are a good filler and a welcome change from bread.

SEA VEGETABLES

Sea vegetables or seaweeds are the Japanese food Westerners are most likely to be prejudiced against, yet in Britain laver bread and other seaweed dishes have been made for centuries. In Japan seaweeds as foodstuffs are commonplace, and their use is taken for granted. In fact kombu seaweed is packaged in fancy boxes which are given as presents by appreciative guests when they go to dinner.

As with land vegetables, the environment of the area in which the seaweed grows affects its quality and taste, but seaweeds are usually rich in vitamins and minerals, they are easily digestible, and provide a good protein source. Perhaps as we exhaust our other food sources they will become more popular. Apart from their nutritive value, they are very useful for seasoning, and this is the way seaweeds are most often used in Japan.

Nori, hijiki and kombu are the types of seaweed usually available in shops in the West. Nori seaweed is dried, pressed into sheets, and wrapped around rolls of rice to make a sort of Japanese sandwich called norimaki. Crumbled over rice or soups nori adds a distinctive flavour. Hijiki is cooked with soya sauce, and eaten as a side dish, and it's also good in salads or fried with rice. Perhaps Kombu is best known as a basic constituent of dashi or Japanese soupstock, but it can also be used to garnish rice dishes, to season vegetables, and in a variety of other ways.

FISH

Japan, surrounded on all sides by the sea, is a great fish-eating nation. In the interior of the country, fish is more scarce, but even here most people eat some fish every day. To satisfy this demand, the Japanese fishing fleets visit waters all over the world. Sadly, their catch still includes the whale, but hopefully with increased world pressure this will stop. The trawlers travel far from home, but the waters around Japan are blessed with fish of all kinds, and the Japanese seem to have mastered the art of cooking each type in the most suitable way. In fact it's possible to have a fine and interesting Japanese meal that contains fish in every course including the dessert!

Fish stories are part of the folklore of Japan, and sashimi or raw fish is part of the folklore of Western attitudes to the Japanese diet. However, contrary to popular imagination, sashimi neither tastes nor smells fishy; it has its own subtle flavour which people usually appreciate once they have tasted it. I wasn't sure whether to include recipes for sashimi in this book, because I do agree that outside the environment of Japan, eating raw fish seems an unlikely thing to do, but trusting to the experimental nature of the reader, I have included information on the preparation of sashimi. These dishes, along with other fish recipes in the book, can be prepared with the sorts of fish available at the local fishmonger.

VEGETABLES AND VEGETABLE CUTTING TECHNIQUES

The Japanese are very appreciative of vegetables, and great care is taken to ensure they are cooked in a manner which retains the different textures and flavours of the various types. They eat more vegetables and less meat than we do in the West, and grow a greater variety. Whether through good luck or good management, their vegetables are of the best quality, and the average Japanese greengrocery shop, with its display of crispy, clean, shiny and delicious-looking vegetables, looks more like a stand at a horticulture show.

Vegetables are not seen as an accompaniment to a main dish, but as an independent part of the meal. They are not generally served plain, but seasoned with soya sauce, miso, sesame seeds, or other ingredients such as tofu. The vegetables are only lightly cooked, and the Japanese make little distinction between salads and vegetables, which are anyway sometimes served cold. Pickled vegetables may be substituted where we may use salads. The vegetables are either cooked quickly in a little oil, or sautéed first and then simmered in a drop of water. Leafy green vegetables and others that contain a lot of water are cooked in their own liquid in a pan with a heavy lid.

Below is a list of vegetables commonly used in Japan. The list is divided into three sections: The first section will be familiar, and contains those vegetables easily available in our own shops. The second includes vegetables not as easy to obtain fresh, but usually on sale at specialist shops, or Indian, West Indian or Chinese grocery stores. The third list is made up of distinctively Japanese vegetables with their English names. Some of these vegetables are available canned, and the others where they appear in recipes will be included as optional ingredients. A brief description of these unusual vegetables is given beneath the lists.

I
Aubergines (egg plants)
Bell peppers – Broccoli
Cucumber
Carrots
Cabbage
Celery
French beans
Lettuce
Leeks
Mushrooms
Onions
Peas
Potatoes
Spring onions
Sprouts
Tomatoes
Turnips

II
Asparagus
Bean sprouts
Chinese cabbage
Corn on the cob
Okra
Pumpkin
Sweet potatoes

III
Daikon – Japanese radish
Gobo – Burdock root
Renkon – Lotus root

Shiitake – Dried mushroom
Shungiku – Chrysanthemum leaves
Takenoko – Bamboo shoots

Daikon – Japanese white radish, it grows to a foot (30 cm) or more in length, and can be used fresh or pickled. Small sweet turnips make a fair substitute.

Gobo – This is the long slender root vegetable, burdock. Peeled and chopped into matchstick shapes, it is used extensively in Japanese cookery.

Renkon – Lotus root is a white sausage-shaped vegetable. Sliced thinly cross-wise, it gives beautiful white slices patterned symmetrically with small holes. The taste is somewhat bland.

Shiitake – Japanese tree mushrooms are cultivated by injecting fungus into the soft barks of water-soaked tree trunks. The mushrooms are dried before being sold. They are quite expensive and the very best varieties are a delicacy only the rich can afford. Large fresh mushrooms or French champignons can sometimes be substituted.

Shungiku – The edible leaves of the chrysanthemum plant impart a subtle fragrance to soups and casseroles. Spinach has the same colour and texture, but it has a stronger flavour, and, if used as a replacement, it should be added carefully in small amounts.

Takenoko – Bamboo shoots are normally only available canned; however, the crisp texture even of the canned variety makes a contrast to soft cooked vegetables.

VEGETABLE CUTTING
In a Japanese kitchen the cutting board is as important as the stove. Vegetables are cut to suit the manner in which they are to be cooked, and each type of vegetable is cut in a uniform fashion to ensure uniform cooking of each piece. An additional factor to be borne in mind is that the meal is to be eaten with chopsticks, and each piece should be small enough to pick up and put into the mouth whole. Further, it is important that the appearance of the cooked or uncooked

vegetable should be pleasing to the eye. Following are sketches of various methods of cutting up vegetables: some are obvious, others may be new to you. There are of course many other techniques, and you may wish to use your own cutting methods to produce other interesting shapes.

Cutting into Rectangles (Tanzaku-Giri)

Circle Cutting (Wa-Giri)

*Half Moons
(Hangetsu-Giri)*

*Quarter Circles
(Icho-Giri)*

*Cutting Rectangles into Thick Strips and
Chopping Coarsely (Sainome-Giri)*

*Cutting Rectangles into Thin Strips and
Chopping Finely (Sen-Giri)*

Alternate Way of Cutting

Pencil Cutting (Sasagaki)

Cutting on the Bias

17

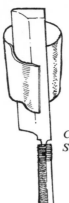

Cutting into Thin Sheets or Bark Shapes (Katsura- Muki)

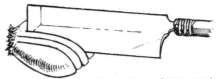

Onion Dicing (Mijin-Giri)

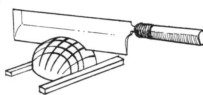

Chrysanthemum Cutting (Kikka-Kabu)

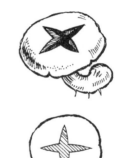

Criss-crossing Mushroom Caps

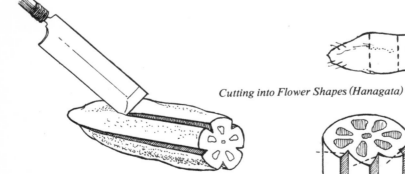

Cutting into Flower Shapes (Hanagata)

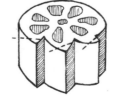

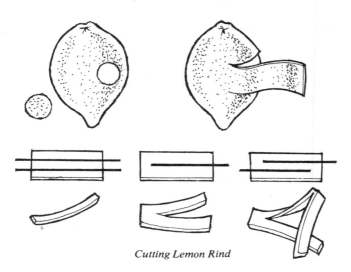

Cutting Lemon Rind

MEAT AND POULTRY

Meat, especially beef, is very expensive in Japan, and it is used sparingly. Steak is popular, but only in restaurants, and it is rarely cooked at home. Beef steak, when it is used, is cooked in very thin slices as part of a sukiyaki-type meal. Where quick cooking is required, pre-cooked meat is cut into small cubes and combined with rice or vegetables. There is nothing in the Japanese diet analogous to the Sunday roast. The meat is, however, of good quality, and beef from the Kobe area of Japan, where they include beer in the cattle diet, is justly famous. Kobe steakhouses are popular all over Japan, even though they sell in total much more steak than the area around Kobe could possibly supply.

Keeping pigs needs much less space than keeping the same number of cows and this has meant with Japan's land shortage that pork is more often a part of the Japanese diet than beef. Again, it is eaten sparingly, although bacon is becoming popular, and a bacon and egg breafast is quite common amongst young people.

Chicken, next to fish, is the animal food most important in Japanese cookery. Other types of fowl are not well-known, although wild game occasionally appears on the menu.

SEASONINGS

We have already mentioned the roles of shoyu, miso and seaweeds as seasonings in Japanese cookery, and the ingredients below complete the list of condiments commonly used by the Japanese cook.

Sesame Seeds (Goma) – Sesame seeds are toasted and then crushed to be used as a seasoning on their own or mixed with salt. This salt mixture is called gomashiso. Sesame seed oil is sometimes added to soya or corn cooking oil, to give a nutty flavour to the cooked food.

Vinegar – Vinegar is called for in a number of recipes. The Japanese use a distilled rice wine that gives a slightly sweet vinegar. Cider vinegar is a suitable substitute.

Mirin – Mirin is a sweet fortified wine, used to sweeten and glaze. Sherry or a sweetened white wine are alternatives.

Aji-No-Moto – This is a seasoning based on monosodium glutamate. It is tasteless, but brings out the flavour of foods. Excessive use can cause stomach trouble, and I have not specified its use in any of the recipes.

Ginger Root (Shoga) – Sliced or grated ginger root is eaten on its own, raw, or pickled as a side

19

dish. It is also used as a spice in cooking, and it has the property of absorbing fishy smells if added to the fish before cooking.

Wasabi – Japanese horse-radish mustard is used in dipping sauces, and in the preparation of sushi rice balls. It is sold in powder form in the same way as English mustard, a fair replacement.

Togarashi – A blend of several spices, which when combined taste like a mixture of black pepper and hot pepper sauce. Either or both the latter can be substituted, but use sparingly.

Dried Bonito (Katsuobushi) – The soup stock dashi, used as the base for various Japanese dishes, is prepared by boiling together flakes of the dried bonito fish called Katsuobushi and Kombu seaweed. It is possible to buy packets of bonito flakes, but in Japan they sell the dried bonito fish whole. The dried fish looks like a combination between a truncheon and a boomerang, and it's as hard as both. On one occasion, scraping flakes off these hard sticks I almost lost a finger, and I wouldn't recommend trying it, not, that is, if you can find a packet of the pre-flaked fish.

There are other soup stocks just as suitable as dashi, and easier to prepare, and since the ingredients for dashi are not readily available in the West recipes for both dashi and substitutes are given.

A complete glossary of Japanese cookery terms is given at the end of the book.

TEA AND SAKE

Green tea or o-cha is drunk on every conceivable occasion. Wherever you go in Japan you will see work people drinking tea from large metal teapots filled with warm o-cha. It's served free in restaurants and snack bars. Tea is drunk without milk or sugar. Powdered green tea is also used to flavour foods such as noodles and ice-cream.

Sake, the light rice wine, is also served on any occasion. It is poured from a sake jug into tiny cups and sipped. Warm sake is served in the winter. It is also used extensively in cooking – white wine or dry sherry may be used as a substitute.

Tea and sake are discussed in greater detail in the chapter on beverages.

KITCHEN EQUIPMENT

You will need very little special equipment for Japanese cookery, and most of the recipes given could be followed adequately in an ordinarily equipped Western kitchen, but to increase your joy in Japanese cooking, and to make the job easier, the following items will be helpful:

Hocho – A Japanese all-purpose cutting knife, with a squared off end. They are excellent for cutting vegetables.

Cutting Board – A thick, unvarnished, heavy chopping board makes all types of cutting jobs easier, and reduces the risk of cut fingers.

Saibashi – Long cooking chopsticks used for handling hot foods, and mixing ingredients at the stove. They are wooden, taper to a point at the end, and are usually joined at the other end by a piece of string.

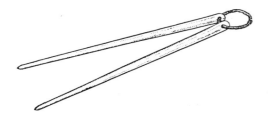

Saucepans – Heavy duty pans with good fitting lids are the most useful for boiling rice, making soups, sautéeing vegetables, etc. At home I have a series of heavy wooden lids that are just laid on top of the saucepan. They are interchangable between pans, and reversed on a work top they make extra chopping boards.

Sudare – A flexible rolling mat constructed of fine bamboo slats, it is used for preparing sushi rice rolls. It's possible to find bamboo squares designed for use as table mats that make a good substitute.

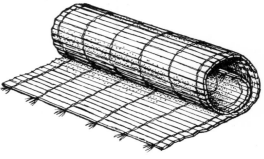

Surikogi and Suribachi – A mortar and pestle. The bowl is earthenware and serrated inside. With the wooden pestle it is effective for grinding sesame seeds, pulses, making purées, etc.

Zaru – A bamboo strainer which doubles as a colander for draining foods, and as a container for serving food at the table. A regular colander and a wicker bread basket will do the jobs separately.

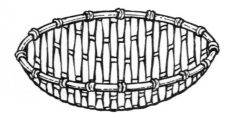

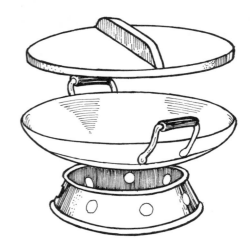

Wok – This Chinese cooking pot is excellent for quick or deep frying. It is fitted with a wooden lid for simmering food, and with one or more bamboo steaming baskets that sit inside the wok one on top of the other, different dishes may be steamed. The wok has a rounded base, and to give it stability on an ordinary gas stove, it is worthwhile using a wok support.

Finally, for cooking meals at the table, an electric frying pan is very useful. Alternatively, use a table-top gas burner of the type used by camping enthusiasts.

RECIPE NOTES

The recipes were prepared with authenticity as a prime consideration, but where a preferred ingredient is specialist, a viable alternative has been suggested. Recipes that include ingredients very difficult to obtain outside Japan have not been included.

The following points are applicable to the recipe section in general, and I have listed them here to save making them in each individual recipe in which they are relevant.

Before starting a recipe, read the notes at the beginning of the chapter in which it appears. There may be useful information applicable to the recipe.

Where the recipe stipulates the use of a pan, you may also use a wok. If the ingredients list mushrooms, this means ordinary fresh mushrooms. Where shiitake are stipulated, Japanese dried tree mushrooms are required (see glossary for alternatives).

Fresh ginger root is called for in a number of recipes. This is now quite generally available, but when you cannot obtain any, ground ginger used sparingly may be used as a replacement. 2 parts ginger powder equals 1 part root ginger.

The best method to steam food is with a wok and Chinese bamboo steamer, but if you do not have this equipment, use the following method: Put 1" water in a large pot, bring to the boil, and carefully place in the pot an inverted bowl. On top of the bowl lay a plate containing the food to be steamed. Cover the mouth of the pot with a clean tea towel, place on the lid and steam at medium heat. The cloth prevents moisture dripping on to the food. A small colander that will fit inside the pot can be used in place of the bowl and plate.

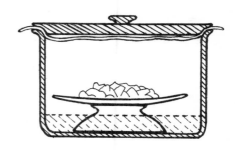

Seaweeds and shiitake are usually only available, in the West, dried. In some recipes they are used in the dried form, and in others pre-soaked. Where the reconstituted variety are required this will be stipulated, otherwise use dried. To reconstitute dried vegetables, soak in warm water approximately 30 minutes. Reserve the soaking liquid for use in stocks, etc.

Sesame seeds appear quite often in Japanese recipes. They are used either whole or partially grounded and roasted. To roast the seeds, heat a heavy frying pan on a medium flame. When the pan is hot enough to evaporate a drop of water instantly, add the seeds and reduce the heat. Shake the pan about, and keep the seeds moving around. They are ready after about three minutes, and should be light brown in colour. Store in a glass jar, and grind as required. A pepper mill will grind small amounts, but for larger quantities use a suribachi and surikogi or pestle and mortar. Where it is more convenient, tahini may be substituted for ground sesame seeds. ½ tablespoon tahini equals 1 tablespoon ground sesame seeds.

Bamboo shoots and lotus roots are required in some of the recipes. They are not generally available fresh, and the recipes always refer to the tinned variety.

French beans are frequently used as a garnishing. They should always be topped, tailed and stringed before use, unless young and fresh. Dwarf French beans, green beans and runner beans may also be used.

Nori seaweed is another popular garnishing. It is sold in paper-thin sheets and for garnishing purposes is usually lightly toasted before use. To toast, wave a sheet of nori over a medium flame or hot electric ring for 30–40 seconds or until crisp and crumbly.

To ease the shelling of prawns and shrimps, drop them into boiling water for one or two minutes before shelling.

The ingredients listed below are basic to the recipes described in this book, and a stock of these ingredients or their alternatives available in the kitchen will be very useful when using the book.

Sesame seeds
Ginger root
Soy sauce (Tamari variety)
Sake or medium dry white wine
Mirin or medium sweet sherry
Cider or mild white vinegar
Young leeks or spring onions or chives or scallions or shallots, all to be used as garnishings
Soup stock, fish or vegetable, or bouillon cubes

WEIGHTS AND MEASURES
Quantities in recipes have been given in both imperial and American measures.

The following table can be used for the conversion of imperial to metric:

Ounces/Fluid Ounces	Grammes or Millilitres to the nearest unit of 25
1	25
2	50
3	75
4	100
5	150
6	175
7	200
8	225
9	250
10	275
11	300
12	350
13	375
14	400
15	425
16	450
17	475
18	500
19	550
20	575

5 fl oz	= $\frac{1}{4}$ pt	= 150 ml
10 fl oz	= $\frac{1}{2}$ pt	= 275 ml
20 fl oz	= 1 pt	= 575 ml
35 fl oz	= $1\frac{1}{4}$ pt	= 1 l
16 oz	= 1 lb	= 450 g
2 lb 3 oz	= 1 kg	

For American readers the following conversions for liquid measurements may be useful.

Imperial	American
8 pt	10 pt
2 pt	5 cups
16 fl oz	1 pt
1 pt	$2\frac{1}{2}$ cups
8 fl oz	1 cup
2 fl oz = 4 tablespoons	$\frac{1}{4}$ cup
$\frac{1}{2}$ fl oz = 1 tablespoon	approx. $1\frac{1}{2}$ tablespoons
1 teaspoon = $\frac{1}{4}$ tablespoon	1 teaspoon = $\frac{1}{3}$ tablespoon

For small amounts of ingredients tablespoon measurements have been used in the recipes. If you prefer to weigh things out, the following table lists commonly used ingredients with their tablespoon measurements and equivalent weight or volume amounts.

Salt, sake, vinegar, soy sauce, miso, mirin	1 teaspoon	$\frac{1}{5}$ oz	5 g
Salt, sake, vinegar oil	1 tablespoon	$\frac{1}{4}$ oz	20 g
Sugar, cornflour, flour	1 tablespoon	$\frac{1}{2}$ oz	15 g
Soy sauce, miso, mirin	1 tablespoon	1 oz	28 g

Bear in mind that there are so many variables in cooking that it is not possible to be exactly precise about every weight and volume. Much depends on personal taste and judgement, and you are your own best judge of when a particular seasoning is just right or when a particular dish is cooked to your liking.

SERVING AND PLANNING A JAPANESE MEAL

If you are planning a Japanese dinner, and not experimenting with a single dish, the following advice will help you do it in genuine style.

First of all, don't buy too much of any one ingredient, but buy the best quality and freshest specimens you can find or afford. Persuade your grocer or fishmonger to select for you the choicest of his stock of vegetables or fish. Plan a menu that is nutritively well balanced. Meat and/or fish, but not too much, cooked vegetables, fresh or pickled vegetables, rice and fresh fruit. Concentrate on eye appeal, and go to some trouble arranging the food before serving. There is no rigid serving order, but generally all the dishes are laid on the table at the same time, and the hot dishes are eaten first. A sensible system for the host who wishes to join the guests during the meal.

How you serve the meal will depend to some extent on the type and quantity of crockery you have, but ideally you need for each person: bowls for soup and rice, small plates for pickles and other titbits, a bowl each for the main courses, wooden chopsticks and small Japanese or Chinese teacups.

Except for whole fish, the food is cut into mouth-size pieces, either before or after cooking, whichever is the most suitable. The dishes that compose the meal are served for each guest in the various bowls, and then taken to the table. Before starting the meal remind your guests to say to you '*Itadakimasu*' to which you reply '*Dozo*', or roughly translated, 'I would like to begin this fine meal'; reply 'oh please do'.

Allow older people to start first, and if a bowl is passed to you take it in both hands as a mark of respect for the food it contains. It you take food from a communal bowl, reverse your chopsticks, and use the blunt end for removing the chosen morsel. If you are going to want more rice, leave a few grains in the bottom of your bowl. This is the signal, and if your guests should do the same, pass them the rice. However, when you have had enough rice, clean the bowl free of all rice grains, otherwise custom has it that you will develop a rash of warts! One thing to remember, if you have a large appetite: it is considered impolite to start first and finish last. At the end of the meal, place your chopsticks neatly on the table (or chopstick rests) not in the bowl. If you have primed your guests sufficiently well, they may say to you '*Arigato Gozaimashito*' or 'thank you for an excellent dinner'. Finally, do remember to keep the teapot topped up with hot water, and the sake cups well filled.

I haven't tried to explain how to use chopsticks. It seems to me more difficult to follow complicated instructions than to pick up a pair and experiment. Just remember one stick stays stationary, and the other moves. Chopsticks do add an extra quality to eating a Japanese meal so, if you cannot yet use them, I hope you will persevere in your efforts.

SOUPS AND STOCKS

One of the things that most surprised me when I arrived in Japan was the custom of having miso soup for breakfast, but I discovered that it was quick to prepare, nutritious and warming on a cold morning. By the time I had established myself in my own apartment, I had begun to start the day with my own bowl of miso soup.

Miso soup, along with many other Japanese soups is based on an all-purpose soup stock called dashi. This is made from dried bonito fish flakes and kombu seaweed. In Japan dashi is a quick and economical stock to make. The ingredients are easily available and cheap. This is not usually the case in the West, and while giving a recipe for dashi, I have also given recipes for chicken, fish and vegetable stocks, which may be substituted for it. Your own ideas and variations on the preparation of soup stock will add a different flavour and greater usefulness to those soup recipes that require a stock base.

The Japanese, as we do, divide their soups into roughly two types. One category is clear soups or suimono, which are appreciated for the distinctiveness, colour and quality of their garnishings, while the second category, the thick soups or sumashi-shiru, is more akin to the Western stew. Most of the sumashi-shiru contain miso as an ingredient. Just as we tend to be casual about the ingredients of a stew, so do the Japanese, and once you have established the taste and style of the thicker soups, you do not need to adhere strictly to the ingredients listed in recipes.

The two categories of soups of course overlap, and I have found it more convenient and practical to divide the soup recipes into clear soups, soups that do not contain miso, and miso soups. The former recipes are given first.

Soups that contain noodles as a major ingredient will be found in the chapter on noodles.

The quantities given in the soup recipes are for four servings. If, however, the soup dish is only one part of a large meal, the amount prepared will stretch to six servings. It is convenient to make large amounts of soup stocks and the quantities given for stocks are sufficient to prepare enough for two soup recipes.

SOUP STOCKS

DASHI

¼ oz (¼ cup) kombu seaweed
4 pt (10 cups) water
¼ oz (¼ cup) bonito flakes (katsuobushi)
Soy sauce to taste (optional)

Clean the seaweed with a damp cloth, then add it to the water and bring to the boil. Boil for three or four minutes, turn down heat and remove, but reserve seaweed. Add the bonito flakes. Re-heat, and as the water just returns to the boil turn off the heat. Leave to stand for five minutes or until the bonito sinks. Strain, reserving the bonito for further use. Season with soy sauce and the dashi is ready for use.

To prepare a weaker stock for cooking vegetables, the reserved seaweed and bonito fish flakes may be boiled for ten minutes in one and a half pints of water. The secondary dashi is strained off and the bonito and kombu are discarded.

CHICKEN STOCK

This is not a fixed recipe and you may use other vegetables apart from those listed.

2 lb chicken bones or left over chicken pieces
4 oz (¼ cup) cabbage, shredded
4 oz (¼ cup) carrots, grated
4 oz (¼ cup) leeks, sliced
4 oz (¼ cup) celery, chopped
4 pt (10 cups) water
Salt and/or soy sauce to taste

Chop the chicken bones into convenient-size pieces and put all the ingredients, except the seasoning, into a pan. Bring to the boil, and then simmer for an hour or more. Occasionally, skim off the fat and other residues that float to the surface. Strain and season the reserved stock to taste.

FISH STOCK

1 lb head, tail and other trimmings of any white fish
1 medium onion, diced
2 oz (¼ cup) finely chopped, fresh ginger root
4 pt (10 cups) water
Salt and/or soy sauce to taste

Put all the ingredients, except the seasoning, in a pan. Bring to the boil and cook for 20–30 minutes. Remove any scum that floats to the surface. Strain and season the reserved stock to taste.

VEGETABLE STOCK

This recipe is not fixed and you may use any combination of the suggested vegetables or any others you think suitable. With stocks nothing need be wasted, and you can use vegetable trimmings, the good parts of partly bad vegetables etc.

6 oz (¾ cup) soya beans, soaked overnight and drained
4 pt (10 cups) water
Soy sauce, salt and black pepper or togarashi to taste
¼ teaspoon yeast extract (optional)

Any three or four of the following chopped vegetables. Total weight 1 lb: carrots, turnips, parsnips, celery, potatoes, onions, cabbage, cauliflower.

Place all the vegetables in one pan, add the water and drained beans. Bring to the boil, simmer for two to three hours. Strain off the stock and season.

CLEAR SOUPS (AND SOUPS WITHOUT MISO)

Most of the soups call for soup stock. If you do not have any available, or the time to prepare any, chicken or vegetable bouillon cubes can be used.

CLEAR SOUP WITH GARNISHINGS

This soup is served in individual bowls, each containing a few tiny pieces of colourful garnishings. It is served with the meal. Chopsticks are used to pick out the garnishings, and the soup is then sipped directly from the bowl.

2 pt (5 cups) clear vegetable soup stock
2 tablespoons (⅛ cup) soy sauce
Garnishings (see recipe and table below)
Salt to taste

The stock and soy sauce are heated together and seasoned to taste with salt. The soup is poured into the bowls, and the garnishings added. Three items different in texture and shape should be used. For something solid use a piece of cooked noodle, diced omelette or tofu; add something delicate and leafy, say a celery leaf or parsley sprig; and finally a carefully cut piece of vegetable, such as a thin slice of carrot or mushroom, chopped spring onion or sliced French bean.

There are many other suitable garnishings and I have suggested some below:

SOLID
Boiled egg
Cooked meat
Cooked fish
Peanuts
Small dumpling
Shell fish

LEAFY
Watercress

27

Cucumber
Leek
Spinach
Chinese cabbage
Chrysanthemum leaves

VEGETABLE
Potato (cooked)
Daikon or turnip
Onion
Bean sprouts
Green pepper
Aubergine

Select one ingredient from each column and cut into delicate shape and size. Add to the clear soup stock as directed above.

CLEAR SOUP WITH LEMON AND TOFU

2 pt (5 cups) clear soup stock or dashi
1 small leek, finely chopped
4 oz (¼ cup) tofu, cut into ½" (1.25 cm) cubes
1 small lemon, sliced thinly

Bring the stock to the boil and add the tofu. Reduce the heat and simmer for a few minutes. Divide the soup and tofu between four bowls, taking care not to crush the bean curd. Decorate each bowl with slices of lemon and leek. Do not crowd the bowls with ingredients. If you have too much lemon or leek, save it for future use.

CLEAR SOUP WITH TOFU AND GINGER ROOT

2 pt (5 cups) clear soup stock or dashi
4 oz (¼ cup) tofu, cut into ½" (1.25 cm) cubes
1 oz (1 tablespoon) spinach, chopped
2 medium spring onions, chopped in ¼" (0.5 cm) lengths
1 oz (1 tablespoon) ginger root, finely chopped
2 teaspoons soy sauce

Boil the stock, add spinach, soy sauce and tofu. Return to the boil, reduce heat and simmer for ten minutes. Sprinkle with ginger, spring onions and serve.

CLEAR SOUP WITH RICE DUMPLINGS

2 tablespoons vegetable oil

1 medium turnip, diced
2 leaves Chinese cabbage, 1" (2.5 cm) wide strips
2 pt (5 cups) clear soup stock or dashi
Salt to taste
1 oz (1 tablespoon) parsley, chopped
8 oz (2 cups) rice flour
5 fl oz (1¼ cups) water, boiling

Sauté the diced turnips in the oil in a heavy saucepan until just soft. Stir in the Chinese cabbage and pour in the stock. Bring to boil, and then simmer for twenty minutes. While the soup is cooking, prepare the rice dumplings. Carefully add boiling water to the rice flour whilst stirring vigorously with a wooden spoon. Add as much water as necessary to produce quite a stiff dough. Knead the dough for three or four minutes, and then remove small portions and roll into dumplings. Season the cooked soup with salt and drop in the dumplings. Initially they will drop to the bottom of the pan, but as they cook through (two to three minutes) they will rise to the surface. Serve and garnish each bowl with a little parsley.

CLEAR SOUP WITH FISH DUMPLINGS

2 tablespoons vegetable oil
1 medium parsnip, cut in matchsticks
1 medium carrot, sliced thinly
2 pt (5 cups) clear soup stock or dashi
4 oz (½ cup) fillet white fish (or tinned sardine, salmon)
1 oz (1 tablespoon) ginger root, finely grated (optional)
2 small spring onions, finely chopped
1 egg white
3 tablespoons flour
1 small bunch watercress, chopped
Salt to taste

Sauté the parsnips and carrot in the oil in a heavy pan until just soft. Cover with stock, bring to the boil, then simmer for twenty minutes. While the soup is cooking prepare the fish dumplings. Grind the fish to a smooth paste in a suribachi or mortar, mix in the ginger root, spring onion and egg white. Carefully blend in the flour until the mixture is stiff enough to form into small dumplings. Season the cooked stock with salt, drop in the dumplings and simmer until cooked through (three to four minutes). Add the watercress and serve immediately.

CLEAR SOUP WITH CABBAGE AND MEAT SQUARES

6 large white cabbage leaves
1 lb minced beef or pork
3 teaspoons soy sauce
3 eggs, beaten
2 pt (5 cups) clear soup stock or dashi
2 oz ($\frac{1}{4}$ cup) somen or vermicelli noodles
Salt and black pepper or togarashi to taste

Carefully remove six leaves from a white cabbage. If you have trouble unpeeling the leaves intact, dip the whole cabbage in boiling water for a few moments and try again. Now soften the removed leaves by immersing in boiling water for a second or two. Layer two of the leaves on the base of a shallow baking tin (approximately 6" × 8", 15 cm × 20 cm). Combine the minced meat with the soy sauce, and spread half the mixture on the cabbage leaves. Paint on half the beaten egg, and cover with two more leaves. Add the remaining meat mixture, top with the last two leaves and coat with remaining egg. Cover tray with baking foil and steam for 25 minutes. Alternatively, place the baking tin in a larger tin containing 1" (2.5 cm) of water and bake in a moderate oven 325°F (160°C) for 45 minutes.

Remove from the oven and allow to cool. While this is happening, bring the stock to boil and add the noodles. Simmer until just cooked. Season with salt and togarashi. Cut the meat and cabbage cake into 2" (5 cm) squares, divide into four bowls and pour over the soup and noodles. Serve.

CLEAR SOUP WITH FLOWER-SHAPED PRAWNS

This is a very Japanese-looking soup. It is a little exotic, but worth the trouble for special occasions.

8 prawns
2 tablespoons cornflour
4 shiitake, pre-soaked in cold water
   (or 4 fresh mushrooms)

8 stalks asparagus, cut into 2" (5 cm) pieces
2 pt (5 cups) clear soup stock or dashi
1 tablespoon mirin or sweet sherry (optional)
Rind of 1 medium lemon

Shell prawns, leaving the tails intact. Make a shallow cut along the outside curve of each prawn and carefully remove the black vein. Now make a small slit in the middle of the body and squeeze the tail through. Pull it out the other side to give the flower shape. Lightly sprinkle the prawns with cornflour. Bring the stock to the boil, add the prawns and shiitake or mushrooms. Reduce heat and simmer until prawns are cooked. Cook the asparagus lengths in lightly salted water. Drain. Add the mirin or sweet sherry to the soup. Divide the asparagus and soup into four bowls and garnish with lemon rind.

CHICKEN AND LEEK SOUP

1 lb boiling chicken
2 pt (5 cups) water
3 peppercorns
1 tablespoon soy sauce
Salt to taste
Juice of 1 lemon
1–2 leeks, sliced
2 oz ($\frac{1}{4}$ cup) somen or vermicelli noodles

Chop the chicken into four pieces and bring to boil in water with peppercorns, soy sauce and salt to taste. Simmer until chicken meat is tender. Skim off rising scum and strain. Reserve both liquid and chicken. Remove meat from the bones and cut into small pieces. Return liquid to pan and skim off fat from the surface. Add lemon juice, leek and return to the boil. Add the chicken and simmer until leeks are just cooked. Meanwhile, cook somen noodles in boiling salted water until soft (approximately five minutes). Put a portion of somen in each bowl and pour over the chicken and leek soup.

SHREDDED CHICKEN SOUP

This is useful for using up left-over cooked chicken.

6 oz ($\frac{3}{4}$ cup) cooked chicken
2 pt (5 cups) clear soup stock or dashi

29

1 tablespoon cornflour
Salt and black pepper or togarashi to taste
2 spring onions, chopped or 1 bunch watercress,
  chopped

Shred the chicken into fine pieces. Blend a little of the cold stock with cornflour. Combine with the remainder of stock and bring to the boil. Add the chicken and season to taste. Serve and garnish with spring onion or watercress.

EGG DROP SOUP

By swirling the soup around as you pour in the beaten egg, you can form beautiful patterns with the strands of cooked egg. The Japanese call these shapes egg-flowers.

2 eggs, beaten
1 tablespoon sake or sweet white wine (optional)
1 pinch salt
2 pt (5 cups) clear soup stock or dashi
2 teaspoons cornflour
1 teaspoon soy sauce
4 small leaves spinach, chopped
4 sprigs parsley

Whisk the eggs, add the sake and pinch of salt. Mix the cornflour to a smooth paste with a little of the cold stock. Bring stock to the boil, pour in the paste and stir in. Add soy sauce and season with salt to taste. Now gradually add beaten egg stirring constantly. Bring to the boil, add spinach and turn off heat. Pour into soup bowls and garnish with parsley.

CUSTARD SOUP (Chawan-Mushi)

This is a thick soup served in the container in which it is cooked. Its custard-like consistency makes it a firm favourite with Japanese children.

2 pt (5 cups) clear soup stock or dashi
4 oz (1 cup) mushrooms, sliced thinly
2 spring onions, chopped
4 oz (1 cup) French beans, sliced, or other
  cooked vegetables
4 eggs beaten
Salt to taste

Boil the stock and add salt to taste. Distribute the other ingredients in four small earthenware or oven-proof bowls (cereal bowls will do). Fill each with boiling stock and cover with baking foil. Stand the bowls in a pan containing 1" (2.5 cm) of water. Bring to the boil, reduce heat, cover pan and gently steam for 20 minutes. Serve bowls straight on to the table.

SUMMERTIME EGG SOUP

4 eggs
2 pt (5 cups) water
1 pinch salt
3 tablespoons vinegar
1 medium cucumber, peeled and diced
4 oz (1 cup) peas, fresh or tinned
2 pt (5 cups) vegetable soup stock
Rind 1 lemon

Place the water, vinegar and pinch of salt in a pan and bring to the boil. Lower the heat and poach the eggs one by one. Reserve the cooked eggs in warm water. While the eggs are cooking bring the stock to the boil, add the vegetables and simmer until cooked. Place one egg in each bowl, pour over the hot soup and garnish with lemon peel.

MUSSEL SOUP

To make the stock tasty enough, this recipe requires more mussels than are actually served with the soup. You can save the remainder and use them in other dishes. This is a beautiful soup with a distinctive flavour.

18 fresh mussels
2 pt (5 cups) water
2 tablespoons mirin or sweet sherry
Salt, black pepper, or togarashi, soy sauce to
  taste
Juice 1 lemon

Thoroughly clean the mussel shells. Boil the mussels in lots of water until the shells open. Drain and rinse mussels in cold water to remove any trapped sand. Bring the water to the boil, add the mirin and the mussels still in their shells. Simmer for 15 minutes and then add the lemon juice. Season with salt, black pepper and soy sauce. Pour clear stock into individual bowls and garnish each with one or two mussels in their shells.

SHRIMP SOUP

6 oz (1 cup) fresh shrimps, peeled, finely chopped
1 egg, beaten
6 oz (1¼ cups) daikon, finely diced (small sweet
turnip may be substituted)
1 pinch salt
2 pt (5 cups) clear soup stock or dashi
4 shiitake, soaked and softened, or 4 oz (1 cup)
mushrooms
4 spinach leaves

Combine the shrimps, egg, radish and pinch of
salt. Boil stock, add mushrooms and simmer for
five minutes. Add spinach, cook for further two
minutes. Divide shrimp mixture between four
bowls. Ladle two mushrooms and a spinach leaf
into each bowl and pour over hot stock.

WAKAME SEAWEED SOUP

Next to kombu, wakame is the seaweed most
often used in soup preparations. Spinach is an
adequate substitute if you cannot obtain
wakame.

2 pt (5 cups) clear soup stock or dashi
2 oz (¼ cup) wakame, soaked, drained and cut in
1" (2.5 cm) lengths
5 oz (1¼ cups) tinned bamboo shoots, sliced
thinly
Soy sauce to taste
12 oz (1¼ cups) tofu cut into 1" (2.5 cm) squares
4 umeboshi (pickled plums) (optional)

Bring stock to the boil, add bamboo shoots,
seaweed and carefully drop in the tofu squares.
Return to the boil, reduce heat and simmer for
two minutes. Season with soy sauce. Place one
umeboshi in each bowl, pour in soup and serve.

PORK AND VEGETABLE SOUP

8 oz (2 cups) lean pork, thin slices
2 pt (5 cups) clear soup stock or dashi
2 small carrots, sliced thinly
5 oz (1¼ cups) tinned bamboo shoots, sliced
thinly into half-moon shapes
8 shiitake, soaked and drained (optional)
2 leaves Chinese or white cabbage
1 oz (1 tablespoon) ginger root, grated
Salt, soy sauce to taste
2 spring onions, finely chopped

Cut pork into 1" (2.5 cm) squares. Boil stock,
add pork and cook for five minutes. Add all the
other ingredients except seasoning and spring
onions. Return to the boil, reduce heat and
simmer for five minutes. Season and serve,
garnished with spring onions.

THICK RICE SOUP

Once sitting in a café in Okinawa, I was
intrigued by the cast-iron soup bowl, with a
wooden lid, laid on the table in front of the man
next to me. When he took the lid off I was more
interested in the contents, a steaming bowl of
rice soup.

2 pt (5 cups) clear soup stock or dashi
3 oz (¼ cup) rice
1 oz (1 tablespoon) ginger root, grated
Salt and black pepper or togarashi to taste
4 oz (¾ cup) peas (fresh or tinned)
1 sheet nori seaweed, crumbled (optional)
1 egg yolk, beaten

Boil stock, add rice and ginger. Lower heat and
simmer until rice is well cooked and starting to
disintegrate (30 minutes for white rice, up to one
hour for brown rice). Season with salt and black
pepper. Add the peas, nori and beaten egg yolk.
Simmer for further ten minutes and serve.

MISO SOUPS
The most convenient way of adding miso to a
pan of hot soup or water is to make a creamy
paste of the miso in a cupful of the hot liquid,
then add the paste to the pan and stir. The sort of
miso to use in the recipes is not stipulated, but
where you have a choice, experiment with the
different types and find the flavour that suits you
most.

If you cannot obtain miso, a substitute for
soups can be prepared from dried soya beans,
vinegar and soy sauce (see below). It is not
satisfactory as an exact copy of miso, but the
substitute has its own flavour that some may
enjoy.

MOCK MISO PASTE

6 oz (¾ cup) dried soya beans, soaked in 2 pt (5
cups) water overnight

6 tablespoons malt vinegar
3 tablespoons soy sauce
1 pt (2½ cups) water
Salt to taste

Drain the soaked beans and discard the water. Boil in fresh water in covered pan until tender (two to three hours). Add the vinegar and soy sauce to beans and cooking liquid, and purée the whole in electric blender. The finished paste should be thick enough just to adhere to a spoon. Adjust water if necessary. Season and store in refrigerator to use as required.

TOFU MISO SOUP

2 pt (5 cups) clear soup stock or water
1 small carrot, grated
1 small onion, diced
4 oz (½ cup) miso
6 oz (1 cup) tofu, cut into 1" (2.5 cm) squares
1 pinch togarashi

Combine the stock, carrot and onions and bring to the boil, reduce heat and simmer for five minutes. Add the creamed miso, stir well, then drop in the tofu. Return to the boil. Turn off heat, add pinch of togarashi, stir and serve.

WINE AND TOFU MISO SOUP

1½ pt (4¼ cups) vegetable stock or water
4 oz (½ cup) miso
10 fl oz (1¼ cups) sake or sweet white wine
4 oz (¾ cup) tofu, cut in 1½" (3.5 cm) squares
1 tablespoon parsley, chopped

Bring stock to the boil. Combine wine with miso into smooth paste, add to stock and stir well. Carefully add tofu, return to the boil, switch off heat and serve garnished with parsley.

VEGETABLE MISO SOUP

2 tablespoons vegetable oil
2 oz (¼ cup) mushrooms, sliced
4 oz (1 cup) daikon or turnip, matchsticks
1 small onion diced
4 oz (½ cup) burdock root, peeled grated (optional)
4 oz (½ cup) miso
2 pt (5 cups) clear soup stock or water

2 tablespoons parsley, chopped or 1 sheet nori, crumbled

Place the oil in a heavy pan and sauté the mushrooms, daikon, onion and burdock. When the onions are soft add the stock and bring to the boil. Cream the miso and stir into the soup. Return to the boil, and serve garnished with parsley or nori.

CHILLED SUMMER VEGETABLE MISO SOUP

2 pt (5 cups) vegetable soup stock, chilled
3 oz (⅓ cup) miso
4 oz (½ cup) cucumber, thinly sliced and chilled
4 oz (½ cup) tomatoes, diced and chilled
Small bunch fresh mint, chopped

Blend the stock and miso together. Divide the vegetables between four bowls, pour on the soup and garnish with mint.

SOYA BEAN MISO SOUP (Gôjiru)

This is a thick winter soup prepared with a purée of well-soaked but uncooked soya beans. Most vegetables can be added to the soup, so do try other types than those suggested.

3 oz (⅓ cup) dried soya beans, rinsed and soaked overnight in ½ pt (1¼ cup) water
2 tablespoons vegetable oil
1 onion, thinly sliced
1 carrot, thinly sliced
1 bamboo shoot, thinly sliced into half moons
1 stick celery, chopped
2 oz (¼ cup) mushrooms, sliced
4 oz (½ cup) auberage (fried tofu) in 1" (2.5 cm) cubes (optional)
1½ pt (2¾ cups) clear soup stock or water
Togarashi or black pepper to taste

In an electric blender liquidise the soya beans and the water they were soaked in. Alternatively, drain beans reserving liquid and pass them through a fine mincer. Re-combine with liquid.

Sauté the vegetables in oil in a heavy saucepan. Add the puréed beans to the softened vegetables, mix well and add stock or water. Bring to the boil, reduce heat and simmer for ten minutes. Cream the miso and stir in. Season with togarashi and serve.

PORK AND WATERCRESS MISO SOUP

2 pt (5 cups) water
8 oz (2 cups) lean pork, diced
1 bunch watercress, chopped
4 oz ($\frac{1}{2}$ cup) miso
1 oz (1 tablespoon) ginger root, grated
1 small leek, chopped and minced

Add the diced pork to the water and bring to the boil. Reduce heat and simmer for ten minutes. Cream the miso and add to the stock, stir well. Add the watercress and return to the boil. Sprinkle with leeks and ginger and serve.

BEEF WITH EGG MISO SOUP

8 oz (2 cups) lean beef, diced
2 tablespoons oil
2 pt (5 cups) water or beef stock
1 parsnip, peeled and sliced
4 oz ($\frac{1}{2}$ cup) miso
2 eggs, lightly beaten
4 chives, finely chopped
4 pinches of togarashi or black pepper

Lightly sauté the beef in oil in a heavy pan, add the stock or water and bring to the boil, then add the parsnip and simmer until meat is tender. Cream the miso and stir into the stock. Return to the boil and slowly pour in the eggs stirring continuously. Boil again, then serve in individual bowls each garnished with chives and a pinch of togarashi.

RICE

Inari, the rice god, is quite naturally held in high esteem by the Japanese farmer, and during the summer growing season she is courted assiduously. If she has behaved well, the farmer and his family are rewarded with a heavy autumn harvest as well as the back-breaking job of bringing it in. But afterwards, when the harvest is gathered, there will be traditional festivities and thanks to Inari over a cup of sake (or just as likely, nowadays, a glass of Johnny Walker whisky). The importance of rice to the farmer and the nation is reflected in the language, and although Japanese for rice is han, it is always given the highest honourable prefix and called go-han.

Most Japanese eat only white polished rice, not unrefined brown rice, just as we in the West eat mainly white bread. The trend toward eating polished rice began in the late fifteenth century, when Japanese aristocrats set the fashion, and it has slowly become standard practice for everyone. Nowadays, in Japan as elsewhere, there is a greater awareness of food values, and some younger people are starting to eat the more nutritious brown rice. But for older people brown rice is too attached in their minds to wartime rations, and the privations of that time, to start eating it now. Some of the following rice recipes can be easily adapted to brown rice, if you wish to use it, but others have been developed for, and taste better with, the lighter, fluffier, Japanese cooked white rice. The chapter on macrobiotic cookery contains recipes for brown rice.

PLAIN BOILED RICE

Short grain Japanese rice is cooked until it is just sticky enough to pick up mouthful amounts with chopsticks. Other types of rice, with practice, can be cooked in the same way just as successfully. The amount of water used in cooking cannot be given precisely, since it depends on the type of rice used, but an approximate water to rice ratio is $1\frac{1}{3}$–$1\frac{1}{2}$ volumes of water for 1 volume of rice. After cooking rice a few times by the following method, you will be better able to judge how much water to use. The recipe specifies a particular volume of water, but this is just for guidance.

BASIC COOKING METHOD

1 lb rice
$1\frac{1}{2}$ pt ($4\frac{3}{4}$ cups) water

Wash the rice well by stirring it vigorously in lots of water. Let the rice settle and carefully pour off all the milky residue. Repeat the process until the water remains almost clear. Drain and place the rice in a heavy bottomed pan with a good lid. Add the cooking water, cover the pan and bring to the boil quickly. Turn the heat right down and allow to simmer for 15 minutes (longer for brown rice). Finally, turn the heat off and allow the rice to stand for 5–10 minutes. Serve rice from the pot using a wooden spoon or rice paddle (samegi). No salt is added.

Please note rice cooked with soy sauce tends to burn easily and takes longer to cook. Thus, when soy sauce is added to the cooking water, the heat should be lower and the cooking time longer than when cooking ordinary rice.

MISO COOKED RICE

Although it is not stipulated in any particular case, miso could be added to most of the following recipes (except those for sushi). Proceed in each case as directed in the recipe, but combine one tablespoon miso with each 1 lb of rice before addition of cooking water.

CHESTNUT RICE (Kuri Gohan)

15–20 chestnuts, skinned and quartered (see below)
1 teaspoon salt
1 lb dry rice, washed and drained
1½ pt (4¾ cups) water
2 tablespoons soy sauce
2 tablespoons sake or sweet white wine (optional)
1 tablespoon sesame seeds, toasted

There are three ways of preparing the chestnuts and each method gives a slightly different flavour to the rice.
(1) Make an incision in the shell with knife and boil for five minutes. Peel and quarter.
(2) Shell and skin the chestnuts uncooked. Soak in water for 30 minutes then cut in quarters.
(3) Fork the chestnuts once or twice and bake in a medium oven for 30 minutes. Peel and cut into quarters.

Put rice, chestnuts, salt, soy sauce and sake into a heavy pan, stir well and cook as for plain rice. Serve sprinkled with toasted sesame seeds.

GREEN RICE (Na-Meshi)

1 lb dry rice, washed and drained
1½ pt (4¾ cups) water
8 oz (2 cups) fresh spinach or chrysanthemum leaves or watercress
Salt to taste

Cook rice by the basic method. Meanwhile, boil the greens in the smallest amount of water (i.e. 1 or 2 tablespoons). Immediately the leaves soften, drain and cool in water. Drain again and press out excess liquid. Cut into shreds, add to freshly cooked rice, salt to taste and mix together. Serve.

RED RICE

This dish is usually made with a variety of rice, called mochi, that is sweeter than the regular kind. It is known as Sekihan when made with mochi, and is a great favourite for festive occasions, especially Hina Matouri or Girls' Day. A red colouring is given to the rice by cooking it with aduki beans. Mochi rice is not readily available in the West, and the recipe given here will be for regular rice. If you cannot obtain aduki beans, use red or kidney beans instead.

Rice and aduki beans eaten together provide a rich protein source as well as a colourful dish.

4 oz (½ cup) aduki beans, soaked in water six hours or more
2 pt (5 cups) water
1 lb dry rice, washed and drained
1 teaspoon salt
2 tablespoons sesame seeds, toasted

Drain the soaked beans. Place in pot with water, bring to the boil, reduce heat and simmer until cooked (about one and a half hours). Drain and reserve liquid. Put rice in pot, add the bean cooking liquid plus, if necessary, enough water to make the volume up to 1½ pt (4¾ cups). Cover and bring to the boil. Add beans, mix and continue to simmer until rice is cooked. Combine salt and toasted sesame seeds. Serve red rice hot or cold, garnished with sesame seed and salt mixture (this mixture is called 'gomashio').

CHICKEN WITH RICE

6 oz (¾ cup) boned chicken breast cut into 1" (2.5 cm) cubes
1 oz (1 tablespoon) ginger root, grated
2 tablespoons sake or sweet wine or medium sherry
2 tablespoons soy sauce
1 tablespoon sugar
1 lb dry rice, washed and drained
1½ pt (4¾ cups) chicken stock
8 oz (2 cups) mushrooms, sliced
2 sheets nori, toasted or
1 tablespoon parsley, finely chopped

Marinade the chicken in the ginger, sake, soy

sauce and sugar for 30 minutes or longer. Add the mushrooms, then gently boil the mixture until the chicken pieces are just tender. Place rice in heavy pan, add the chicken stock and any marinating liquid not absorbed by the chicken and mushrooms during cooking. Bring to the boil, stir in chicken and mushroom, reduce heat, cover pot and carefully simmer for 15 minutes. Turn off heat, allow to stand 15 minutes. Serve garnished with crumbled toasted nori or parsley.

TEA AND RICE (Chazuke)
This is a quick snack and a favourite Japanese way of using left-over rice. Green tea is normally used, but there is no reason why you should not try your own favourite flavour or brand of tea.

8 oz (1½ cups) cooked rice, per person
8 fl oz (1 cup) hot green tea per person
1 sheet nori, toasted, per person

Place the rice in individual bowls, pour over the hot tea and garnish with crumbled, toasted nori.

MUSHROOM AND RICE (Matzuke Gohan)

1 lb dry rice, washed and drained
1½ pt (4¼ cups) water
4 shiitake or 6 oz (1¾ cups) mushrooms, thinly sliced
1 tablespoon vegetable oil (sesame seed oil is best)
1 tablespoon soy sauce
¼ teaspoon salt
2 tablespoons water

Soak the shiitake for 20 minutes in cold water, remove any hard stems and thinly slice. Cook the rice by the basic method. While the rice is simmering, cook the mushrooms. Heat a small heavy pan, coat with oil and lightly sauté the shiitake or mushrooms. Add the soy sauce, salt and water. Cover pan and simmer five minutes. Uncover and reduce liquid, by gentle simmering, until the mushrooms are only just moist. Combine the hot, cooked rice and mushrooms, cover and leave to stand for five minutes. Serve.

GREEN PEAS WITH RICE (Aomame Gohan)

1 lb dry rice, washed and drained
1½ pt (4¼ cups) clear soup stock or dashi
1 tablespoon sake or sweet white wine (optional)
1 teaspoon salt
10 oz (2 cups) peas (fresh, frozen or tinned)

Put rice into pot with soup stock, sake and salt, allow to stand one hour. Add peas, cook by basic method for plain rice. Before serving, gently fluff up the rice with a fork or wooden spoon.

EGG AND CHICKEN TRIANGLES ON RICE
Part of the appeal of this dish is its colourful attractive presentation, and it is a good addition to a dinner party meal or buffet table.

1 lb dry rice, washed and drained
1½ pt (4¼ cups) water
2 tablespoons soy sauce
1 lb cooked chicken, diced
1 oz (1 tablespoon) ginger root, grated (optional)
2 tablespoons mirin or sweet sherry
1 teaspoon sugar
3 eggs, beaten
Pinch of salt
1 bunch parsley, chopped

Cook the rice by the basic method. While it is simmering put chicken in small heavy pan with soy sauce, ginger root and mirin or sherry. Gently boil for two to three minutes with constant stirring. Cover and simmer. Add pinch of salt to eggs and scramble. Lay a bed of rice in a shallow square or rectangular serving dish. Join two corners of the dish with a line of chopped parsley. Two triangles are formed, in one arrange the chicken and sauce, and in the other the scrambled eggs.

WHITE FISH WITH RICE

1 lb sole or halibut
2½ pt (6¼ cups) water
1 lb dry rice, washed and drained
1 tablespoon vegetable oil
1 clove garlic, crushed

4 oz (1 cup) mushrooms, sliced
4 spinach leaves, chopped
Pinch of salt
1 tablespoon soy sauce
1 tablespoon watercress or parsley, chopped
1 sheet nori, toasted (optional)

Cut the fish into three or four pieces, and boil in water until tender. Strain, reserve the liquid. Remove flesh from bones and shred into small pieces. Cook rice by basic method using 1½ pt (4¼ cups) of fish stock instead of water. Just before you set the rice to simmer, stir in the flaked fish and then proceed as normal. Lightly sauté garlic in pan with oil, then add mushrooms, spinach and pinch of salt. Cover, lower heat and simmer until mushrooms are soft. Now pour in the remaining fish stock and soy sauce, and heat to boiling. Place rice and fish mixture in individual bowls, pour over the mushroom and spinach broth, and garnish with watercress or parsley and sprinkle with toasted nori.

DEEP FRIED RICE BALLS WITH BARBECUE SAUCE

Deep fried food seems to have universal appeal, and this rice ball dish is no exception. You may add other ingredients to the recipe than those suggested, e.g. minced beef, flaked fish, chopped vegetables, etc.

1½ lb (4½ cups) cooked rice
1 medium leek, finely chopped
2 tablespoons vegetable oil
2 tablespoons miso
2 cloves garlic, crushed
1 oz (1 tablespoon) ginger root, grated
2 oz (½ cup) plain flour, sieved
Oil for deep frying (including, if possible, 25% sesame seed oil)

BARBECUE SAUCE

4 fl oz (½ cup) soy sauce
4 fl oz (½ cup) mirin or sweet sherry
1 tablespoon sugar

Combine barbecue sauce ingredients and gently simmer uncovered, until reduced to half original volume. Meanwhile, thoroughly mix all the other ingredients except the flour. Lightly wet hands and shape mixture into small balls (1"–2", 2.5–5 cm in diameter). Heat deep frying oil in wok or other pan, to about 350°F (175°C), roll rice balls in flour and deep fry (6–8 at a time) until brown and crisp. Drain well. If you are making a large quantity, keep the fried rice balls hot in a medium oven. Serve with barbecue sauce. Dip hot balls in sauce before eating.

FRIED RICE I

2 tablespoons vegetable oil
1 clove garlic, crushed
1 medium onion, diced
4 oz (1 cup) mushrooms, sliced
4 oz (1 cup) celery or French beans, chopped
1 lb (3 cups) cooked rice
1 egg or 1-egg omelette, cut in strips
2 tablespoons soy sauce

Heat the oil in a heavy frying pan. Add the crushed garlic and onion. Sauté until onions are just soft, and then add the mushrooms and celery. Fry gently for two or three minutes retaining the texture of each vegetable. Stir in the rice and tofu. Heat through, stirring constantly. Break the egg over the rice mixture, sprinkle on the soy sauce and mix well. Serve. Alternatively, for a fried rice with a less creamy texture, replace the egg with strips of omelette.

FRIED RICE II

2 tablespoons vegetable oil
1 medium leek or 2 spring onions, finely chopped
1 bunch parsley, finely chopped
5 oz (¼ cup) bamboo shoots, thinly sliced
1 lb (3 cups) cooked rice
Peel of 1 lemon, grated
2 tablespoons soy sauce
Togarashi or black pepper to taste

Heat the oil in a heavy frying pan. Add the leeks and parsley, and sauté until just soft (about three minutes). Meanwhile, boil the bamboo shoots in the water in which they were tinned. Drain. Add rice, bamboo shoots, lemon peel, soy sauce and togarashi to frying pan. Stir gently and serve when heated through.

DONBURI

Donburi dishes are large bowls of rice or noodles combined with vegetables or meat, and served topped with egg and perhaps a sauce. Alternatively, the vegetables and meat are mixed with the egg and the whole is fried, before topping the rice. Donburi means 'big bowl'. They can be rich dishes filled with many ingredients or simply cooked rice combined with left-over vegetables topped with an omelette.

CHICKEN DONBURI

For four to six people.

1 small chicken or chicken pieces weighing 1–2 lb
1 lb dry rice, washed and drained
1½ pt (3½ cups) water
8 fl oz (1 cup) chicken stock
2 tablespoons mirin or sweet sherry (optional)
2 tablespoons soy sauce
8 oz (2 cups) mushrooms, sliced
4 oz (1 cup) peas (fresh, frozen or tinned)
3 eggs, beaten
1 teaspoon salt

Cut the chicken into four or five pieces and boil in the minimum of water until tender. Strain and reserve liquid. Remove the bones and skin from the chicken pieces and cut the flesh into small pieces. Cook rice by the basic method. Place part of the reserved chicken stock in a large pan and add the mirin or sherry, soy sauce, mushrooms and peas. Cook until vegetables are just soft. Gently mix into the pan the rice and chicken. Combine the egg and salt and pour over rice mixture. Stir well and maintain low heat until egg is just set. Serve in 'big bowl'.

TOFU AND SHRIMP DONBURI

1 lb dry rice, washed and drained
1½ pt (3½ cups) water
1 medium onion, diced
2 medium carrots, grated
1 bunch parsley, chopped
4 oz (¼ cups) cooked shrimps (tinned)
6 oz (1 cup) tofu, diced into 1" (2.5 cm) squares

3 tablespoons soy sauce
Salt to taste
2 teaspoons sugar
2 eggs, beaten

Cook rice by the basic method. Meanwhile, heat the oil in a heavy pan and sauté the carrots, onion and finally parsley until just soft. Add the shrimps, tofu, soy sauce and salt to taste. Stir, heat through and then pour beaten eggs over the mixture. Cook until eggs just set. Put cooked rice in serving bowl, top with shrimp tofu mixture and serve.

VEGETABLE DONBURI

4 shiitake or 4 oz (¼ cup) mushrooms, sliced
1 lb dry rice, washed and drained
2 tablespoons vegetable oil
2 small leeks or 2 spring onions, thinly sliced
1 medium carrot, grated
4 leaves spinach, chopped
2 sticks celery, chopped
2 tablespoons soy sauce
2 teaspoons sugar
Salt to taste
Pinch of togarashi or black pepper

Soak the shiitake for 20 minutes in cold water, remove any hard stems and thinly slice. Cook the rice by the basic method. Meanwhile, heat the oil in a heavy pan and sauté the vegetables and mushrooms until just soft. Add the soy sauce, sugar and salt to taste. Pour over the beaten eggs, add a pinch of togarashi, stir and cook until eggs just set. Put cooked rice in serving bowl, top with egg and vegetables and serve.

CHICKEN KEBAB DONBURI AND SAUCE

1 lb boned chicken, cut in cubes
2 tablespoons soy sauce
1 tablespoon sugar
1 clove garlic, crushed
1 lb dry rice, washed and drained
1½ pt (3½ cups) water

SAUCE
2 tablespoons mirin or sweet sherry
1 tablespoon soy sauce
4 fl oz (½ cup) clear soup stock

Marinate chicken in mixture of soy sauce, sugar and garlic for one hour or more. Cook rice by basic method. Combine sauce ingredients and heat to boiling. Reduce heat and simmer. Put the marinated chicken cubes on skewers and grill under medium heat, turning two or three times to ensure even cooking. Prepare bed of rice in a large dish, arrange skewers of chicken on the top and pour over the sauce. Serve.

The sauce used in this recipe can also be used for other donburi dishes, either to pour over the top or as a dipping sauce.

TEMPURA DONBURI

Tendon, an abbreviation of tempura and donburi, is the name used for this dish, which is a bed of rice topped with tempura (fish or vegetables and meat dipped in batter and deep fried). Recipes for tempura are given in the chapter on tempura and fried foods (see p. 116).

JAPANESE CURRIED RICE

See curried noodles (p. 52).

SUSHI

Sushi is the word used to describe a variety of dishes in which cooked rice seasoned with vinegar and sugar is the basic ingredient. The sushi shop is very popular in Japan, where it is used as a casual bar where one can relax and sit down to a snack or meal and drink. Sushi is prepared with all sorts of ingredients in a variety of combinations. It serves the same purpose as, and can be compared to, the Western sandwich. A box of assorted sushi is convenient for lunchtimes, picnics or travelling, and they are sold from take-away booths at airports, train stations, etc.

There are three main types of sushi. The simplest but somehow most difficult to make perfectly is nigiri-sushi. As with many processes, the simplest method requires the most skill if it is to be executed perfectly. The vinegared rice is moulded with wet hands into an oval, round, square, etc. shape and topped with a slice of fish, vegetable, egg or pickle. For sashimi or raw fish garnish, the rice patties are first dabbed with a little wasabi (green Japanese mustard). An alternative way of making nigiri-sushi is to mix the garnish and rice before shaping. The patty is then sprinkled with toasted nori or sesame seeds.

In the nigiri category we will include oshi-sushi, which are rather like double-decker rice sandwiches, in which layers of rice and filling are pressed together in a mould.

Norimaki-sushi is rice and other ingredients wrapped in a thin sheet of nori seaweed. The resulting swiss roll shape is cut into thick slices and each piece displays the colourful filling.

The nori seaweed may be replaced by a thin egg omelette cut into a rectangle shape. Egg-wrapped sushi or yushiki-sushi as they are called, are an excellent replacement for nori-maki-sushi if nori is not available.

Chirasushi, our third category, is a sort of rice salad, in which various ingredients and sushi rice are mixed.

An assortment of various sushi served with thin slices of fresh ginger and soy sauce makes a fine meal.

SUSHI RICE – BASIC METHOD

The quantities given in this recipe may not be suitable for all types of rice, and you may need to experiment a little to find the exact combination of cooking water and sugar/vinegar mixture to give the best sushi rice. Do remember the success of the dish depends on the quality of the sushi rice. It should be tasty, sticky enough to mould, but not the least bit squashy or mashed up.

The quantities given for the sushi dressing will make enough for several preparations of sushi rice. Reserve what you do not use and store in the refrigerator.

SUSHI RICE (for four people)

1 lb dry rice, washed and drained
1½ pt (4¼ cups) water
2–3 tablespoons sushi dressing

SUSHI DRESSING
4 fl oz (½ cup) vinegar
6 oz (¾ cup) sugar
1 tablespoon salt

To prepare sushi dressing, combine vinegar, sugar and salt and bring to the boil. Turn off heat and leave. Use hot or cold; either way it gives the same result.

Cook the rice by the basic method for plain rice, then turn it into a wooden or non-metallic bowl. Pour dressing over the hot rice until a little remains unabsorbed in the bottom of the bowl. Now stir the rice gently with a wet rice paddle or wooden spoon, while the other hand fans the rice with a flat pan lid or rolled up newspaper. This cools the rice quickly and gives it an authentic shine.

NIGIRI-SUSHI

Prepare the sushi rice by the basic method (see above) and while it is still warm, prepare rice patties as follows: Wet your hands and using about one heaped tablespoon of rice, form a shape (e.g. oval, ball, square, etc.) in the palm of your hands. Continue until all the rice is used up. Wet your hands as necessary to prevent the rice sticking to them. Arrange the rice shapes on a serving dish and garnish with one or more of the suggested toppings below.

GARNISHINGS FOR NIGIRI-SUSHI

Quantities have not been given, since the amount needed will depend on how much sushi rice you have prepared, and how many different toppings you want to use.

(1) Thin egg omelette cut into strips and brushed with soy sauce
(2) Fresh uncooked slices of sashimi (see p. 80), sparingly spread with wasabi or English mustard
(3) Smoked salmon in small pieces, sprinkled with fresh lemon juice
(4) Anchovies
(5) Cooked shrimps
(6) Sardines
(7) Prawns, shelled: leave tail intact and lightly cook
(8) Mussels, cooked
(9) Sliced pickled herring

(10) Fresh cucumber, sliced and sparingly spread with wasabi or English mustard
(11) Sliced mushrooms, lightly cooked in equal parts of soy sauce and sugar
(12) Cooked vegetables, cut into suitable shapes
(13) Cooked chicken or meat, thinly sliced
(14) Sesame seeds, toasted
(15) Fish paste: grind cooked fish and garlic in a suribachi or mortar and spread on sushi
(16) Nori seaweed, toasted and crumbled

Remember you may mix the garnishing with rice before moulding into shape. The filled sushi is then garnished with toasted nori or sesame seeds.

NORIMAKI-SUSHI

Norimaki-sushi traditionally has six different fillings, but of course you may use as many as you wish. The fillings are prepared before the sushi is rolled in the seaweed wrapping. This is not a recipe that can be written out in a regular fashion, and for clarity I have divided it into two parts. The first describes how to assemble the norimaki, and the second gives a list of fillings. The amounts given for each filling will, in combination with three or four other components, make enough norimaki for four to six people. See page 43 for egg-wrapped sushi.

ASSEMBLY OF NORIMAKI-SUSHI

Sushi rice for four people (see p. 40)
Fillings (see below)
4 sheets of nori

Hold nori seaweed over a direct heat source to crispen it. Place on a bamboo screen or mat (called a sudare) approximately 8" × 8" (20 cm × 20 cm), or a damp cloth of the same size (this makes the wrapping process a little more difficult, but nothing insurmountable). Divide the rice into four portions and spread one portion over the sheet of nori, leaving a 1" (2.5 cm) gap at the top and bottom ends to allow for overlap. Lay the fillings in horizontal rows down the middle of the rice. Slightly moisten the exposed edges of the nori and then roll up the mixture in the mat or cloth. Make sure the ingredients are tightly encased by the seaweed and then unroll carefully. Trim the ends and cut roll into 1" (2.5 cm) thick slices. Repeat for each sheet of nori. See diagram.

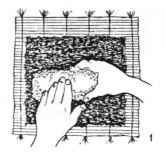

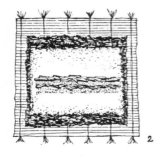

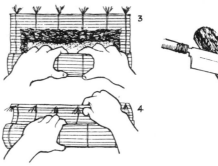

Assembling Norimaki-Sushi

NORIMAKI-SUSHI FILLINGS

(1) CARROT
1 medium carrot, quartered lengthwise and cut into sticks ¼" (0.5 cm) thick
1 tablespoon vegetable oil
1 tablespoon water
Pinch of salt

Sauté the carrot sticks in oil for two minutes. Add water and pinch of salt. Simmer until carrots are just soft.

(2) LOTUS ROOT
1 medium lotus root, quartered lengthwise and cut into sticks ¼" (0.5 cm) thick
1 tablespoon soy sauce
1 tablespoon water

Combine ingredients and heat through.

(3) SPINACH
4 oz (¾ cup) spinach
2 tablespoons water
Pinch of salt
1 tablespoon sesame seeds, toasted

Boil spinach lightly in salted water for two to three minutes. Drain, chop and mix with sesame seeds.

(4) FRENCH BEANS
4 oz (¼ cup) French beans
Water to cover
Pinch of salt

Cover beans in water, bring to the boil, add a pinch of salt. Simmer for three or four minutes. Drain and store in cold water.

(5) EGG
Beat 2 eggs. Prepare paper thin omelettes and cut into ¼" (0.5 cm) wide strips.

(6) FISH
2 oz (½ cup) prawns, peeled and cooked *or* filleted salmon, halibut or plaice
2 eggs, beaten
1 tablespoon sake or white wine
Pinch of salt
2 tablespoons oil

Pound prawns or fish in suribachi or mortar,

add beaten egg, sake and pinch of salt. Mix well. Heat oil in heavy frying pan, pour mixture in and quickly fry on both sides. Cut into thin strips.

(7) SHIITAKE OR MUSHROOMS

4 shiitake or 4 oz (¼ cup) mushrooms, thinly
   sliced
4 tablespoons water
¼ tablespoon sugar
¼ tablespoon soy sauce

Soak the shiitake for 20 minutes in cold water. Remove any hard stems and thinly slice. Omit this for fresh mushrooms. Cook mushrooms in remaining ingredients until soft.

(8) WATERCRESS

1 bunch watercress, chopped

(9) SASHIMI

4 oz (¼ cup) sashimi (see p. 80) cut into lengths
   ¼" (0.5 cm) square

(10) CUCUMBER

½ medium cucumber, peeled and cut into long
   matchsticks
Wasabi or English mustard to taste

Sparingly dab cucumber strips with wasabi before laying in norimaki.

The above suggestions should be supplemented with your own ideas. Make full use of left-over cooked vegetables, fish, meat, etc.

YUSHIKI-SUSHI

To make yushiki-sushi proceed in exactly the same way as for norimaki-sushi, but substitute paper-thin omelette sheets for the nori. The recipe given below for thin omelettes makes the equivalent of eight sheets of nori.

PAPER-THIN OMELETTES

4 eggs, beaten
½ teaspoon salt
2 tablespoons vegetable oil

Add salt to beaten eggs, mix well. Coat a large, heavy frying pan with a little oil and heat well. Pour in one-eighth of the egg, tilt the pan to spread egg evenly and cook over medium heat.

Turn omelette over when fairly hardened on bottom side. Cook both sides.

For norimaki cut omelette into squares approximately 8" × 8" (20 cm × 20 cm). Use the trimmings for filling.

CHAKIN-SUSHI

This recipe also makes use of egg-wrapped sushi, but utilises a different shape wrapping than yushiki-sushi. Chakin-sushi consists of rice-filled egg pouches garnished with shrimps and green peas. See diagram.

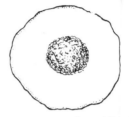

Assembling Chakin-Sushi

1 lb sushi rice (see p. 40)
8 paper-thin omelettes (see above)
4 oz (¼ cup) shrimps, cooked
2 oz (¼ cup) green peas, cooked
2 tablespoons parsley, chopped

Spread out a roughly circular paper-thin omelette and place one-eighth of the sushi rice in the centre. Gather the edges of the omelette together, and draw to the centre. Fold back the edges, leaving an opening at the top. Tie the pouch into shape by fastening coloured string or cotton under the folds. Garnish the top of the rice in each pouch with shrimp, peas and parsley.

CHIRA-SUSHI

This vinegared rice salad, or 'Vinegared Rice with Fish and Vegetable Mingled' as I've seen it described on a Japanese menu, can be prepared with a multitude of ingredients. Traditionally, it requires nine different garnishings, but you may wish to use less. Again there is no absolutely specific recipe, but I have given a fixed recipe as a guide, and followed it with a list of alternative ingredients. If you add or replace or subtract ingredients from the given recipe you will need to adjust amounts accordingly. The recipe is authentic but straightforward for the Western cook. If you wish to try more exotic garnishings see the alternatives suggested at the end of the recipe. The quantities given will prepare chira-sushi for 4–6 people.

Sushi rice for 4 people (see p. 40)
3 tablespoons vegetable oil
1 medium carrot, finely diced
1 medium onion, finely diced
1 stick celery, finely chopped
2 oz ($\frac{1}{3}$ cup) mushrooms, chopped
1 teaspoon sugar
2 teaspoons soy sauce
1 egg, beaten
2 oz ($\frac{1}{4}$ cup) salmon, tinned or fresh boiled
2 oz ($\frac{1}{3}$ cup) green peas, cooked
1 oz (1 tablespoon) ginger root, finely sliced
1 tablespoon sesame seeds, toasted
Salt to taste

Sauté the carrot, onion and celery in 2 tablespoons of oil until just soft. Combine the beaten egg with 1 teaspoon of soy sauce, a pinch of salt and prepare a pancake-thin omelette with the mixture, cut into strips. Cook mushrooms in 1 tablespoon of oil, stir in sugar and remaining soy sauce. Flake the salmon and season with salt. Gently mix the sushi rice with cooked vegetables, strips of omelette and salmon. Transfer the mixture to serving bowl, heaping it to a point in the middle. Garnish the top with green peas, slivers of ginger root, and sprinkle with sesame seeds. Serve hot or cold.

ALTERNATIVE INGREDIENTS FOR CHIRA-SUSHI
(1) 2 oz ($\frac{1}{4}$ cup) filleted white fish (halibut, cod, plaice, hake, etc.), fried and flaked.
(2) 2 oz ($\frac{1}{4}$ cup) shrimps (fresh or tinned). If you use fresh shrimps leave shell on and boil in a little water. Remove shell and soak shrimps in vinegar before use.
(3) 2 oz ($\frac{1}{4}$ cup) sashimi (see p. 80)
(4) 2 oz ($\frac{1}{4}$ cup) anchovies
(5) 2 oz ($\frac{1}{4}$ cup) mussels (raw or poached)
(6) 2 oz ($\frac{1}{4}$ cup) pickled herring, sliced
(7) 2 oz ($\frac{1}{4}$ cup) sardines

(8) 4 shiitake. Soak in cold water for 20 minutes, remove any hard stems and slice.
(9) 4 oz ($\frac{3}{4}$ cup) tofu cut into 1" (2.5 cm) cubes
(10) 2 oz ($\frac{1}{2}$ cup) French beans, lightly boiled in salted water
(11) 2 oz ($\frac{1}{2}$ cup) bamboo shoots, thinly sliced or cut in half moon shapes
(12) 2 oz ($\frac{1}{2}$ cup) lotus root, thinly sliced, quartered
(13) 3 oz ($\frac{1}{2}$ cup) chestnuts, cooked, peeled and chopped (see p. 35)
(14) 2 oz ($\frac{1}{2}$ cup) fresh bean sprouts

OSHI-SUSHI
The name of this sushi derives from the special wooden moulds, with removable frames, in which it is made. They are called oshiwaku. The moulds come in various shapes, but rectangular is the most popular. Sushi rice is layered on to the base of the mould followed by a layer of filling, another layer of rice, and finally a topping of a suitable garnish. The whole is pressed, the frame removed and the resulting sandwich cut into small squares.

A small, round or square cake tin with removable bottom can be used in place of the oshiwaku. Alternatively, you could drape the base and sides of a small rectangular or square tin with damp cheesecloth. Prepare the oshi-sushi on top of the cheesecloth and remove by drawing up the edges of the overhanging material.

In the recipes that follow the number of oshi-sushi that you make from the quantities given will depend on the size of the mould you use, but the amounts given will, in total, serve 4 to 6 people.

CHICKEN, SHRIMP AND CUCUMBER OSHI-SUSHI

8 oz sushi rice (see p. 40)
$\frac{1}{4}$ medium cucumber, thinly sliced
1 teaspoon salt
2 tablespoons vinegar
2 teaspoons sugar
4 oz ($\frac{1}{4}$ cup) shrimps (fresh or tinned; if fresh shrimps, shell, devein, lightly boil)
4 oz ($\frac{1}{4}$ cup) cooked chicken, thinly sliced

1 pinch togarashi or black pepper
1 teaspoon wasabi or English mustard
Peel of 1 lemon, grated

Sprinkle the cucumber slices with salt and leave to soften (about 10 minutes). Drain off the liquid, add vinegar and sugar, leave to marinate until needed. Lightly wet sides of cake tin, cover the base with rice ⅔" (1.5 cm) thick and top with layer of chicken smeared with wasabi, cucumber and grated lemon peel. Add another layer of rice ⅔" (1.5 cm) thick, garnish with shrimps and pinch of togarashi. Cover top with greaseproof paper or suitable flat plate and weigh it down with a pan of water. Leave for 30 minutes or more, remove weight and run wet knife around the edge of the pressed rice. Push sandwich out of the cake tin using removable base and cut into 2" (5 cm) squares.

MUSHROOM, EGG AND HAM OSHI-SUSHI

8 oz sushi rice (see p. 40)
2 shiitake or 2 oz (⅓ cup) mushrooms, sliced
1 tablespoon sake or sweet white wine
1 teaspoon sugar
1 tablespoon soy sauce
3 oz (⅓ cup) cooked ham, sliced
Pinch of salt
1 egg, beaten
1 teaspoon wasabi or English mustard
2 sheets of nori, toasted *or* 1 tablespoon sesame seed, toasted *or* 1 oz (1 tablespoon) ginger root, grated

Soak the shiitake for 20 minutes in cold water, remove any hard stems, thinly slice. Combine the sake, sugar and soy sauce, add shiitake or mushrooms and bring to the boil. Simmer until mushrooms are soft. Drain and reserve mushrooms are soft. Drain and reserve mushrooms. Add pinch of salt to egg and prepare a pancake-thin omelette. Mould sandwiches as for chicken, shrimp and cucumber oshi-sushi but substitute mushrooms, ham and mustard and omelette for the filling, and for the garnish or topping use a combination of nori, sesame seeds and ginger root or only one of these.
the suggested fillings and toppings for nigiri (see p. 41) and norimaki-sushi (see p. 41) to provide ideas for devising your own varieties of oshi-sushi.

NOODLES

Italy is usually most associated with pasta dishes, but in the shape of noodles pasta has been eaten in the Far East for thousands of years. Noodles, one of Japan's most basic foodstuffs, lend themselves to a wide range of dishes and methods of preparation. Noodles in steaming hot soup topped with chicken, pork or vegetables, stir fried with vegetables, served alone with a simple dipping sauce or garnishing, or in the summer chilled in a salad or mixed with cold sautéed vegetables, are a few of the 'oodles of noodles' dishes.

Udon, somen and soba are the three main types of Japanese noodles. Udon and somen are made from wheat flour, and they are related in the way spaghetti is to vermicelli (two suitable substitutes respectively). That is, udon is a fat noodle and somen a thin one. Soba are buckwheat flour noodles; they tend to be a little chewier and tastier than the wheat flour variety, and are perhaps the Japanese' favourite noodle. They are often eaten on festive occasions and especially at New Year to ensure a happy and lucky year ahead, the length of the noodle representing longevity and continuity.

It is not difficult to make your own noodles, and recipes are given for preparing udon and soba. Otherwise, packets of both these noodles and somen are available in health/wholefood stores. Alternatively, other types of pasta can be used.

Traditionally in the East, flour has been used to prepare noodles – not to make bread. Flour in noodle form is easily digestible, and noodles made with some or all wholewheat or buckwheat flour are nutritious as well as delicious.

The chapter is arranged in the following order: preparation and cooking of noodles, noodles in soup stock, dipping sauces and garnishings for noodle dishes, fried noodles, other hot noodle dishes and finally chilled and salad noodles. Where a recipe specifies just noodles either udom, somen or soba may be used. Soup stock is called for in a number of recipes; if you do not have any available, bouillon cubes are a good substitute.

PREPARATION AND COOKING OF HOME-MADE NOODLES
One pound of noodles serves five to six people.

UDON (Wheat flour noodles)

4 oz (1 cup) wholewheat flour and 12 oz (3 cups)
   strong, plain white flour
   or 1 lb (4 cups) plain white flour
1 teaspoon salt
5 fl oz ($\frac{1}{4}$ cup) water, approximately

Mix flour and salt in a large bowl, then gradually add water to form a slightly dry dough. Knead for 10 to 15 minutes. Flour a board and roll out dough into a thin (approximately $\frac{1}{4}$" [0.25 cm] thick) rectangular sheet. Fold the two narrow ends of the sheet into the middle, fold again at the middle to divide dough into quarters. See diagram on page 47.
With a sharp knife, cut folded sheet crosswise into $\frac{1}{4}$" (0.25 cm) strips. Unroll noodles and spread on floured board to await cooking.

Boil 4 pt (10 cups) water, carefully lower in noodles and return water to boil. Add 8 fl oz (1

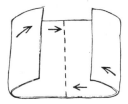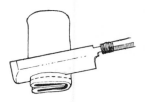

cup) cold water and bring to the boil a second time. Reduce heat and simmer until noodles are cooked but still just hard at the core (approximately 10 minutes). This method of cooking ensures that both the inside and outside of the noodle are evenly cooked. Drain noodles and rinse under cold running water separating any noodles that are stuck together. To reheat pour boiling water over the noodles. Note, the water in which the noodles were cooked may be reserved and used for preparing soup stock.

SOBA (Buckwheat Flour Noodles)

1 lb (4 cups) buckwheat flour
1 teaspoon salt
1 egg, beaten
4 fl oz ($\frac{1}{2}$ cup) water, approximately

Place the flour and salt in a large mixing bowl, thoroughly mix, add beaten egg and stir in. Gradually add water to form a slightly dry dough. Proceed as for udon noodles on previous page.

NOODLES IN SOUP STOCK

HOMEMADE NOODLES WITH MISO

This recipe makes use of the water in which noodles are cooked to make a thick miso noodle soup. Follow recipe as for homemade udon or soba but do not drain cooked noodles. Instead add to the pot four tablespoons of miso, creamed with a little water and two small leeks cut into 1½" (3.75 cm) pieces. Bring pot back to the boil and simmer for 10 minutes. Switch off heat and allow to stand for two to 12 hours. Serve cold or reheated, garnished with chopped chives, parsley or spring onion. For a thick noodle and vegetable soup add other cooked or parboiled vegetables as well as the leeks.

TO COOK DRIED NOODLES

For four people:

12 oz (1½ cup) dried noodles
5 pt (12½ cups) water

Either follow instructions on the packet or use following method: Bring water to boil, add noodles and stir gently. Return to the boil, reduce heat until water is just bubbling. Cook uncovered until noodles are cooked, but still just hard at the core (approximately five minutes). Drain, and if not to be used immediately, rinse under cold running water. Stand to drain well. Use as required. If storing add a little soft butter or oil to stop the noodles sticking together. To reheat, pour boiling water over noodles.

SIMPLE UDON OR SOBA

This is a basic method. For more elaborate and more filling udon or soba, try some of the toppings suggested below.

12 oz (3 cups) udon or soba, cooked and drained
2 pt (5 cups) hot soup stock
2 tablespoons chives or spring onions, chopped and/or other garnishings (see below)
Soy sauce to taste

Divide noodles among four bowls, pour over soup stock and garnish with chives or spring onions.

Other possible toppings are: parboiled carrot slices; bamboo shoots or lotus root slices, cooked; fresh or frozen garden peas or other vegetables; slices of mushroom or soaked shiitake sautéed in oil; pieces of cooked chicken or pork; whole shrimp; hard boiled egg slices; abalone slices. Also see garnishings suggested for Noodles with Egg and Vegetables (p. 48) and Soba Noodles with Dipping Sauce (p. 49).

NOODLES WITH EGG AND VEG-ETABLES

This is a basic recipe. For a more elaborate dish, see suggestions below.

12 oz (3 cups) udon, parboiled and drained
2 pt (5 cups) soup stock or water
4 fl oz (½ cup) soy sauce
4 tablespoons mirin or sweet sherry
1 tablespoon sugar
2 oz (⅓ cup) small mushrooms, whole
2 small leeks, cut into 2" (5 cm) pieces
4 eggs
2 tablespoons parsley, minced
Togarashi or black pepper to taste

Place parboiled noodles in large casserole, bring stock or water, soy sauce, mirin and sugar to the boil and pour over noodles. Arrange mushrooms and leeks on top and carefully break in four eggs, separately. Cover and bring to the boil. Reduce heat and simmer until eggs are cooked. Serve garnished with parsley and togarashi to taste. Below are suggested alternatives and/or additions to ingredients in the recipe. They should be added before the eggs.

(1) 4 oz (¾ cup) cooked chicken, cut into small pieces.
(2) 4 shiitake, soaked in cold water for 20 minutes. Remove hard stems, criss cross the tops with sharp knife. Cook in 2 tablespoons sugar and 2 tablespoons soy sauce until liquid is absorbed.
(3) 8 oz (1½ cups) French beans, parboiled in salted water 3 to 4 minutes, drained.
(4) 1 medium carrot, thinly sliced, parboiled in salted water 3 to 4 minutes, drained.
(5) 4 stalks spinach or chrysanthemum leaves, parboiled in little salted water, drained, chopped in 1" (2.5 cm) lengths.

RAMEN (Chinese Noodles)

Ramen are short, crunchy, yellowish noodles, Chinese in origin (and available in Chinese provision stores) but popular in Japan where ramen is a favoured small restaurant meal. A bowl of ramen with vegetables in hot soup stock is good, but it's even better with a crisp side salad, that will complement the noodles. Make up your own salad or try the cucumber and radish salad suggested below. Somen may be used in place of ramen if you wish.

1 tablespoon vegetable oil
1 clove garlic, crushed
4 oz (½ cup) bean sprouts, rinsed
2 spring onions chopped *or* 1 medium onion, sliced
3 tablespoons miso
1½ pt (4¼ cups) soup stock
Pinch of 7-spices, pepper or cayenne
8 oz (1 cup) ramen, cooked as for dried noodles (see p. 47), reheated

Sauté garlic in oil in heavy pan, add bean sprouts and onion and sauté a further few minutes. Cream miso in a little of the soup stock and stir into the pan with the remainder of stock. Season with 7-spices, pepper or cayenne and bring to the boil stirring constantly. Divide hot ramen among four bowls and pour over vegetables and stock. Serve with chilled side salad.

SIDE SALAD
4 tablespoons vinegar
2 tablespoons vegetable oil
Pinch of salt and black pepper
4 oz (¾ cup) cucumber, sliced
2 oz (⅓ cup) radish, halved

Combine oil, vinegar, salt and pepper, mix well. Arrange cucumber and radish in an attractive pattern in a bowl, cover with dressing and chill.

SEAFOOD, CHICKEN AND VEGETABLES WITH NOODLES

2 pt (5 cups) soup stock (chicken is best)
2 small leeks, cut into 2" (5 cm) pieces
1 oz (1 tablespoon) ginger root, grated
4 oz (¾ cup) chicken, thin strips
4 oz (¾ cup) prawns, shelled, deveined (see p. 79), cut into ½" (1.25 cm) pieces or use tinned
4 oz (¾ cup) shrimps, shelled, deveined (see p. 79) or use tinned
2 oz (⅓ cup) mushrooms, sliced
3 tablespoons soy sauce
Salt to taste
12 oz (1½ cups) noodles, cooked and drained

Bring soup stock to the boil. Add all the other ingredients except the noodles. Return to the boil, cover, reduce heat and simmer for 10 minutes. Adjust seasoning with salt and serve noodles divided between four bowls.

FIVE COLOUR NOODLES – GOMOKUSOMAN

4 shiitake or 4 oz (1 cup) mushrooms
2 tablespoons sugar
2 tablespoons soy sauce
2 eggs
4 oz (¾ cup) French beans, parboiled in a little salted water
1 tablespoon vegetable oil
1 green pepper, de-seeded, cut into ½" (1.25 cm) strips
½ medium cucumber, thinly sliced
4 oz (½ cup) cooked ham, thinly sliced
12 oz (1½ cups) somen, cooked and drained

Soak shiitake in cold water 20 minutes. Remove hard stems, criss cross the tops with a sharp knife. Cook shiitake or mushrooms in sugar and soy sauce until the liquid is absorbed. Prepare four paper-thin omelettes (see p. 43) and cut into narrow strips. Heat oil in a heavy pan and lightly sauté green pepper. Heat noodles by pouring boiling water over them. Drain and distribute noodles among four bowls. Decorate the top of the noodles with the five prepared ingredients and serve.

NOODLES WITH DIPPING SAUCES AND GARNISHINGS

SOBA NOODLES WITH DIPPING SAUCE

This is a dish in which the noodles are cooked, topped with a wide range of garnishings and served either with a separate dipping sauce or with the sauce poured over. A basic recipe is given with three different dipping sauces. Additions and alternatives to the recipe follow. This dish can also be made with udon, but it is not quite as tasty as with soba.

12 oz (1½ cups) soba, cooked and drained
4 tablespoons leeks, chives or spring onions, finely chopped

SAUCE I
3 fl oz (⅓ cup) vinegar
4 fl oz (½ cup) soup stock
2 tablespoons sugar

SAUCE II
4 fl oz (½ cup) soy sauce
4 fl oz (½ cup) mirin or sweet sherry
8 fl oz (1 cup) soup stock
Pinch of togarashi or black pepper

SAUCE III
4 tablespoons soy sauce
2 tablespoons mirin or sweet sherry
12 fl oz (1½ cups) soup stock
2 tablespoons miso
2 tablespoons sesame seeds, toasted and pounded to paste in suribachi or mortar

Combine ingredients of whichever sauce you choose to make, and bring to the boil. Place soba on one large plate or bowl. Divide sauce among four bowls and garnish each with leeks, etc. Dip noodles into sauce before eating. Both noodles and sauce can also be served cold. The other way to serve the dish is to divide the noodles among four bowls, pour over the sauce and garnish.

ALTERNATIVE GARNISHINGS
(1) The garnishings suggested for Simple Udon or Soba (see p. 47) and Noodles with Egg and Vegetables (see p. 48).
(2) 2 paper-thin omelettes (see p. 43), cooled, cut into strips.
(3) ½ medium cucumber, peeled, cut into half lengthwise and thinly sliced. Marinate in 1 tablespoon vinegar and 1 tablespoon sugar before using.
(4) 2 tablespoons sesame seeds, toasted.
(5) 2 sheets nori, toasted and crumbled.

Keep garnishes separate when arranging on top of noodles.

SOBA WITH NORI AND MUSTARD

12 oz (1½ cups) soba, cooked and drained
2 sheets nori, toasted and crumbled
2 spring onions, thinly chopped
2 teaspoons wasabi or English mustard
8 fl oz (1 cup) Sauce II (see above)

The soba can be served either hot or cold. For hot soba, pour boiling water over noodles before serving. Divide noodles among four bowls, garnish with nori. Serve dipping sauce in four individual bowls, and wasabi and spring onions in small central bowls. Invite your guests to season their dipping sauce with wasabi and spring onion. Dip noodles into sauce before eating.

NOODLE AND BEEF OR CHICKEN CUSTARD

4 oz ($\frac{1}{2}$ cup) beef or chicken, cooked, thinly sliced
1 tablespoon soy sauce
1 tablespoon sugar
12 oz (1$\frac{1}{2}$ cups) noodles, cooked and drained
1$\frac{1}{2}$ pt (4$\frac{1}{4}$ cups) soup stock, cold
2 eggs, beaten
4 oz ($\frac{3}{4}$ cup) peas (fresh, frozen or tinned)
4 oz ($\frac{3}{4}$ cup) shrimps (tinned)
2 tablespoons parsley, chopped
4 small heat-proof bowls with lids

Marinate beef or chicken in soy sauce and sugar. Meanwhile prepare the other ingredients. Divide noodles among four bowls. Combine egg and stock and pour over noodles. Top with beef or chicken, peas, shrimps and parsley in pleasing pattern. Steam bowls as for Custard Soup (see p. 30) until custard sets. Serve immediately. Try this dish with vegetables, fish or meat other than those given.

NOODLES COOKED WITH MISO

This is equally delicious hot or cold. If you obtain Cha soba (green noodles made with green tea powder) they go particularly well with the miso sauce. Spinach-based pasta is an effective substitute.

2 tablespoons miso
1 pt (2$\frac{1}{2}$ cups) soup stock
2 tablespoons mirin or sherry or white wine
1 tablespoon sugar
2 tablespoons soy sauce
2 tablespoons sesame seeds, toasted (optional)
2 tablespoons vegetable oil
1 medium onion, thinly sliced

2 oz ($\frac{1}{2}$ cup) mushrooms, thinly sliced
1 oz (1 tablespoon) ginger root, grated
12 oz (1$\frac{1}{2}$ cups) noodles, cooked and drained

Cream the miso with a little stock, then combine first seven ingredients, mix well and bring to the boil. Sauté onion, mushrooms and ginger in oil in heavy pan. Stir in the miso mixture and noodles and bring to the boil. Reduce heat and simmer for 10 minutes. Serve hot or cold.

FOX NOODLES (Kitsune Udon or Soba)

Japanese legend has it that the wily fox particularly enjoys the fried tofu contained in this dish, hence the name.

6 oz ($\frac{2}{3}$ cup) tofu, cut into $\frac{1}{2}$" (1.25 cm) cubes
Vegetable oil for deep frying
4 fl oz ($\frac{1}{2}$ cup) soup stock or water
1 tablespoon sugar
2 tablespoons soy sauce
1 tablespoon mirin or sherry (optional)
Pinch of salt
1$\frac{1}{2}$ pt (4$\frac{1}{4}$ cups) soup stock
1 medium onion, cut into wedges or crescents
12 oz (1$\frac{1}{2}$ cups) soba or udan, cooked and drained
4 pinches 7-spices pepper or cayenne

Pour enough oil into a heavy-bottomed saucepan or frying pan to come 1–1$\frac{1}{2}$" (2.5–3.75 cm) up the sides. Heat the pan on a high flame until a small piece of tofu dropped into the fat immediately bubbles (300–350°F, 150–175°C). Deep fry the tofu pieces, a few at a time, for one minute. Drain on absorbent paper. If you are on a low fat diet, lightly dip the drained tofu in boiling water and drain again. This removes excess oil. Combine the tofu, sugar, soy sauce and mirin in a small pan, bring to the boil, reduce heat and simmer uncovered until the tofu has absorbed most of the liquid, or it has evaporated. In the meantime add the onion slices to the soup stock and heat to boiling. Add the noodles and return to the boil. Serve soup and noodles in individual bowls and top each with tofu. Season each with pinch of 7-spices pepper or cayenne.

FRIED NOODLES

There are two ways of frying noodles: soft fried in a little oil or deep fried. Udon, somen and soba can be fried by either method. In each case the noodles are pre-cooked, drained and cooled. To soft fry noodles, heat 2 to 3 tablespoons oil, per 8 oz (1 cup) cooked noodles, in a heavy frying pan. Add the noodles and sauté with constant stirring for 4 to 5 minutes. To deep fry, separate the cooked noodles into single strands, fill heavy pan or deep frying pan with 3 to 4 inches (7–10 cm) oil and heat to 350°F (175°C). Drop in the noodles, a handful at a time, and fry until medium brown in colour. Remove with chopsticks and drain on absorbent paper.

SOFT FRIED UDON OR SOBA

This is a basic recipe; more elaborate additions are suggested below.

4 tablespoons vegetable oil
1 clove garlic, minced
1 oz (1 tablespoon) of ginger root, grated (optional)
½ medium carrot, grated
4 oz (¼ cup) Chinese cabbage, chopped
1 medium green pepper, diced
12 oz (1½ cups) udon or soba, cooked and drained
Togarashi or black pepper to taste
Soy sauce to taste

Heat the oil in a heavy frying pan, sauté the garlic and ginger for 2 to 3 minutes, then add the other vegetables. Fry until just soft cooked. Stir in the noodles, heat through, season with soy sauce and togarashi. Other ingredients that can be fried with noodles are:

(1) 2 paper-thin omelettes (see p. 43), cut into 1" (2.5 cm) strips
(2) 4 oz (¼ cup) French beans, cut into 1" (2.5 cm) pieces
(3) 2 stalks celery, chopped
(4) 1 medium onion, diced
(5) 2 spring onions, chopped
(6) 4 oz (¼ cup) bean sprouts
(7) 4 oz (¼ cup) cooked meat, sliced
(8) 4 oz (¼ cup) cooked fish, whole or sliced
(9) 1 medium lotus, sliced, or bamboo shoots
(10) 2 oz (¼ cup) mushrooms, sliced
(11) 4 shiitake, soaked for 20 minutes, hard stems removed, sliced
(12) 6 oz (¾ cup) tofu, 1" (2.5 cm) cubes
(13) 6 oz (¾ cup) fried tofu (see Fox Noodles p. 50)
(14) 4 oz (¾ cup) cheese, grated
(15) 4 oz (¼ cup) beans (soya, aduki, kidney, etc.) cooked. Combine with 2 tablespoons soy sauce, separate beans into equal portions, mash one portion, salt, recombine
(16) 4 oz (¼ cup) shrimps or prawns, shelled, deveined and cooked (see p. 79) or tinned

FRIED SOBA WITH SPINACH

This is not as far as I know, a traditional Japanese recipe, but I was given it by an American friend living in Japan. It looks Japanese, but tastes a little too much of garlic to be really authentic. My friend's mother was Italian. Anyway it's delicious.

2 tablespoons oil
4 cloves garlic, crushed
1 lb fresh spinach, washed, coarsely chopped and drained
12 oz (1½ cups) noodles, cooked
Salt and black pepper to taste

Heat the oil in a heavy pan. Add the garlic and sauté until light brown (about 3 minutes). Drop in the spinach, cover pan and lower heat. Stir occasionally. Simmer until spinach is completely wilted. Now stir in noodles, season with salt and black pepper and heat through. Serve.

FRIED SOBA WITH EGGS

3 tablespoons vegetable oil
4 eggs, beaten
Pinch of salt and black pepper
6 oz (¾ cup) Chinese cabbage, chopped
1 medium onion, thinly sliced
3 tablespoons soy sauce or 2 tablespoons miso
12 oz (1½ cups) soba, cooked and drained

Coat a heavy pan or frying pan with 1 tablespoon oil, heat and pour in the eggs. Season with salt and black pepper and scramble until well cooked. Remove eggs from pan and reserve. Add remaining oil to pan and lightly sauté cabbage and onion for about 3 minutes.

Stir in the soy sauce or miso, mix well, add noodles and eggs and heat through. Serve.

DEEP FRIED NOODLES (YAKI SOBA)

Yaki soba was the first dish I learned to order in Japanese. The name rolls off the tongue and the pronunciation is easy, but that is not the only reason for asking for it. The Japanese are masters at deep frying and yaki soba allows this talent full expression. For a special treat, try it with ginger and garlic or sweet and sour sauce. See recipes below.

2 tablespoons vegetable oil
½ medium carrot, cut into matchsticks
1 medium onion, cut into thin wedges
1 green pepper, cut into ½" (1.25 cm) strips
2 oz (¼ cup) mushrooms, sliced
2 tablespoons cornflour (blended with 4 table-spoons water)
1 tablespoon soy sauce
Oil for deep frying
8 oz (1½ cups) noodles, cooked and drained

Heat oil in a heavy pan, add all the vegetables and sauté for 4 to 5 minutes. Add water until the vegetables are just covered, cover pan, simmer for 5 minutes, then stir in cornflour and soy sauce and simmer a further 5 minutes. Deep fry noodles according to method given (see p. 51), drain on absorbent paper and divide among four bowls. Pour over vegetable sauce and serve.

DEEP FRIED NOODLES WITH SAUCE

Ingredients as for Deep Fried Noodles (above)

FOR GARLIC AND GINGER SAUCE

2 tablespoons soy sauce
2 tablespoons vinegar
1 oz (1 tablespoon) ginger root, grated
1 clove garlic, crushed
3 tablespoons water
3 tablespoons sugar

FOR SWEET AND SOUR SAUCE

3 tablespoons tomato purée
1 tablespoon soy sauce
3 tablespoons vinegar
2 tablespoons sugar
3 tablespoons water or fruit juice

Combine sauce ingredients and bring to the boil. Remove from heat. Follow recipe for Deep Fried Noodles, but, after sautéeing vegetables, add one of the sauces instead of water. Simmer for 2 minutes, stir in the cornflour and soy sauce and simmer, with frequent stirring, for a further five minutes. Deep fry noodles according to method given (see p. 51), drain on absorbent paper and divide among four bowls. Pour over vegetables and sauce and serve.

OTHER HOT NOODLE DISHES

CURRIED NOODLES

The ubiquitous curry has even reached Japan, although in a much milder version than the traditional Indian variety. It is popular served over noodles or rice. Modern youngsters eat curry with a spoon rather than chopsticks, and I remember sitting in a café near Okinawa University eating a bowl of soba, feeling proud because of my deftness with the chopsticks, when all around me sat students shovelling down curry and rice with spoons!

2 tablespoons vegetable oil
8 oz (1 cup) chicken, lean pork ot beef, diced into small cubes
1 medium onion, thinly sliced
2 medium potatoes, diced
1 medium carrot, thinly sliced
4 fl oz (½ cup) water
1–2 teaspoons mild curry powder
Pinch of salt
12 oz (1½ cups) noodles, cooked and drained
1 oz (1 tablespoon) ginger root (grated), chutney *or* 2 tablespoons finely chopped spring onion

Brown the meat or chicken in oil in a heavy pan, add the vegetables and sauté until soft. Make a paste with a little of the water and curry powder and add it with remaining water to pan. Add salt and ginger and cook while stirring for 5 to 10 minutes. The consistency should be quite thick; simmer to reduce liquid if necessary. Either stir in the noodles and warm through or heat noodles by pouring boiling water over them and serve curry sauce over the noodles. Garnish with chutney or, more authentically, with chopped spring onions.

MOON NOODLES (Tsukimi Udon)

This is not really my favourite dish. Raw eggs on hot soup I quite enjoy, but a full moon, in the shape of a raw egg, on a rice paddie, that is, a bowl of cold noodles, is too Japanese even for my palate. However, if you are a poetic or adventurous soul, try moon noodles; you never know, the dish may be just to your taste.

1½ pt (4½ cups) soup stock, chilled (remove all fat if meat or chicken-based stock)
4 tablespoons soy sauce
2 tablespoons sugar
12 oz (1½ cups) noodles, cooked and drained
4 eggs
1 bunch parsley or watercress, chopped

Combine the soup stock, soy sauce and sugar, mix well. Divide the noodles among four bowls, carefully break an egg, keeping the yolk intact, over each. Pour in the soup mixture and surround each egg with a garnishing of chopped parsley or watercress. Serve.

CHILLED AND SALAD NOODLES

SUMMER NOODLES (Hiyashi Somen)

The Japanese enjoy many foods cold that in the West we expect to eat hot. Chilled noodles are a great favourite, particularly in the summer, when stallholders appear on the streets selling bowls of hiyashi somen. Chilled noodles make a welcome change, for a summer meal, from our usual salads and sandwiches.

This recipe gives the basic method. You can elaborate upon it by using different garnishings.

12 oz (1½ cups) somen (or udon), cooked, drained and chilled
1½ pt (3¼ cups) soup stock, chilled (remove all fat if meat or chicken-based stock)
3 tablespoons mirin or sweet sherry (optional)
2 tablespoons soy sauce
Pinch 7-spices pepper or cayenne
1 oz (1 tablespoon) ginger root, grated
4 tablespoons parsley or watercress or spring onion or young spinach leaves

Divide soba among four bowls. Combine stock, mirin, soy sauce and 7-spices pepper and divide among four small bowls. Place ginger and parsley in central bowls and invite each guest to garnish his/her own bowl of noodles. Dip noodles into individual bowls of sauce and eat.

SUMMER NOODLES WITH SHRIMP AND EGG OR MUSHROOMS, CHICKEN AND FISH

Proceed as for Summer Noodles, but additionally garnish each bowl of noodles with a quarter portion of the following:

4 oz (½ cup) shrimps, tinned or fresh. If fresh use 8 shrimps in shells, drop into boiling water and cook until they turn pink (about 3 minutes). Drain, rinse in cold water, shell and devein.
2 paper-thin omelettes (see p. 43) cut into strips
4 shiitake, soaked for 20 minutes in little cold water. Remove any hard stems, cook in soaking water, uncovered, with ½ teaspoon sugar and one tablespoon soy sauce. Simmer until liquid is almost absorbed or evaporated.
6 oz (¾ cup) cooked chicken, sliced thinly
6 oz (¾ cup) cooked, filleted white fish

SUMMER NOODLES WITH MUSTARD AND MISO DRESSING

3 tablespoons miso
1 tablespoon sugar
1 tablespoon oil
4 tablespoons water
1 tablespoon vinegar
½ tablespoon English mustard
12 oz (1½ cups) noodles, cooked, drained and chilled
½ medium cucumber, sliced
2 tomatoes, quartered
2 eggs, hard boiled, sliced

Combine miso, sugar, oil and water and bring to the boil. Reduce heat and gently simmer for 4 to 5 minutes. Stir in vinegar and mustard, cool and chill. Divide noodles among four bowls, top each with miso and mustard dressing and surround in an attractive pattern with cucumber, tomato and egg. Serve. Try the following salad toppings and miso sauces as an alternative to those given in the recipe.

ALTERNATIVE SALAD TOPPINGS
2 stalks celery, chopped
1 bunch parsley, chopped
4 lettuce leaves, chopped
4 oz (1 cup) grated cheese

ALTERNATIVE DRESSINGS
Onion Miso Dressing:

1 tablespoon onion, minced
1 tablespoon vegetable oil
3 tablespoons vinegar

3 tablespoons lemon
2 tablespoons miso

Mayonnaise Miso:

4 tablespoons mayonnaise
2 tablespoons miso
1 tablespoon lemon juice
Pinch togarashi or black pepper

Combine dressing ingredients and mix well. Ordinary mayonnaise or French dressing also goes well with cold noodle salads.

PICKLES AND SALADS
(Tsukemono and Sunomono/Aemono)

For many foreigners, more than anything else, the distinctive and appetising smell of pickled vegetables or tsukemono reminds them of Japanese market places and households. Every sort of vegetable is pickled, although the most popular are Chinese cabbage and daikon. The pickles have a slightly crisp texture and tangy flavour, a good contrast to the blandness of white rice, and the two are often eaten together as a lunchtime snack.

A variety of pickling agents are used, including neat miso, but the most common are salt or a rice bran and salt mixture. Rice bran is the brown skin that surrounds each grain of rice and which is removed to give white rice. The vegetables to be pickled are left whole or cut into suitable shapes, layered in a wooden tub with lots of salt and pressed down with a heavy weight. The longer they are pressed, the more they come to resemble pickles. After four or five days the vegetables will have lost much of their water content and be submerged in a brine solution. The pickles are removed as required, rinsed in plenty of water, chopped up and served in small amounts with soy sauce and grated ginger. For a crispier and longer-lasting pickle, the vegetables are air dried before pickling. Daikon, particularly, is pickled in this way when it is known as 'all winter long' takuan. This salt-pressing pickling process is easily applied in a Western kitchen, and it is a useful way of preserving surplus garden vegetables.

The Japanese are great salad eaters, but not in the Western sense of the word. Instead they use a combination of pickles, vinegar-dressed salads called sunomono and partially-cooked vegetable salads known as aemono.

Most sunomono or vinegared salads are prepared at the time they are required, but some call for marinating for up to 24 hours. These salads are also called pickles, but they shouldn't be confused with the salt-pressed variety. Sunomono can be used to accompany a main meal or in larger amounts as a lunchtime salad.

Aemono, which means 'dressed things' are used like sunomono. They fill a gap between fresh salads and cooked vegetables not often explored in Western cookery. Aemono utilise a variety of dressings, most of which are excellent accompaniments to Western-style salads. They have none or almost no oil, and could be helpful in planning a low cholesterol diet.

There is considerable overlap between tsukemono, sunomono and aemono, and I am not going to try and strictly categorise them into different sections. Instead the recipes start with a general method for salt-pressing vegetables, followed by more specific pickling recipes, then a selection of sunomono and aemono salad dressings and finally a variety of recipes for vegetable and fish salads, both cooked and uncooked. Many of the methods described are widely applicable, and you do not need to be limited to those ingredients specified in particular recipes.

TSUKEMONO AND OTHER PICKLED VEGETABLES
In all the salt-pressing techniques the vegetables will continue to ferment in the tub for as long as you leave them. Thus when they become as sour as you wish, drain off the liquid and either store the pickles in a container in the refrigerator or bottle them in air-tight jars.

The quantities given in recipes that require vinegar are for malt or wine vinegar. The Japanese use a mild rice vinegar and if you use this type, increase the volume of vinegar stipulated in the recipes by one and a half times.

SALT PRESSED PICKLE OR SALAD – A GENERAL METHOD
Whether salt-pressed vegetables are called pickles or salads depends upon the duration of the pressing time. Many vegetables are delicious prepared this way, and, particularly in winter, they are more satisfying than a regular cold salad. Try cabbage, turnip, carrot or onion to start with.

Cut root vegetables into matchsticks or slices and chop or shred green vegetables into fine pieces. Place the vegetables in a large wooden tub, bowl or non-metallic container and generously sprinkle with salt. Place a wooden lid or plate directly on top of the vegetables and weight down with water-filled pan, stone, etc. Leave for one hour to five days. Pour off excess liquid as it collects or leave for more sour pickles. Use pickles as required and rinse in cold water if too salty. A small amount of pickles accompanying another dish is the best way to eat these salt-pressed vegetables.

MIXED VEGETABLE TSUKEMONO

4 medium carrots, thinly sliced
2 small turnips, quartered and sliced
1 small cabbage, cut in strips
2 cucumbers, thinly sliced
1 lb French beans (leave whole)
Salt
4 to 5 small chilli peppers (optional)

Place vegetables in colourful layers in a wooden tub or earthenware container. Generously sprinkle each layer with salt. Place a wooden lid or plate (about 2 lb) directly on the top of the vegetables and weigh down. Leave to ferment for four to five days, then use as required. Serve with soy sauce and/or vinegar or sesame seed oil. To prepare hot pickles, distribute the chilli peppers in the layers of vegetables before adding the salt. Soak the pickles in cold water if too salty for your taste.

Any of the vegetables used in the recipe can be prepared in the same way singly or in any convenient combination. Other suggestions are lettuce, daikon, spinach, cauliflower or aubergine.

An alternative method of salt pickling is as follows: Sterilise a number of large preserving jars and carefully load the vegetables in a colourful neat pattern. Boil a solution of salt and water (1 pint [2½ cups] water to 1 lb salt), cool and pour over vegetables. Cover and leave for a week. Remove pickles with fork or chopsticks, sterilised in boiling water.

VARIOUS PICKLING RECIPES

QUICK PICKLE
These pickles are ready two to 24 hours after preparation.

2 small turnips, quartered and diced
2 medium carrots, matchsticks
4 cabbage leaves, finely chopped
Peel of 1 lemon, grated
2 tablespoons salt

Sprinkle the cabbage leaves with a little of the salt, allow to stand for five minutes, then squeeze out the excess liquid by gently pressing. Mix all the ingredients in a salad bowl. Place a wooden lid or plate (1½ lb) directly on the top of the vegetables and weigh down for two to 24 hours. Store unused pickle in the refrigerator.

DAIKON OR TURNIP TSUKEMONO
This is another quick method of preparing fresh daikon or turnip pickles.

2 lb daikon or small white turnip
Salt
8 oz (1 cup) sugar
4 fl oz (½ cup) vinegar

Wash the vegetables and slice crosswise into neat ¼" (0.15 cm) thick circles. Place in colander and sprinkle with salt, ensuring it is evenly distributed throughout. Leave for one hour, then rinse and squeeze dry in a clean cloth. Transfer to a storage jar and pour over vinegar and sugar. Stir well. Refrigerate and use as required.

VINEGAR-PRESSED VEGETABLES

1 lb vegetables
10 fl oz (1¼ cups) vinegar
2 tablespoons sugar
2 teaspoons salt
4 tablespoons sesame seeds, toasted and crushed (optional)

Suggested vegetables – alone or in combination:

Carrots, thinly sliced
Cabbage, finely shredded
Cucumber, thinly sliced
Red or green pepper, deseeded, cut into 1" (1.5 cm) strips
Aubergine, sliced, salted, rinsed and drained

Combine vinegar, sugar and salt, and bring to the boil. Add the crushed sesame seeds and cool. Place vegetables in salad bowl or other non-metallic container with wide mouth, and pour on vinegar mixture. Stir well, then place a wooden lid or plate (about 2 lb) directly on top of vegetables and weigh down. Leave two to three hours. The vegetable can now be served. Leave whatever is not used in the pickling liquid and store in the refrigerator.

MISO PICKLED VEGETABLES

Vegetables buried in a tub of miso preserve very well and last indefinitely. Nowadays, however, it is an expensive method of pickling. It is still used in Japan, but not to the same extent as in the past. If you would like to try it on a small scale, here is the method for a number of vegetables, although miso pickling is applicable to many more. Fill a tub or other container with miso and prepare the vegetables as follows:

CARROT

Use whole or cut into lengths that will fit the tub. Boil for 30 seconds in lightly salted water and cool. Bury in miso. Ready in ten days.

CUCUMBER

Use whole or cut into lengths that will fit the tub. Sprinkle with salt and press in a bowl for one to two days. Discard excess liquid, bury in miso. Ready in one month.

DAIKON OR TURNIP

Air dry for two to three days. Quarter, bury in miso. Ready in two weeks.

GREEN PEPPER

Remove seeds and stem, cut into 1" (2.5 cm) strips. Sprinkle with salt and press in bowl for one to two days. Drain off liquid, bury in miso. Ready in one month.

Remove vegetables from miso as required. Clean off and return miso to container. Rinse pickles in water and cut to shape. Serve.

The miso can be used normally after all the pickles have been removed although it will be softer than usual due to moisture absorbed from the vegetables.

PICKLED MUSHROOMS I

This is not a pickle in the sense that it can be preserved over a long period. It does, however, keep well in the refrigerator. Serve hot or cold.

1 lb mushrooms, whole, halved or quartered (depending on size)
4 spring onions, finely chopped
6 oz (¾ cup) sugar
8 fl oz (1 cup) soy sauce
Salt to taste

Bring the sugar and soy sauce to the boil. Add the spring onions and simmer for two minutes. Toss in the mushrooms and return to the boil. Boil for three minutes, remove from the heat and allow to stand for ten minutes. Drain off the liquid, reserve for further use. Serve mushrooms hot or cold.

PICKLED MUSHROOMS II

1 lb small mushrooms, whole
6 oz (1¼ cups) turnips
3 tablespoons sake or white wine or sherry
3 tablespoons vinegar
2 tablespoons sugar
1 tablespoon soy sauce
1 tablespoon salt

Wash mushrooms and discard the stalks. Thread on to skewers and brush lightly with oil. Grill until well browned. Remove from skewers. Boil turnip in a little water until tender.

Drain and cool. Slice into rings and mix with mushrooms. Combine the other ingredients and pour over the mushrooms and turnips. Allow to stand for one hour in refrigerator before serving.

SWEET AND SOUR PICKLED CUCUMBERS

4 medium cucumbers, washed and thinly sliced
Salt
4 fl oz (⅓ cup) vinegar
2 tablespoons soy sauce
6 oz (¾ cup) sugar

Salt cucumber and place in a colander. Cover with plate plus weight, and press for 30 minutes. Rinse and squeeze dry in clean cloth. Combine other ingredients and stir until sugar is dissolved. Transfer cucumber to jar and pour over sweet and sour dressing. Chill and serve. Store unused pickle in a refrigerator.

PICKLED MELON

Once when I visited a friend's house in Japan, his father invited me to taste his home-made wine. It turned out to be a jar full of garlic cloves covered with sake, sealed and left for a year or two. I had a small glass. The taste is hard to describe, but I can still remember it. Fortunately, pickled melon has a much different taste, even though it uses the same pickling agent.

1 small melon, peeled, seeded and cut into 1"
    (2.5 cm) cubes
½ pt (1 cup) sake or medium sherry
2 tablespoons brandy
Pinch of salt

Put melon cubes into a sterilised preserving jar. Add the other ingredients, seal and leave for at least three days. Serve as a dessert. You may need to add more sake and brandy if the amount given does not cover the melon.

PICKLED AUBERGINE SALAD

1 large aubergine
Salt
3 tablespoons soy sauce
3 tablespoons sugar
3 tablespoons mirin or sweet sherry
1 teaspoon dry English mustard

Quarter the aubergine and cut each quarter into thin slices. Sprinkle salt generously over slices and lay in colander to drain. Leave 30 minutes to soften, rinse thoroughly, press out excess moisture and pat dry on a clean cloth. Prepare a thin paste of the other ingredients and coat aubergine with it. Cover and chill for two hours before serving.

KOMBU PICKLES

3" by 12" (7.5 cm by 30 cm) piece kombu, cut
    into 1" (2.5 cm) squares
Soy sauce

Cover the kombu in water and leave to soak for four hours or more. Drain and transfer to a heavy pan. Just cover the kombu in soy sauce, bring to the boil, reduce heat and very gently simmer until all the liquid has evaporated or been absorbed. Store in a sealed jar and use as required.

AEMONO AND SUNOMONO SALAD DRESSINGS
The dressings are named after the most dominant seasoning employed.

VINEGAR, SUGAR AND SOY DRESSING

This is a basic sunomono dressing and can be used with most vegetable or fish salads.

3 fl oz (⅓ cup) vinegar
1 teaspoon soy sauce
2 tablespoons sugar

Mix all the ingredients together, stir well and pour over salad

MISO AND VINEGAR DRESSING

This dressing can be made in endless variations. Do not stick to the quantities given in the recipe, but try different ratios of miso to vinegar to sugar. The consistency should be quite thick; add more miso if it is not. Experiment with adding herbs and spices to the dressing. It is a basic dressing, good with both cooked and uncooked salads.

2 tablespoons miso
1 tablespoon vinegar

2 teaspoons sugar
1 teaspoon lemon juice (optional)

Mix miso into a smooth paste with vinegar and sugar. Add lemon juice and stir well. Serve on salad or in individual bowls for each guest.

SESAME, VINEGAR AND SUGAR DRESSING

This is another general dressing, good with many salads.

3 tablespoons sesame seeds, toasted *or* 1½ tablespoons tahini
2 tablespoons vinegar
2 tablespoons sugar or mirin or sweet sherry
1 tablespoon soy sauce
1 tablespoon lemon juice

Pulverise sesame seeds in suribachi or mortar, add the other ingredients and continue to pound. When mixed well, pour over salad or serve in individual bowls for each guest. If you use tahini just combine all the ingredients and mix well.

MISO, SESAME AND VINEGAR DRESSING

This dressing goes well with green vegetables, seafoods and mushrooms.

2 tablespoons sesame seeds, toasted *or* 1 tablespoon tahini
2 tablespoons miso
2 tablespoons vinegar
1 tablespoon sugar

Prepare and use in the same way as the Sesame, Vinegar and Sugar Dressing (see above).

EGG DRESSING

A smooth yellow dressing, which complements light-coloured foods such as potatoes, aubergines, white fish, etc.

4 tablespoons vinegar
2 tablespoons sugar
1 teaspoon salt
1 tablespoon mirin or sherry (optional)
2 egg yolks, well beaten

Bring all the ingredients to the boil except the egg yolks. Take the mixture off the heat and add the yolks and stir briskly until the mixture is smooth and blended. Cool and serve over salad.

MUSTARD DRESSING

Good with cabbage, French beans, aubergines and seafood.

1 teaspoon dry English mustard
2 tablespoons vinegar
1 tablespoon soy sauce *or* 1 tablespoon miso paste
1 teaspoon sugar

Mix ingredients and blend well.

TOFU DRESSING

A good accompaniment to cooked vegetables such as potato, turnip, carrot, etc.

3 tablespoons sesame seeds, lightly toasted *or* 1½ tablespoons tahini
6 oz (¾ cup) tofu
3 tablespoons sugar
½ teaspoon salt
1 teaspoon soy sauce

Pound sesame seeds in a suribachi or mortar into a fine paste, or use tahini. Press excess moisture out of the tofu and add with the other ingredients to sesame seeds. Grind mixtures smooth. Gently mix dressing into salad and serve.

VEGETABLE AND FISH SALADS

RED AND GREEN PEPPER SALAD

Bell peppers are a relatively new vegetable to the Japanese, but just as the potato has been adopted in Europe, so has the pepper in Japan.

3 tablespoons soy sauce
1 teaspoon sugar
1 tablespoon mirin or sweet sherry
½ teaspoon togarashi or black pepper
2 tablespoons vegetable oil (sesame is best)
2 large red peppers and 2 large green peppers, deseeded, cut into ½" (1.25cm) strips

Combine the first four ingredients and mix well. Heat the oil in a heavy pan until very hot. Add the strips of pepper and cook for two minutes.

59

Pour in the soy mixture and stir; fry for 30 seconds to a minute. Serve immediately.

You may vary the above dish by adding 6 oz (1¼ cups) finely-sliced bamboo shoots or 8 oz (1¼ cups) cauliflower flowerettes to the peppers before frying.

FRIED AUBERGINE SALAD

1 lb aubergines, thinly sliced
Salt
2 tablespoons vegetable oil
4 tablespoons Mustard Dressing (see p. 59)

Generously salt aubergine, layer in a colander and leave to drain. Rinse, press out excess moisture and pat dry with a clean cloth. Heat oil in frying pan and fry aubergine slices until nicely brown on both sides. Serve hot with Mustard Dressing.

CARROT AND DAIKON OR TURNIP SALAD

1 lb young carrots, cut into matchsticks
8 oz (2 cups) daikon or small turnips, grated
Salt
4 tablespoons Sesame, Vinegar and Sugar Dressing (see p. 59)

Parboil carrot for two minutes in a little salted water. Drain, separately salt carrot and daikon or turnip. Leave for one hour, rinse and pat dry on a clean cloth. Combine vegetables and serve with dressing in individual bowls.

BEAN AND MUSHROOM SALAD

4 shiitake or 4 oz (1 cup) mushrooms, sliced
2 oz (½ cup) beans, cooked (aduki, kidney, broad beans, haricot, etc.)
One pinch salt
4 tablespoons Tofu Dressing (see p. 59)
4 tablespoons water or clear soup stock

Soak shiitake in cold water for 20 minutes. Remove hard stems and slice. Alternatively, use fresh mushrooms. Combine with beans, the pinch of salt and water or stock. Bring to the boil. Serve hot in individual bowls with tofu dressing separately.

SPINACH SALAD I

This recipe is suitable for other greens, such as lettuce, cabbage, broccoli, etc.

1 lb spinach, washed
3 tablespoons sesame seeds, lightly toasted or 1¼ tablespoons tahini
2 tablespoons soy sauce
¼ teaspoon salt
1 teaspoon vinegar
1 teaspoon dry mustard
2 spring onions, finely chopped (optional)
1 oz (1 tablespoon) ginger root, grated
½ teaspoon togarashi or black pepper

Pick over spinach and cut away any coarse stems. Boil in small amount of salted water until tender (about three minutes). Drain, cut into mouthful lengths, wrap in cloth and press to remove water. Pulverise the sesame seeds in a suribachi or mortar. Add the other ingredients, except spinach, and pound to a smooth mixture. Serve spinach and dressing in separate individual bowls.

A variation on this dish is to lightly stir fry 8 oz (2 cups) bamboo shoots (cut into matchsticks) and add to cooked spinach. The contrasting colours and textures complement one another.

SPINACH SALAD II

1 lb spinach, washed
Salt
Miso, Sesame and Vinegar Dressing (see p. 59)
2 sheets nori, toasted

Bring a large pan of salted boiling water to the boil. Collect spinach into four bunches with stems together, discard any coarse leaves or stems. Now holding each bunch by the stems, dip in and out of boiling water until spinach is just cooked. Repeat for each bundle. Put them together to form a cylinder, wrap in a cloth and squeeze out excess moisture. Cut into 2" (5 cm) lengths and, over them, pour over Miso Dressing. Garnish with crumbled nori and serve.

CUCUMBER SALAD

4 tablespoons vinegar
2 teaspoons sugar
1 teaspoon salt
1 oz (1 tablespoon) ginger root, grated
1 medium cucumber, cut in half lengthwise, thinly sliced

Combine first four ingredients, pour over cucumber and marinate for one hour. Chill and serve.

CUCUMBER AND WAKAME SALAD

4 oz (¼ cup) wakame seaweed
1 medium cucumber, thinly sliced
4 tablespoons vinegar
2 tablespoons soy sauce
2 teaspoons sugar
½ teaspoon salt

Rinse wakame and soak in cold water for 20–30 minutes. Drain, squeeze out excess moisture, and cut into 1½" (3.75 cm) lengths. Mix with cucumber. Combine last four ingredients and pour over vegetables. Serve.

GREEN BEAN AND CARROT SALAD

12 oz (2½ cups) French beans, cut in 1½" (3.75 cm) lengths
2 medium carrots, cut into matchsticks
Salt
2 tablespoons soy sauce
1 tablespoon sugar
Miso, Sesame and Vinegar Dressing or Tofu Dressing (see p. 59), both optional

Parboil the beans and carrots separately in a little salted water. Drain. In a small saucepan combine the carrots, beans, soy sauce and sugar. Simmer over a low heat until the vegetables have absorbed all the liquid. Remove from heat and cool. Serve on their own or with one of the suggested dressings.

BAMBOO SHOOT OR LOTUS ROOT SALAD

4 tablespoons vinegar
2 tablespoons sugar
2 tablespoons mirin or sherry
½ teaspoon salt
1 tinned bamboo shoot, drained, cut into matchsticks or 1 tinned lotus root, drained, cut into half-moon slices
4 lettuce or Chinese cabbage leaves

Combine the first four ingredients and heat in a small pan until the sugar dissolves. Pour mixture over the bamboo shoot or lotus root. Allow to cool. Arrange lettuce leaves in individual bowls, spoon on the vegetables and serve.

WHITE SALAD

White salad is a popular tofu dish. It usually contains konnyaku, a starchy substance made from the devil's tongue plant, but this is a difficult ingredient to obtain, and I have not included it in the recipe. If you do wish to include konnyaku in the salad, instructions on how to do so are given at the end of the recipe.

4 shiitake or 4 oz (1 cup) mushrooms, sliced
2 medium carrots, cut into matchsticks
4 fl oz (½ cup) soup stock or water
1 teaspoon salt
1 teaspoon soy sauce
Tofu Dressing (see p. 59)
2 tablespoons mint leaves, chopped (optional)

Soak the shiitake in cold water for 20 minutes. Cut off any hard stems and slice. Alternatively, use fresh mushrooms. Combine the carrots, mushrooms, stock, salt and soy sauce in a small saucepan and bring to the boil. Simmer until all the liquid has evaporated or been absorbed. Allow to cool. Stir in tofu dressing, garnish with chopped mint and serve.

To add konnyaku, cut one block into small rectangles, parboil and add to the simmering carrots and mushrooms.

ASPARAGUS AND CUCUMBER SALAD

This salad may be prepared with French beans, broccoli or Brussels sprouts if asparagus is not available.

2 tablespoons vegetable oil
2 tablespoons sesame seeds
3 tablespoons vinegar

3 tablespoons sugar
1 teaspoon soy sauce
½ teaspoon togarashi or black pepper
12 oz (3 cups) asparagus
¼ medium cucumber

Heat the oil in a frying pan, and fry the sesame seeds until brown. Cool and add seeds to vinegar, sugar, soy sauce and togarashi. Stir. Remove the base and tough stringy part of the asparagus, then cut them on the bias into 1" (2.5 cm) long pieces. Parboil in a little salted water for four to five minutes. Drain. Cut cucumber in half lengthwise and then into 3" (7.5 cm) long matchsticks. Combine cucumber and asparagus, pour over sauce, and carefully mix in. Chill for 30 minutes. Serve.

Bean sprouts or bamboo shoots, lightly stir fried, make an interesting variation.

CHRYSANTHEMUM SALAD

The following is an extract from an old book on salad making, published in Britain in the 1920s (*A Book of Salads* by Alfred Suzanne and C. Herman Senn). Those 'eccentric' Japanese greengrocers still sell bunches of fresh, cleaned chrysanthemum leaves in Yokohama and elsewhere.

Chrysanthemum Salad

Knowing the eccentric manners and tastes of the Japanese, it is not astonishing to find that they use chrysanthemum flowers as a salad, seasoning them like lettuce with salt, pepper, oil and vinegar after having washed and drained them. It seems that this is a popular dish, and at Yokohama when the chrysanthemum is in flower all the greengrocers sell them carefully washed and picked. The most appreciated variety is that with dark yellow flowers.

One other extract from the book. It's for a 'Japanese Salad'. Except for the truffle it could be true.

Japanese Salad

Alexandre Dumas *fils* invented this salad, and one of the characters in *Frarcillon* gives the recipe. Cook some new potatoes in meat stock. Cut them into slices and put them into a salad bowl with cooked mussels and a few sprigs of celery heart. There should be rather more potatoes than mussels. Add some fresh truffles cut in slices, salt, pepper, oil, vinegar, and a little chopped tarragon.

VINEGARED MUSSELS

If you have any chrysanthemum flowers in bloom, pluck off a few petals and use to garnish this dish or any of the fish salads.

2 lb mussels in shells, washed and rinsed
1 tablespoon soy sauce
2 tablespoons sugar
2 tablespoons vinegar
2 tablespoons sake or white wine

Boil the mussels in plenty of water until shells open. Extract the mussels and allow to cool. Bring last four ingredients to the boil and cool. Pour dressing over mussels and marinate in the refrigerator for four to five hours.

Miso and Vinegar Dressing (see p. 58) also goes well with mussels.

MACKEREL IN VINEGAR DRESSING

A different way of preparing mackerel which gives it an exciting new flavour. The mackerel are not cooked, but you would never tell from the taste.

1 lb mackerel, cleaned, scaled and filleted
Salt
5 fl oz (⅝ cup) vinegar
1 tablespoon sugar
2 tablespoons fresh parsley, chopped
1 oz (1 tablespoon) ginger root, grated (optional)
2 tablespoons lemon juice
1 tablespoon soy sauce

Rub salt into the fish on both sides and leave covered in refrigerator for six hours or longer (overnight is fine). Combine vinegar, sugar and water and marinate salted fish in mixture for 30 minutes. Now cut mackerel into very thin slices (½" or 1.25 cm) and arrange in individual bowls. Garnish each bowl with parsley and serve with a dipping sauce of ginger, lemon and soy sauce.

SHELLFISH (CUCUMBER) SALAD

French beans may be used in place of cucumber. See Abalone and French Bean Salad recipe below for preparation of beans. Both effectively complement the shellfish in colour and texture.

4 oz (¼ cup) cooked shellfish (lobster, prawns, crab, shrimp, etc.)
2 tablespoons sake or sweet white wine *or* 2 tablespoons vinegar and 1 tablespoon sugar
1 medium cucumber
Salt
2 hard boiled egg yolks
2 teaspoons sugar
1 tablespoon vinegar
1 teaspoon salt

Cut up the shellfish meat or leave small items, like shrimps, whole. Marinate in sake, or alternative, for one hour. Partially peel cucumber leaving little strips of green to add colour to the dish. Cut into half lengthwise and thinly slice each half crosswise. Sprinkle with salt, leave 30 minutes. Rinse in cold water and squeeze dry in a clean cloth. Mash the egg yolks with sugar, vinegar and salt. Combine the shellfish and cucumber and serve in individual dishes with side bowls of yolk dressing.

ABALONE OR SHRIMP AND FRENCH BEAN SALAD
Cucumber may be used in place of French beans. See Shellfish (Cucumber) Salad above for preparation of cucumber.

1 lb French beans cut into 1½" (3.75 cm) pieces
Salt
1 tablespoon cornflour
2 tablespoons water
1 tablespoon sugar
4 fl oz (½ cup) vinegar
3 tablespoons sesame seeds, toasted
8 oz (1¼ cups) tinned abalone or shrimps

Parboil beans in a little salted water for five to six minutes. Immediately plunge into cold water to retain vivid green colour. For slightly softer beans, boil a minute or two longer. Mix the cornflour and water into a smooth paste, add the sugar and vinegar, bring to the boil, stirring constantly. Reduce heat and simmer for five minutes. Add sesame seeds and cool. Cut abalone into thin strips. Combine with beans and dressing. Chill and serve.

SALMON AND VEGETABLE SALAD IN LEMON SHELLS

3 tablespoons vinegar
1½ tablespoons sugar
½ teaspoon salt
8 oz (1¼ cups) daikon or small sweet turnips, grated *or* 4 oz (¼ cup) small red radish, thinly sliced
4 oz (¼ cup) salmon, fresh boiled or tinned
2 large lemons, cut in halves
1 tablespoon parsley, chopped

Combine vinegar, sugar and salt with vegetables and salmon. Scoop out the lemon halves and fill skins with mixture. Decorate with parsley and sprinkle with lemon juice squeezed from the lemon flesh.

PIG'S EAR AND PEANUT SALAD
This intriguing recipe was given to me by a Japanese friend with a sense of humour, who knew I was interested in peasant dishes. I am told by people who have eaten jelly fish that they taste similar to pig's ear! Whatever, this salad should surprise your friends and the butcher.

4 oz (½ cup) pig's ear
Pinch salt
4 tablespoons peanut butter
1 tablespoon miso
2 tablespoons vinegar
1 tablespoon sugar
1 small cucumber, thinly sliced

Singe the ear over a flame and scrape off any hairs with the edge of a knife. Rinse ear under running water, place in a pan and just cover with water. Bring to the boil and gently boil until cooked tender (about 30 minutes). Drain. Score across ear with shallow knife cuts and sprinkle with salt. Set aside. Combine peanut butter, miso, vinegar and sugar, and pour over cucumber in a bowl. Rinse the ear under cold water, drain, cut into pieces and stir into bowl. Serve.

VEGETABLES

For general information on Japanese cooked vegetables, see the Introduction. The vegetable recipes have been arranged in alphabetical order, with the first letter of a vegetable's best-known English name deciding its position. The methods used in the preparation of vegetable dishes are designed to retain and highlight the individual taste, texture and colour of each vegetable. Recipes containing vegetable ingredients are to be found in nearly every chapter in the book but in this chapter, with one or two exceptions, the recipes will be solely vegetable dishes.

AUBERGINES (EGG PLANT)
Japanese aubergines are smaller and a little tenderer than the Western variety, but the two are interchangeable. Before cooking aubergines should be sliced, or cut into whatever shape is required for the recipe, placed in a colander, sprinkled with salt and left for 30 minutes to an hour, then rinsed and drained. This process removes excess moisture and bitter juices. Aubergines are not normally peeled before use. Remember that aubergine dishes often improve when reheated and are usually as good cold as hot.

AUBERGINE WITH MISO AND SESAME (Goma Nasubi Miso)

1 lb aubergines, cut into ¾" (2 cm) cubes, salted, rinsed and drained
2 tablespoons sesame seeds, toasted
6 tablespoons oil
3 tablespoons miso
3 tablespoons sugar

1 tablespoon soy sauce
2 tablespoons mirin, white wine or sherry
3 fl oz (⅓ cup) soup stock or water

Heat oil in a heavy pan, add aubergines and sauté for three to four minutes. Stir frequently. Grind sesame seeds to a paste in suribachi or mortar, and combine with next five ingredients. Pour mixture over aubergines and simmer gently until heated through. Serve hot over noodles or rice, or chilled in a bed of lettuce.

GRILLED AUBERGINE
This is an excellent way to prepare aubergines for people on a low-fat diet. In Japan they would be cooked over a charcoal fire; if you have a barbecue grill try it this way, otherwise a preheated oven grill will do.

1 lb aubergines, cut into 1" (2.5 cm) thick slices, salted, rinsed and drained
Salt
Soy sauce to taste

Preheat grill. Dry aubergines on a clean cloth. Very lightly sprinkle with salt. Grill until soft (two to three minutes each side). Serve with soy sauce.

SPICY AUBERGINES (Korai Nasubi)

1 lb aubergines, cut into ¾" (2 cm) cubes, salted, rinsed and drained
4 tablespoons oil
1 oz (1 tablespoon) ginger root, grated
1 clove garlic, crushed
Good pinch 7-spices pepper or cayenne or hot pepper sauce
1 medium leek or onion, thinly sliced

3 fl oz (⅓ cup) soup stock or water
1 teaspoon sugar
1 tablespoon chopped chives or parsley or spring onion *or* 1 sheet nori, toasted, crumbled

Heat oil in a heavy pan, add aubergine and sauté for three to four minutes. Stir frequently. Remove aubergines from the pan, drain and reserve excess oil. Put aubergines to one side and return reserved oil to pan. Add ginger, garlic, leek, and 7-spices pepper and sauté over high flame for 30 seconds. Reduce heat, pour in stock and sugar and mix well. Add the aubergines, bring to the boil. Turn off heat and serve garnished with chives, etc.

BEEF-STUFFED AUBERGINES

2 large or 4 small aubergines
Salt
6 oz (¾ cup) minced beef
1 egg
2 oz (1 cup) breadcrumbs
½ medium onion, diced
2 teaspoons soy sauce
Pinch salt and togarashi or black pepper
2 tablespoons sesame seeds, toasted
2 to 3 tablespoons cornflour
Oil for deep frying
2 oz (2 tablespoons) ginger root, grated

Cut aubergines lengthwise down the middle, but do not cut completely in half; leave about 1" (2.5 cm) of stem end intact. Soak in lightly salted water. Meanwhile, combine beef, egg, breadcrumbs, onion, soy sauce, salt and pepper and mix well. Drain aubergines, pat dry on clean cloth and open them out as much as possible. Sprinkle cornflour on inside surfaces and stuff beef mixture between. At this point it may be necessary to clamp edges together with toothpicks. Sprinkle bulging edges of stuffing with any remaining cornflour. Pour oil 3–4" (7.5–10 cm) deep into a heavy pan, heat to 350°–360°F(175°–185°C), and carefully lower in stuffed aubergines. Deep fry four to five minutes. Remove with slotted spoon and serve with grated ginger. Minced pork or chicken or shrimps may be used in place of beef.

BAMBOO SHOOTS (Takenoko)
Even tinned bamboo shoots retain the crunchy texture of the fresh plant, and they contrast well with softer vegetables if the two are served together.

BOILED BAMBOO SHOOTS

8 oz (1½ cup) bamboo shoots, cut into ½" (1.25 cm) thick matchsticks
1 pt (2½ cups) soup stock
2 teaspoons soy sauce
1 tablespoon sugar

Combine all the ingredients in a heavy pan. Bring to the boil, reduce heat and simmer for approximately 15 minutes. Drain, reserve liquid for further use if required. Serve.

GRILLED BAMBOO SHOOTS

2 tablespoons soy sauce
1 tablespoon vinegar
1 tablespoon sake or white wine or dry sherry
1 teaspoon sugar
Pinch 7-spices pepper or cayenne
2 tablespoons soup stock or water
8 oz (1½ cups) bamboo shoots cut into ¼" (0.5 cm) thick slices

Combine first six ingredients and bring to the boil. Remove from heat, add bamboo shoots and marinade for one hour. Drain and reserve liquid. Grill bamboo shoot slices under low flame for five to six minutes each side. Brush each side two to three times with marinade liquid during grilling.

BAMBOO SHOOTS WITH TOFU

2 tablespoons vegetable oil
1 oz (1 tablespoon) ginger root, grated
6 oz (⅓ cup) tofu, cut into 1" (2.5 cm) cubes
2 tablespoons soy sauce
½ teaspoon sugar
6 oz (1 cup) bamboo shoots, thinly sliced
4 fl oz (½ cup) water

Heat oil in a heavy pan, add ginger and sauté for two to three minutes. Add tofu and gently fry for a few minutes on both sides. Add remaining ingredients, lower heat and simmer in

65

uncovered pan for 20 minutes or until most of the liquid has been absorbed or evaporated.

BAMBOO SHOOTS WITH STEAMED DOUGH

Proceed as for Bamboo Shoots with Tofu (see p. 65), but replace tofu with steamed dough prepared as follows:

3 oz (¾ cup) plain flour
2 fl oz (¼ cup) water

Mix flour and water. Knead for five minutes. Cover and allow to stand 30 minutes. Roll out on floured board into 1" (2.5 cm) diameter sausage shape. Cut into ½" (1.25 cm) thick rings, lay on greased waxed paper and steam for 30 minutes.

BEAN SPROUTS (Moyashi)

More often used in conjunction with other vegetables or fresh in salads, bean sprouts are nevertheless tasty just quick fried with garlic and ginger. They are normally grown from mung beans. For a plant food they have a very high protein to calorie content ratio.

FRIED BEAN SPROUTS

2 tablespoons vegetable oil
1 clove garlic, crushed
2 tablespoons soy sauce
1 oz (1 tablespoon) ginger root, grated
1 lb bean sprouts
Togarashi or black pepper to taste

Heat oil in a heavy pan, add garlic and sauté for two to three minutes. Add soy sauce, ginger and bean sprouts. Toss about in pan and fry until bean sprouts have softened but not completely wilted (about three minutes). Serve sprinkled with togarashi or black pepper.

BEAN SPROUTS WITH TOFU

Bean sprouts and tofu combined are a rich source of vegetable protein.

2 tablespoons oil
1 clove garlic, crushed
1 medium onion, diced
12 oz (2¼ cups) tofu, cut in 1" (2.5 cm) cubes

12 oz bean sprouts
1 teaspoon salt
1 tablespoon soy sauce

Heat oil in a heavy pan, add garlic, sauté for two to three minutes. Add onion and tofu. Fry, stirring constantly, until tofu is lightly browned on both sides. Add bean sprouts, salt and soy sauce. Mix well, heat through and serve very hot.

BROCCOLI

This hardy vegetable thrives well in colder, mountainous areas, of which there are many in northern Japan. Substitute cauliflower, cut into small flowerettes or Brussels sprouts, left whole if small, otherwise halved, for broccoli in any of the following recipes.

BROCCOLI WITH MISO

3 pt (7½ cups) water
1 teaspoon salt
1 lb broccoli cut into flowerettes
2 tablespoons miso
1 tablespoon water
Pinch togarashi or black pepper

Bring water to boil, add salt and drop in broccoli. Cook, uncovered, until broccoli is bright green and tender (about five minutes). Drain and quickly submerge flowerettes in cold water (this seals in colour and stops further cooking), drain and arrange in serving bowl. Cream miso, water and pinch of togarashi. Dip broccoli into miso sauce before eating.

BROCCOLI WITH SOY SAUCE AND SESAME SEEDS

3 pt (7½ cups) water
1 teaspoon salt
1 lb broccoli, cut into flowerettes
2 tablespoons sesame seeds, toasted
2 tablespoons soy sauce

Cook broccoli as described in Broccoli with Miso recipe (above). Serve sprinkled with sesame seeds and soy sauce.

BROCCOLI WITH MUSTARD SAUCE

3 pt (7½ cups) water
1 teaspoon salt
1 lb broccoli, cut into flowerettes
2 tablespoons dry English mustard
2 tablespoons water
2 tablespoons soy sauce
2 tablespoons sugar

Bring water to boil, add salt and parboil broccoli for three to four minutes. Drain. Combine other ingredients, pour over broccoli and leave to marinate for one hour. Serve cold or drain off marinade, heat to boiling, toss in broccoli, heat through and serve.

BURDOCK (Gobo)

Burdock is a dark brown root vegetable, long, thin, and tapering to a point at one end. In Japanese markets they are sold in bunches or at stalls that specialise in burdock and they can be bought in bags, already peeled, soaked and chopped. This work is all done by hand, in between serving the customers and is fascinating to watch. Unfortunately, burdock is no longer generally available in the West (although more available in America than Europe), but in Japan it is an important and widely used vegetable. It has a tough texture, and the larger ones are sometimes pounded with a heavy wooden roller before use. To prepare burdock for cooking, hold the root under running water and scrape off the dark peel. Cut into 2" (5 cm) long pieces and cut these individually into thin matchsticks. Alternatively, thinly slice into rounds. Soak burdock pieces in cold water for 20 minutes to remove slightly alkaline taste. Drain and proceed as below.

BURDOCK WITH FRENCH BEANS

1 medium burdock root, prepared as described
  above
Water
2 tablespoons vegetable oil
1 tablespoon miso
2 teaspoons grated lemon peel

Heat oil in a heavy pan, add burdock and sauté for three to four minutes. Just cover with water and simmer until tender. Add more water if necessary. Cream miso with a little of the cooking water and stir paste into pan. Add lemon peel, mix in well and simmer, uncovered, over a very low heat until all liquid has been absorbed or evaporated. Stir frequently. This is good served with parboiled spinach or fresh watercress.

BURDOCK COILS (Gobo Machi)

Burdock roots, wrapped in sheets of pork and poached.

4 burdock roots
1 lb lean pork, thinly sliced
1 pt (2½ cups) water
2 tablespoons sugar
4 tablespoons sake or white wine
4 tablespoons soy sauce

Trim the skin off the burdock roots and soak in water for one hour. Drain and wrap roots in pieces of pork, secured in place with toothpicks. Place in a heavy pan and pour over the water. Bring to the boil, add sugar, sake and soy sauce, reduce heat and simmer, uncovered, for one hour. Serve.

CABBAGE (Chinese and White)

Chinese cabbage either pickled, quick fried, or in soups, salads or stuffed is most popular in Japan. It is now generally available in the West, but if you have any trouble obtaining it, ordinary white cabbage is a good substitute. Chinese cabbage takes a slightly shorter time to cook than white cabbage, so in the recipes allow a slightly longer cooking time for the latter. The recipes, unless otherwise stated, are good for both types of cabbage.

PLAIN BRAISED CABBAGE

1 lb cabbage, coarsely chopped
2 tablespoons vegetable oil
Soy sauce and togarashi or black pepper to taste

Heat oil in a heavy pan, add cabbage and sauté briskly over a high heat. Stir frequently. After two to three minutes, reduce heat, cover and simmer for 10 to 15 minutes. Stir occasionally. Serve seasoned with soy sauce and togarashi to taste. To add colour to the dish, add one medium carrot, cut into matchsticks, to cabbage before cooking.

CABBAGE WITH MISO AND MUSTARD SAUCE

1 lb cabbage, finely shredded
8 fl oz (¼ cup) water
2 tablespoons miso
1 tablespoon English mustard
2 tablespoons sugar
2 tablespoons vinegar

Boil water in a large pan, toss in cabbage, return to the boil. Reduce heat, cover and simmer until just tender (about five minutes). Drain and squeeze cabbage. Combine other ingredients into a smooth paste, pour over cabbage, stir in and serve hot.

CABBAGE ROLLS

8 large cabbage leaves
4 shiitake or 4 oz (1 cup) mushrooms
2 tablespoons vegetable oil
1 medium onion, finely diced
½ medium carrot, grated
4 tablespoons soy sauce
1 teaspoon salt
1 teaspoon sugar
2 oz (⅓ cup) cooked somen or (5 cm) vermicelli cut into 2" lengths
1 pt (2 cups) soup stock or 1 pt (2 cups) water and 2" (5 cm) piece of kombu
2 tablespoons parsley

Place cabbage leaves in a colander and pour boiling water over them. Reserve water and repeat process with the same water until leaves just soften up. Put aside. Soak the shiitake in cold water for 20 minutes. Drain, cut away any hard stems and thinly slice. Alternatively, use thinly sliced mushrooms. Heat oil in a heavy frying pan, add onion and fry until light brown, drop in carrots, then mushrooms. Stir fry each one for two minutes after addition. Add noodles, 2 tablespoons sauce, ½ teaspoon salt and sugar, mix well and remove from heat.

Lay one cabbage leaf flat and, on one end, spoon 2–3 tablespoons of sautéed vegetables and noodles. Roll the leaf up, tucking in the ends and secure with toothpick or twine. Repeat for each leaf. Put stock or kombu and water in pan, add remaining soy sauce and salt and bring to the boil, lower in cabbage rolls, return to the boil, reduce heat, cover and simmer for ten minutes. Lift rolls out with slotted spoon, arrange in serving dish, pour over some of the cooking liquid, garnish with parsley and serve. For variety add minced meat or chicken to the stuffing mixture, or enclose stuffing in fried tofu before wrapping in leaves as described below.

Aburage or fried tofu is normally sold in Japan in small rectangular blocks. It is available at Chinese provision stores, or you can make your own (see p.00). Slit along three sides of a block, repeat for total of four blocks. Open up into flat sheets. Douse aburage sheets with boiling water to remove excess oil and drain. Place half a sheet below and half above vegetable and noodle stuffing before wrapping up in cabbage leaves.

CHINESE CABBAGE AND SPINACH ROLLS

This is a good method of serving greens. Even children enjoy the colours and taste.

8 Chinese cabbage leaves
8 oz (1½ cups) spinach
Salt
2 tablespoons soy sauce
1 tablespoon lemon juice

Place cabbage leaves in a colander and pour boiling water over them. Reserve water and repeat process with same water until leaves just soften up. Pour over cold water and set aside. Collect the stems of the spinach leaves together and tie spinach into four bunches with twine. Cook bunches in a little salted water until stems are just soft. Drain, rinse in cold water. Place two cabbage leaves flat and overlapping. Remove twine from one bunch of spinach and lay the spinach horizontally across cabbage leaves. Roll into a tight bundle and squeeze out excess moisture. Repeat with remaining ingredients and allow rolls to stand for 20 minutes. Cut into 1" (2.5 cm) thick sections. Serve sprinkled with soy sauce and lemon juice. Replace spinach with watercress if it is more easily available or for variation.

CARROTS
Did you ever as a child turn your nose up at boiled cabbage or spinach? Well, Japanese children seem to reserve this reaction for the poor carrot, but don't let that put you off the recipes.

CARROT WITH SESAME

2 tablespoons vegetable oil
2 medium carrots, grated
Salt to taste
2 tablespoons sesame seeds, toasted

Heat the oil in a heavy pan, add the carrots and sauté for five minutes. Stir frequently. Season with salt to taste, stir in the sesame seeds, sauté for a further five minutes and serve.

BOILED CARROTS
As for Boiled Bamboo Shoots (see p. 65), but substitute 2 medium carrots, cut into flower shapes, for the bamboo shoots.

CARROTS WITH MASHED TOFU

2 tablespoons vegetable oil
2 medium carrots, thinly sliced
Pinch of salt
6 oz (⅓ cup) tofu, squeezed and drained
4 oz (¼ cup) French beans, parboiled in lightly salted water

Heat oil in a heavy pan, add the carrots and sauté for five minutes. Add pinch of salt and leave to cool. Mash tofu in a serving dish and mix in carrot and green beans. Serve.

To make the dish more filling, stir in 4 oz (⅔ cup) cooked somen or vermicelli and garnish with sesame seeds and soy sauce.

CELERY
Celery is a rarity in Japan, and is considered a special treat. It is cooked very lightly.

4 fl oz (½ cup) water
4 stalks celery, cut on the bias into thin slices
Salt

Bring water to the boil, add salt, drop in celery and cook over high heat for one minute. Drain. Serve with either of these sauces:

SESAME SEED SAUCE
3 tablespoons sesame seeds
1 tablespoon soy sauce
2 tablespoons water

Grind sesame seeds to a paste in suribachi or mortar. Stir in soy sauce and water. Mix well. Pour over celery.

SOY AND GINGER SAUCE
3 tablespoons soy sauce
1 teaspoon sugar
2 oz (2 tablespoons) ginger root, grated

Combine and pour over celery.

CORN ON THE COB
A regular sight during the summer in the southern islands of Japan are roadside venders selling corn on the cob grilled over an open charcoal fire. Served very hot and a touch blackened, they are handed to the buyer with a toothpick stuck in either end. A lovely snack and excellent barbecue meal. To barbecue simply coat corn with oil and cook over charcoal fire, rotating regularly to ensure even cooking. Serve with soy sauce or butter if you wish.

More conventionally you may cook corn on the cob in the oven. Preheat oven to 450°F (230°C). Wrap corn in aluminium foil and bake for 10–15 minutes.

CUCUMBER
The Japanese do not normally cook cucumber, but rather serve it chilled with other vegetables and a dressing (see Pickles and Salads, p. 55). The following recipes have been heavily influenced by Chinese cooking, which does make use of cooked cucumbers.

CUCUMBER, CARROT AND WATER-CRESS RICE CASSEROLE

2 tablespoons vegetable oil
8 oz (1¼ cups) cucumber, cut into ¼" (0.5 cm) thick slices and then quartered
2 medium carrots, cut into ¼" (0.5 cm) thick slices and then quartered
1 bunch watercress, cut into 1" (2.5 cm) lengths
1 lb (2¼ cups) rice, washed and drained
1 teaspoon salt
1½ pt (3¼ cups) soup stock or water
1 sheet toasted nori, optional

Coat base of a casserole dish with oil. Arrange vegetables in the bottom. Cover with rice, add stock or water and bring to the boil. Gently stir, but keep vegetables below rice. Cover, reduce heat and simmer for 15 minutes. Remove from heat and allow to stand a further 15 minutes. Serve garnished with crumbled nori.

CUCUMBER AND MUSHROOMS

1 medium cucumber, thinly sliced
Salt
2 tablespoons vegetable oil
4 oz (¼ cup) mushrooms, sliced
2 tablespoons sesame seeds
3 tablespoons soy sauce
1 tablespoon sugar

Layer cucumber slices in colander and salt each layer. Allow to stand 30 minutes, rinse, drain and dry on clean cloth. Heath oil in a heavy pan, add mushrooms and cucumbers. Cook over a high heat stirring constantly until both vegetables are tender (two to three minutes). Remove from heat. Stir in soy sauce and sugar and serve sprinkled with sesame seeds.

FRENCH BEANS

Young French beans topped and tailed parboiled in a little salted water for four to five minutes, drained, immersed for a few moments in cold water, to preserve their colour, and served on their own make an excellent side dish. French beans are also used in many Japanese recipes as a garnishing or as an ingredient in pickles or cold cooked salads.

FRENCH BEAN CUSTARD

4 fl oz (½ cup) soup stock
2 tablespoons soy sauce
Pinch of salt
8 oz (1¼ cups) French beans, cut in half crosswise
3 eggs, beaten

Bring stock, soy sauce and salt to the boil in an 'oven-to-table' style casserole dish. Add French beans, return to the boil, cover, reduce heat and simmer for five minutes. Pour in beaten egg, cover again and simmer on very low heat until eggs set. Serve straight on to table.

FRENCH BEANS WITH SESAME AND MIRIN SAUCE

8 oz (1¼ cups) French beans, cut diagonally into ¼" (0.5 cm) pieces, parboiled in little salted water
Pinch of salt
1 tablespoon mirin or sherry
4 tablespoons sesame seeds, toasted
1 tablespoon sugar
1 tablespoon soy sauce
2 tablespoons stock or water

Arrange French beans in four individual bowls. Combine salt and mirin and sprinkle lightly over beans. Pound sesame seeds to a paste in suribachi or mortar, add sugar, soy sauce and stock or water. Mix well and pour over beans. Serve.

JAPANESE RADISH (Daikon)

The name means large root, and these vegetables can indeed be up to two feet (60 cm) in length and a foot (30 cm) in circumference. They have quite a sharp flavour when fresh and grated. Fresh daikon is used to add bite to a dish either as a garnish or in a dipping sauce. Cooked or salted the flavour becomes milder. Small white turnips make a good substitute. With young daikon the greens can be cooked in a little salted water and served with soy sauce. They are a rich source of Vitamin C.

Daikon is not generally available in the West, except at specialist shops, but it is worth trying to obtain if you know a stockist. Substitute daikon in any of the turnip recipes (see pp. 76–77) also see Pickles and Salads (p. 55).

LEEKS

The flavour of the Japanese leek is milder than the Western variety, and more akin to the taste of young leeks. Both the green stem and white root section are used. Thinly sliced leek is particularly popular as a garnishing in clear soups or dipping sauces. Scallions or spring onions or young leeks can be used in any of the recipes that specify leeks.

GRILLED LEEKS

4 leeks, sliced into 1½" (3.75 cm) lengths
2 tablespoons vegetable oil

2 tablespoons miso
2 tablespoons sugar
2 tablespoons mirin or sherry (optional)
OR
4 tablespoons soy sauce
Pinch of 7-spices pepper or cayenne

Pre-heat grill. Divide leek pieces on to four skewers. Brush with oil. Combine miso, sugar and mirin or soy sauce and 7-spices pepper. Grill leeks until lightly browned all over. Remove from the grill and brush with either miso or soy sauce mixture. Return to the grill and cook a further two minutes. The sauce-brushed leeks will burn easily so take care. Serve hot.

SKEWERED VEGETABLES

This follows the same method and uses the same brushing sauces as for Grilled Leeks (above), but utilises a variety of vegetables.

1 leek, sliced into 1½" (3.75 cm) lengths
4 oz (¼ cup) tofu cut into four pieces, deep fried (see p. 77)
1 small carrot cut into four pieces, parboiled in lightly salted water for four to five minutes
1 small lotus root, cut into four pieces

Pre-heat grill. Skewer vegetables in a colourful pattern on each of four skewers. Now follow exactly the same method as for Grilled Leeks, using the same basting sauces.

LOTUS ROOT (Renkon)

The fresh variety is not generally available, but tinned lotus root retains the slightly sweet flavour and slightly crunchy texture of the fresh vegetable. The hollow spaces that run its length form lovely patterns when it's sliced, and lotus root adds to the visual impact of any cooked or salad dish to which it is added.

LOTUS ROOT AND LEMON

8 oz (1½ cups) lotus root, thinly sliced
2 tablespoons vegetable oil
Juice of 1 lemon
2 tablespoons water
Pinch of salt

Heat oil in a heavy pan, add lotus root and gently sauté on both sides for two to three minutes. Squeeze in lemon juice, water and pinch of salt, cover and simmer for five minutes. Serve.

LOTUS ROOT AND SEAWEED

2 tablespoons vegetable oil
1 medium onion, thinly sliced
1 medium carrot, grated
4 oz (¼ cup) lotus root, thinly sliced
4 oz (¼ cup) hijiki, reconstituted (see p. 15)
2 tablespoons miso
6 fl oz (¼ cup) water

Heat oil in a pan, add the onion, followed by carrot and lotus root; sauté each for one minute after addition. Dry the hijiki on a clean cloth, add to vegetables and sauté for three minutes. Cream miso in a little of the water and add with remaining water to pan. Cover and simmer for ten minutes. Serve hot or cold.

DEEP FRIED LOTUS ROOT AND BAKED CHESTNUTS

2 oz (⅓ cup) lotus root, cut into paper-thin slices
Oil for deep frying
4 oz (¼ cup) baked chestnuts (see p. 35)
Salt and togarashi or black pepper to taste

Soak lotus root in lightly salted water for one hour. Drain, rinse in cold water, drain again and dry in a clean cloth. Heat oil to 350°F (175°C).

THE JAPANESE COOKBOOK

Deep fry lotus root until crisp. Drain on absorbent paper. Skewer chestnuts and serve one skewer per person with a portion of deep fried lotus root. Season to taste with salt and togarashi or black pepper.

MARROW AND PUMPKIN

Kabocha are Japanese pumpkins. They are small with a green bumpy skin, and very cheap and popular in the autumn when they are harvested. The flesh is similar in colour and taste to the English marrow or American pumpkin, either of which makes a good substitute.

BOILED MARROW AND PUMPKIN

1¼ lb marrow or pumpkin, peeled, de-seeded, cut into 1" (2.5 cm) cubes

STOCK I
2 tablespoons sake or white wine
2 tablespoons sugar
2 tablespoons soy sauce
1 pt (2½ cups) soup stock or water

STOCK II
3 tablespoons soy sauce
2 tablespoons sugar
1 teaspoon salt
1 pt (2½ cups) soup stock or water

Bring the ingredients of Stock I or Stock II to the boil, add the marrow or pumpkin, return to the boil, cover, reduce heat and simmer until tender (10–15 minutes). Drain and serve hot with or without cooking liquid. For a more elaborate dish, top boiled marrow or pumpkin with cooked shrimps and Miso Dressing (see p. 58).

MARROW OR PUMPKIN WITH ONION AND MISO

2 tablespoons vegetable oil
2 medium onions, thinly sliced
1 lb marrow or pumpkin, peeled, de-seeded, cut into 1" (2.5 cm) cubes
4 oz (¼ cup) miso

Heat the oil in a heavy pan, add the onions and sauté until light brown. Drop in the marrow or pumpkin and sauté a further two or three minutes. Stir in water or stock, bring to the boil,

cover, reduce heat and simmer until tender (10–15 minutes). With a little of the cooking liquid cream miso and add to pan. Simmer uncovered intil all liquid has been absorbed or evaporated. Serve.

This method may be used for other vegetables, for example, turnip, daikon, potatoes, sweet potatoes, bamboo shoot, lotus root (cooking time will be less for tinned vegetables), etc.

STUFFED MARROW OR PUMPKIN

Japanese kabocha or pumpkin are small enough to allow one stuffed pumpkin per person. If these are not available you can use one large pumpkin or marrow cut into thick rings.

2–3 lb marrow, cut into 2" (5 cm) thick rings, de-seeded or 2–3 lb pumpkin (cut slice off stem end and hollow out seeds and fibre)
Salt
2 tablespoons oil
1 medium onion, thinly sliced
1 medium carrot, grated
2 oz (¼ cup) mushrooms, sliced
2 oz (¼ cup) green peas or 2 oz (¼ cup) French beans, parboiled
8 oz (1 cup) cooked chicken or pork, diced
4 oz (¼ cup) shrimps, cooked
3 tablespoons sake or white wine (optional)
1 tablespoon soy sauce
1 tablespoon sugar
1 tablespoon cornflour
3 eggs, beaten

Pre-heat oven to 350°F (175°C). Lightly salt marrow slices and arrange on a greased baking tin or lightly salt inside of pumpkin. Heat oil in a heavy pan, add onions and sauté until lightly browned. Add carrots and then mushrooms, sautéeing each lightly as added. Combine sautéed vegetables and remaining ingredients and stuff marrow slices or pumpkin with the mixture. If you are using pumpkin, place sliced stem back on top, brush oil on the outer skin and place on a greased baking tin. Bake marrow or pumpkin for 30–40 minutes or until tender.

Alternatively, either marrow or pumpkin can be steamed in a covered steamer for 30–40 minutes or until tender.

72

MUSHROOMS

There are a number of cultivated tree mushrooms unique to Japanese cookery, but only shiitake in dried form are generally available in the West. Shiitake are not cheap but worth the expense for a special treat. Otherwise substitute large fresh Western mushrooms.

SHIITAKE SIMMERED IN SOY SAUCE

12 shiitake or 4 oz (¼ cup) large mushrooms
12 fl oz (1½ cups) water
2 tablespoons sugar
3 tablespoons vegetable oil (sesame is best)

Soak shiitake in water for 20 minutes. Drain and reserve the liquid. Cut away any hard stems and gently squeeze excess moisture from shiitake back into soaking liquid. Criss-cross the caps with light knife cuts. Heat 2 tablespoons oil in a heavy pan, add shiitake and sauté over a high heat until they are browned. Add remaining ingredients and soaking liquid and simmer over low heat until all liquid has been absorbed or evaporated and the shiitake look shiny (about 30 minutes). Serve hot or cold.

Alternatively, use 4 oz (¼ cup) large fresh mushrooms, miss out soaking section and substitute 6 oz (¾ cup) water for soaking liquid where it is added to sautéed mushrooms.

GRILLED SHIITAKE OR MUSHROOMS

8 shiitake or 8 oz (1½ cups) large mushrooms
3 tablespoons soy sauce
3 tablespoons mirin or sweet sherry
Pinch 7-spices pepper or cayenne

Soak shiitake in water for 20 minutes. Drain, reserve liquid for soup stock. Cut away any hard stems. Combine soy sauce and mirin and marinade shiitake or mushrooms in mixture for one hour. Drain, reserve liquid. Grill shiitake or mushrooms lightly, top side up, for two to three minutes, and brush with marinade twice. Turn over and repeat. Serve sprinkled with 7-spices pepper or cayenne. This dish goes well with turnip or daikon salad (see p. 56).

ONIONS

ONION WITH SESAME SEED

2 tablespoons vegetable oil
2 medium onions, cut into thin wedges or crescents
1 teaspoon salt
2 tablespoons sesame seeds, toasted

Heat the oil in a heavy frying pan, add the onions and fry light brown, reduce heat, season with salt and gently cook a further ten minutes. Serve sprinkled with sesame seeds.

ONIONS AND FRENCH BEANS IN SPICED SAUCE

2 tablespoons vegetable oil
1 clove garlic, crushed
2 medium onions, thinly sliced
4 oz (¼ cup) French beans, parboiled in lightly salted water
1 tablespoon miso
4 fl oz (½ cup) soup stock or water
½ teaspoon 7-spices pepper or hot pepper sauce
1 tablespoon cornflour

Heat oil in a heavy pan, add the garlic, sauté for one minute, add the onions, sauté until lightly browned. Stir in the beans and gently heat. Cream miso in a little of the stock or water and add with remaining liquid and 7-spices pepper or hot pepper sauce to pot. Cream cornflour in 2 tablespoons of liquid from the pot and stir in. Simmer, stirring constantly until sauce is thickened and creamy. Serve as side dish or over rice or noodles.

CHRYSANTHEMUM ONIONS

Serve this unusual and exotic-looking onion preparation as an accompaniment to a main meal.

4 medium-sized onions
1 pt (2½ cups) soup stock or water
1 teaspoon salt
1 medium carrot, grated
2 tablespoons sesame seeds, toasted or 2 tablespoons Miso and Mustard Dressing (see p. 76)
1 tablespoon parsley, chopped

Quarter the onions, but do not cut right through. Leave the root end intact. Place in pot, pour in stock or water, season with salt and bring to the boil. Gently boil until onions are cooked (about 15 minutes). Lift out onions and transfer to four small bowls. Spread onions open and fill each with grated carrot. Sprinkle with sesame seeds or Miso and Mustard Dressing and garnish with parsley.

PEAS

Fresh garden peas served on their own in individual bowls with a sweet or savoury dressing is the favourite Japanese way of serving them.

SWEET PEAS

12 fl oz (12 cups) water
1 lb (2½ cups) fresh peas
Pinch of salt
2 oz (¼ cup) sugar
1 teaspoon cornflour (optional)

Bring water to the boil, add peas and pinch of salt. Return to the boil, reduce heat and simmer until peas are just tender. Stir in the sugar, and for a thicker sauce add cornflour, creamed before addition in a little of the cooking liquid. Simmer very gently for a further 15 minutes. Serve.

SAVOURY PEAS

12 fl oz (1½ cups) soup stock
1 lb (2½ cups) fresh peas
Pinch of salt
1 tablespoon soy sauce
1 tablespoon sake or white wine
1 teaspoon cornflour (optional)

Repeat procedure for Sweet Peas, but replace water by soup stock, and sugar by soy sauce and sake.

GREEN PEPPERS

SAUTEED GREEN PEPPERS

4 medium green peppers
2 tablespoons vegetable oil
2 tablespoons soy sauce
1 teaspoon sugar

Cut peppers into sixths, remove seeds and membranes. Heat oil over high heat, add peppers, soy sauce and sugar. Stir continuously and cook until peppers are just crisp. Serve.

GRILLED GREEN PEPPERS

4 medium green peppers
2 tablespoons vegetable oil

Pre-heat grill. Quarter peppers, remove seeds and membranes. Brush with oil and grill for four to five minutes. Turn three to four times during grilling. Do not overcook; the peppers should remain semi-crisp.

GREEN PEPPER WITH DEEP FRIED TOFU

6 fl oz (¾ cup) soup stock
2 teaspoons sugar
1 teaspoon soy sauce
Salt to taste
2 tablespoons vegetable oil
1 clove garlic, crushed
1 medium onion, thinly sliced
4 medium peppers, cut into sixths, seeds and
    membranes removed
6 oz (¾ cup) tofu, deep fried (see p. 77), cut into
    ½" (1.25 cm) cubes

Combine first four ingredients, bring to the boil and remove from heat. Heat oil in a heavy pan, add garlic and sauté for one minute. Add onion and pepper and stir. Fry over high heat for three to four minutes. Drop in tofu, mix well and pour in the stock mixture. Bring to the boil, stirring continuously. Remove from heat. Serve.

POTATO

Not as common as in the West, but widely used and available, due to some extent to the increase of hamburger cafés in Tokyo.

POTATOES WITH MISO

2 tablespoons vegetable oil
1 lb potatoes, peeled, thinly sliced and cut into
    half or quarter moons
4 fl oz (½ cup) water
2 tablespoons miso
Salt and togarashi or black pepper to taste
2 tablespoons chives, chopped

Heat the oil in a heavy frying pan, add potatoes
and sauté, frequently stirring, for five minutes.
Pour in water, cover and simmer a further five
minutes. Cream miso with a little cooking liquid
and stir into pan. Simmer uncovered until most
of the liquid has been absorbed or evaporated.
Season and garnish with chopped chives.

SWEET AND SOUR POTATOES

2 oz (¼ cup) sugar
2 tablespoons vinegar
1 teaspoon salt
6 fl oz (¾ cup) water
1 lb potatoes, peeled, cut into ½" (1.25 cm) cubes

Combine first four ingredients and bring to the
boil. Add potatoes, return to the boil, cover,
reduce heat and simmer until potatoes are
cooked (about 15 minutes).

BOILED POTATOES

1 pt (2½ cups) water
8 small potatoes, washed
Egg Dressing (see p. 59) or Tofu Dressing (see p.
59)

Bring water to boil, add potatoes, return to the
boil and cook until potatoes are tender but not
soft. Quarter, cutting three quarters of the way
down potato. Open out, arrange in serving dish
and pour over dressing. Alternatively, top with
grated cheese and butter.

SEASONED RICE WITH POTATOES

This is a popular Okinawan country dish.

8 oz (1¼ cup) rice, washed
4 oz (½ cup) lean pork, thinly sliced
2 pt (5 cups) soup stock or water
1 lb potatoes, peeled, sliced and cut into half
    moons

2 tablespoons miso
1 young leek or 2 spring onions, finely chopped
2 tablespoons vegetable oil (preferably sesame
    seed)

Place rice, pork and stock in a heavy pan, bring
to the boil and add potatoes. Return to the boil.
Cover, reduce heat and simmer for 30–40
minutes. Cream the miso with a little liquid
from the pot and stir into the rice and potatoes.
Remove pan from the heat and allow to stand
for ten minutes. Stir in leeks, sprinkle oil over
surface of food and serve.

SPINACH (HORENSO)

The Japanese tend to use young spinach leaves,
and they normally leave the stems on. Steaming
is the cooking method most favoured, since it
retains the fresh green look of the young
spinach. Chrysanthemum leaves (shungiku) are
sometimes used where in the West we would
use spinach. Shungiku is more fragrant and
easier to overcook than spinach, but otherwise
interchangeable. If you use shungiku in recipes
that specify spinach, add one third more in
weight than the amount of spinach required.

STEAMED SPINACH

1 lb (4½ cups) young spinach leaves
Soy sauce and vinegar to taste

Lay spinach in steam basket, cover and steam
for three to four minutes. Remove with
chopsticks, cut into 1" lengths and sprinkle with
soy sauce and vinegar. Serve.

Alternatively, boil spinach in very small
amount of water (½" in a heavy pan) for three to
four minutes. Continue as for steamed spinach.

SPINACH WITH SAUCE

Prepare 1 lb cooked spinach as above and dress
with one of the following sauces:

MISO AND EGG SAUCE
1 tablespoon miso
1 hard boiled egg, mashed
4 tablespoons stock or water
Pinch 7-spices pepper or cayenne

Combine into a smooth paste. Mix with spinach.

LEMON SAUCE

3 tablespoons soy sauce
1 tablespoon sugar
Juice of 1 lemon
Pinch of salt

Combine and pour over spinach.

SPINACH NORIMAKI

4 oz (¾ cup) spinach
2 sheets nori, lightly toasted
1 tablespoon soy sauce

Steam or boil spinach as described above. Gently squeeze cooked leaves to remove excess moisture. Cut nori seaweed sheets into two and lay one half on a sudare (bamboo mat) or flat surface. Sprinkle spinach with soy sauce and divide into four portions. Lay one portion on nori and with sudare, or by hand, roll spinach up in it. Repeat for each portion of spinach. Cut each roll into two pieces and serve.

SWEET POTATOES

Apart from the amplified musical box noise that heralded the arrival of the dust cart (into which we all tipped our own bins), the sound that most intrigued me when I arrived in Japan was the loud shout and accompanying noise of the sweet potato man. He would arrive on the street wheeling a device that looked like a Victorian rocket launcher and then make yodelling noises to attract the attention of the locals. His machine was a charcoal-fired cylinder lined with four long tubes, each stuffed with baking sweet potatoes. I soon became one of his best customers and much enjoyed the charcoal-braised sweet potatoes.

GRILLED SWEET POTATOES

Unfortunately, we cannot simulate the sweet potato baking machine, but sweet potatoes are such delicious vegetables that they taste good just grilled in a straightforward manner.

1 pt (2½ cups) water
Salt
8 small sweet potatoes or 4 medium sweet potatoes
2 tablespoons vegetable oil

Salt water, add potatoes and bring to the boil. Cover, reduce heat and gently boil for ten minutes. Drain, split potatoes in half. Criss-cross open faces with sharp knife, brush with oil and grill, open side up, until browned and tender. Serve with butter or on their own.

Sweet potatoes can be substituted for potatoes in any of the potato recipes.

GREEN SWEET POTATOES

This is a great party dish for children. Use ordinary potatoes if sweet potatoes are not available.

4 oz (1½ cups) sweet potato, peeled
1 pt (2½ cups) water
8 oz (1 cup) sugar
1 tablespoon green powdered tea

Boil sweet potatoes in water until soft. Drain. Return potatoes to pan and over a low heat stir in the sugar. Mash and beat mixture until it starts to take on a glossy sheen. Add powdered tea and beat in. Serve.

Alternatively, squeeze mashed potatoes through an icing bag into a variety of shapes.

TURNIPS

Japanese turnips are small and mild in flavour. Substitute small white turnips.

BOILED TURNIPS

4 small tender turnips
1 pt (2½ cups) soup stock or 1 pt (2½ cups) water plus 4 tablespoons sugar
Soy sauce to taste

Quarter turnips to just over half their depth. Boil stock or water and sugar and turnips until tender (10–15 minutes). Drain, serve sprinkled with soy sauce. Alternatively, if stock is used, retain after draining and thicken up with a little cornflour (2 teaspoons), add soy sauce to taste and pour over turnips.

TURNIP WITH MISO AND MUSTARD SAUCE

Prepare boiled turnips as described above, and dress with following sauce:

3 tablespoons miso
3 tablespoons vinegar
3 tablespoons sugar
1 tablespoon dry English mustard

Combine and mix well.

TURNIP CHAWANMUSHI

2 small turnips, grated
2 egg whites, beaten
Pinch of salt
1 medium carrot, cut into flower-shape slices, parboiled in little salted water
2 small leeks, sliced into 1" (2.5 cm) lengths, parboiled in little salted water
4 oz (¼ cup) tofu, deep fried (see recipe at foot of page), cut into 1" (2.5 cm) cubes (optional)

Combine turnip, egg whites and pinch of salt. Divide mixture amongst four small bowls. Decorate each with carrot, leek and tofu pieces. Cover bowls and steam (see Chawanmushi recipe, p. 30) for 15–20 minutes. Serve straight on to table.

CHRYSANTHEMUM TURNIPS

Turn the poor plain turnip into a flower!

2 small turnips
Salt
3 tablespoon vinegar
1 tablespoon sugar
1 red bell pepper, minced *or* peel of 1 lemon, grated
Chrysanthemum leaves or lettuce

Cut stems off turnips and very finely peel. Stand on stem end and place a chopstick on each side of turnip. Now cut as though you were cutting whole turnip into thin slices but stop each stroke as knife meets chopsticks. Repeat across the other way to give a pine needle effect. Soak turnips in salted water until softened (30 minutes to 1 hour). Rinse, wipe dry on clean cloth, and stand in individual bowls. Combine vinegar, sugar and pinch of salt and pour over turnips. Allow to stand for two to three hours. Decorate by topping with small circles cut out of red pepper for red-centred, or lemon peel for yellow-centred chrysanthemums. Stand in bed of chrysanthemum or lettuce leaves to give flower effect.

TOFU

The nutritional and culinary merits of tofu are discussed on page 13. It is made commercially by finely grinding dry soya beans, then cooking the coarse flour in water. The milky liquid formed is drained off and treated with a controlled amount of calcium sulphate which congeals it into a soft milky substance. This is poured into moulds and further drained through a fine cloth. The congealed solid is now lightly pressed and finally cut into small blocks for selling. Tofu is stored under cold water. It will keep for several days if the water is changed daily.

If you cannot find a source of buying fresh tofu, experiment with the following recipe until you can satisfactorily make your own.

1 lb soya beans
3 tablespoons fresh lemon juice

Cover the soya beans with water and leave to soak for at least 12 hours. Change water once during soaking. Drain and grind the beans either in an electric grinder or hand mill. Transfer to a heavy pot and add 2½ times as much water by volume as beans. Bring to the boil, reduce heat and simmer for one hour. Arrange three to four layers of cheesecloth inside a colander placed over a large pan. Strain the contents of the pan through this. Finally, gather the cheesecloth around the collected pulp and squeeze out as much liquid into the pan as possible. Transfer the liquid to a glass bowl. Use the pulp in soups and stews. Add lemon juice to the liquid, stir once, cover with a damp cloth and leave in a warm spot (80°F, 120°C is perfect) for 8–12 hours or until tofu sets. Drain through cheesecloth to remove excess liquid. The tofu may now be used. For a professional look, pour it into a square mould, put a light weight on top and press for four hours. Store under water in a refrigerator.

For flavoured tofu, simmer a block of it or small squares in oil and soy sauce with mint, garlic, nutmeg, cinnamon, cloves, fennel or black pepper, or whatever seasoning you wish.

DEEP FRIED TOFU (Aburage)

Deep fried tofu or aburage is regularly used in

casseroles and other dishes where long cooking would cause fresh tofu to disintegrate. The amount of fresh tofu given in this recipe yields 8 oz of aburage.

18 oz (3 blocks or 3¼ cups) tofu
Oil for deep frying

Before deep frying tofu, it must first be pressed to remove excess moisture. Slice the tofu blocks in half crosswise to give two thin slices each (six slices in total). Place the slices between two absorbent towels and place a cutting board or other weight on top. Leave for 30 minutes and then proceed to deep fry.

Pour enough oil into a heavy-bottomed pan or frying pan to come 1"–1½" (1.25 cm–1.75 cm) up the sides. Heat pan on a high heat until a small piece of tofu dropped into the fat immediately bubbles (300–350°F, 150–175°C). Reduce heat slightly and carefully drop in half the tofu slices. Deep fry for one to two minutes or until tofu floats to the surface of the oil. Turn slices over and fry another two minutes. Lift from oil and drain on a rack for several minutes before using.

MIXED VEGETABLE AND TOFU
Tofu is an excellent ingredient in mixed vegetable dishes. It absorbs the flavours of other ingredients and links them together. This recipe is for 6–8 people.

2 tablespoons vegetable oil
1 clove garlic, crushed
1 medium onion, thinly sliced
4 oz (¾ cup) cabbage, coarsley chopped
4 oz (¾ cup) broccoli, cut into flowerettes and/or
    4 oz (¾ cup) sprouts, quartered
1 small aubergine, salted, rinsed and drained
2 stalks celery, cut in ½" (1.25 cm) lengths
4 oz (¾ cup) French beans, cut in 1" (2.5 cm) lengths
1 medium green pepper, 1" (2.5 cm) strips
1 bamboo shoot, sliced into half moons
1 lotus root, sliced into half moons
2 oz (⅓ cup) mushrooms, sliced
1 teaspoon salt
1 teaspoon togarashi or black pepper
2 tablespoons soy sauce
10 fl oz (1¼ cup) soup stock or water

6 oz (⅓ cup) tofu, cut into 1" (2.5 cm) cubes and deep fried (see p. 77)
2 tablespoons mirin or sherry (optional)

Heat oil in an 'oven-to-table' type casserole, add garlic and sauté for one minute, add onions and lightly brown. Add all the remaining vegetables and stir fry for three to four minutes. Add remaining ingredients except tofu and mirin and bring to the boil, reduce heat and simmer for ten minutes. Drop in tofu and simmer for a further ten minutes. Finally pour in mirin or sherry and serve from casserole.

This recipe can be altered to include or exclude whichever vegetables are available or otherwise.

ODEN
Oden is a popular winter casserole, often prepared for festive occasions when people can help themselves out of the oden pot, which can bubble away all evening without spoiling. In some big cities, they have vendors in the streets selling oden. From experience I can tell you they are not keen on customers who want to pick and choose from the oden pot. They believe in pot luck. The recipe is for 6–8 people.

2 pt (5 cups) soup stock
1 teaspoon salt
1 tablespoon sugar
1 tablespoon soy sauce
8 oz (1½ cups) daikon or small turnip cut into 1" (2.5 cm) cubes
1 medium carrot, cut into 2" (5 cm) lengths
1 kamabako (a white fish cake, see p. 136) thickly sliced (optional)
1 lb (3 cups) tofu, deep fried (see p. 77)
8 leaves cabbage, coarsely chopped
3 bamboo shoots, cut in half, crosswise
6 small new potatoes
6 hard boiled eggs

Combine the first four ingredients in a large pot and bring to the boil. Add daikon, carrot and kamabako. Cook for 30 minutes, uncovered. Replenish evaporated liquid with soup stock or water. Add all the other ingredients and simmer slowly for 30 minutes. Invite each guest to ladle out some cooking liquid and a selection of vegetables, tofu, etc.

FISH

For a general discussion on fish see page 15.

Buy fresh fish if you can, or, as a second best, buy frozen fish. Look for shiny skin, bright eyes and firm flesh. Reject fish with any smell of staleness. Do not overcook. The inside flesh should remain moist, and it will just come away from the bones when the fish is perfectly cooked.

To clean round fish, work from tail to head, and scrape scales off both sides. Make a 2" (5 cm) slit in belly below pectoral fin, and remove entrails, clean off scales and entrails cavity under cold running water. For flat fish remove gills, cut off fins, slice belly, remove entrails and wash under cold running water. Alternatively, ask your fishmonger to clean the fish and similarly if you require it filleted. Always ask for the bones, head, tail, etc., and use them for preparing fish stock.

For grilled fish, the most popular Japanese cooking method, great care is taken to retain the shape of the fish during cooking. This is accomplished by 'stitching' the fish with skewers. A skewer is inserted near the eye of the fish and threaded along its length by bending the skewer up towards the top of the fins and then down again to the centre. Do not pierce the skin of the fish. Bring the skewer out at the tail end on an upward movement. This causes the tail to stand up when cooked. Insert a second skewer near mouth and repeat process, bringing this skewer out below the tail. For 'swimming' fish, push a skewer completely through fish at a point just below the head. Force it back through to the other side near the centre of body and finally out again near the tail. See diagrams.

To prepare prawns or shrimps for cooking,

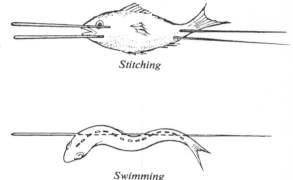

Stitching

Swimming

wash well, remove shells, but, in order to give a natural look, leave tails intact, and, if you wish to devein, make a shallow cut down the back of the shellfish and remove the vein (or intestine tract) with a pointed knife or toothpick. To keep shrimps straight during cooking, insert a toothpick between the shell and flesh, starting at the head end and emerging at the tail end.

The Japanese use five main methods to cook fish: grilling, frying, baking, boiling and steaming. Then there is sashimi or uncooked fish. The chapter is arranged by cooking method, starting with sashimi.

Please note that in the recipes a particular type of fish is not always specified. Instead a category of fish such as white or red (oily) flesh is recommended. This is because the price and availability of fish are always fluctuating, and it is often wiser in terms of freshness and price not to have a fixed shopping list. The recipes can be used to suit the type of fish that is of best value at any particular time.

SASHIMI (see p. 15)

Take an absolutely fresh fish, remove skin and bones, cut the finest of the fillets into thin slices or cubes, serve in an attractive arrangement with garnishings, and there you have sashimi. A simple process but for some reason surrounded by mystique.

For the Western cook the most suitable fish for sashimi are salmon, tuna, seabream, halibut and red or grey mullet, although sole, smelt, trout and turbot are almost as good. Shellfish such as shrimps, prawns and lobster are also served in sashimi dishes. Ideally, they should be killed immediately before use and rinsed under cold water until firm.

Initially, it may be wiser to ask your fishmonger to prepare the filleted fish steak for you, but give him precise instructions. It should be as fresh as possible, free of all bones, and have no smell of fish. To cut white fleshed fish steak for serving, chill first and then cut, holding the knife at angle of about 30°, into slices ½" (1.25 cm) thick and 1½" (3.75 cm) wide. Traditionally, the cuts are made from right to left, and the slices laid on top of another to the right. For red (oily) fish, cut straight down pulling the knife towards you; into pieces ½" (1.25 cm) thick and 2" (5 cm) wide. (Do not cut in a sawing fashion). For small fish such as smelt or trout, shave off thin symmetrical slices of flesh. To keep sashimi fresh, handle the fish as little as possible.

The sashimi is arranged in a dish in overlapping pieces and decorated with fresh raw vegetable garnishing. More than one type of fish may be used. Each person is given a small dish of soy sauce and one containing wasabi (Japanese mustard). The wasabi is mixed into soy sauce to taste and the pieces of sashimi are dipped into the mixture before eating. English mustard or horseradish sauce may be used in place of wasabi.

TO PREPARE SASHIMI

1 lb fresh filleted salmon steak (or tuna, halibut, seabream, red or grey mullet, etc.) *or*
4 large fresh prawns, cut into 3 pieces *or*
8 oz (1¼ cups) fresh shrimps *or*
A combination of the above

GARNISHING

4 oz (¼ cup) cabbage, thinly shredded
1 medium carrot, shredded
½ bunch watercress
4 sprigs parsley

ADDITIONAL OR ALTERNATIVE GARNISHINGS

½ medium cucumber, shredded
½ bunch radishes, cut in shapes
2 small leeks, finely sliced
2 spring onions, finely sliced
4 oz (¼ cup) daikon, shredded

DIPPING SAUCE

1 tablespoon wasabi powder
1 tablespoon water
2 tablespoons soy sauce per guest
or
1 tablespoon English mustard powder
3 teaspoons water
2 tablespoons soy sauce per guest
or
2 tablespoons prepared horseradish sauce
2 tablespoons soy sauce per guest

Prepare and slice fish or shellfish according to the notes given above. Chill until ready for use. Combine cabbage and carrot and store in iced water until ready for use. Blend wasabi or English mustard and water into a smooth paste or use prepared horseradish sauce. In individual bowls arrange a layer of sashimi slices in a neat regular row (traditionally there are an uneven number of slices) or make a small mound of shellfish. Add a pinch of shredded carrot and cabbage, a few leaves of watercress and a sprig of parsley to each bowl. Serve with dishes of wasabi and soy sauce.

Alternatively, the sashimi can be arranged on one large serving dish and surrounded with garnishings. Each guest is given separate bowls of wasabi and soy sauce and helps him/herself to sashimi from the central dish.

GRILLED FISH

Yakimono, or grilled things, are traditionally cooked over a charcoal brazier or hibachi, and these recipes are excellent for barbecue-style cooking. However, they can be as equally well cooked and with less chance of things going wrong under a gas or electric grill. There are two characteristically Japanese methods of preparing the fish for grilling. In the first method called shioyaki, the fish is well salted before grilling, and in the second called terriyaki the fish is marinated in a sauce before or after grilling or basted with a sauce during grilling.

SHIOYAKI

Salted, grilled fish is the simplest of dishes. The salt helps to keep the flesh moist and, without any other adornment, the natural flavour of the fish can be appreciated to the full.

TROUT GRILLED WITH SALT (AYU SHIOYAKI)

4 fresh trout (see below)
Salt
Oil

Clean and scale fish, but leave on head and tail. Skewer fish as described and lightly salt all over (the correct amount of salt is 2–3% of the weight of fish). Allow to stand for 30 minutes. Pre-heat grill. Cover fish tails in silver foil to prevent burning. Brush grill rack lightly with oil and grill the trout six minutes on each side. Do not turn more than once. Towards the end of grilling the second side, turn grill up and brown fish. Remove skewers and serve.

Almost any fish or fish fillet (with skin left on) can be cooked in this way. Seabream if you can obtain it, is particularly good.

BASIC TERRIYAKI

Small whole fish of the red (oily) kind (for example, mackerel, herring, etc.) are best for this recipe. If you use filleted fish make sure the skin is left on.

1 lb whole fish, cleaned, or filleted fish
Soy sauce
1 lemon, thinly sliced
2 oz (2 tablespoons) ginger root, grated (optional)

Pre-heat moderate grill. Skewer fish as described. Brush fish with soy sauce and grill for total of five to ten minutes on each side, depending on size of fish. Turn fish three to four times during cooking and each time brush with soy sauce. The fish is cooked when the centre flesh flakes if prodded with a fork. Remove skewers and serve fish hot, garnished with lemon slices and grated ginger.

TERRIYAKI FISH WITH LEMON JUICE AND POPPY SEED

1 lb whole fish, cleaned, or filleted fish, skin left on
2 tablespoons lemon juice
2 tablespoons vegetable oil
2 tablespoons soy sauce
3 tablespoons poppy seeds

Clean and skewer whole fish as described or use filleted fish. Combine lemon juice, vegetable oil and soy sauce. Brush fish with this mixture and grill as for Basic Terriyaki, substituting the lemon sauce for soy sauce. Serve sprinkled with poppy seeds. Sesame seeds may also be used.

MARINATED TERRIYAKI

1 lb small whole fish or filleted fish, skins left on
1 lemon, cut into 4 wedges

MARINADE I
4 fl oz ($\frac{1}{2}$ cup) sake or white wine
4 fl oz ($\frac{1}{2}$ cup) soy sauce
1 tablespoon sugar
1 clove garlic, crushed

MARINADE II (SWEET)
3 tablespoons mirin or sherry
3 fl oz ($\frac{1}{3}$ cup) soy sauce
3 fl oz ($\frac{1}{3}$ cup) sake or white wine
2 tablespoons sugar

Combine ingredients of marinade I or marinade II together and bring to the boil. Remove from heat. Marinade fish in mixture for one hour (or more in a refrigerator). Occasionally move fish around to ensure each piece is well marinated. Pre-heat moderate grill. Cook fish flesh side up for five to ten minutes, depending on size of fish. Carefully turn fish over and baste top side with marinade. Grill another three to four minutes.

In the meantime bring remaining marinade to the boil. Serve fish in individual bowls and pour over a little hot marinade sauce. Garnish with a wedge of lemon.

MISO MARINATED HADDOCK OR PLAICE

4 oz (¼ cup) miso (white is best)
1 tablespoon sugar
1 tablespoon mirin or sherry (optional)
1 lb filleted haddock or plaice, skin left on
1 tablespoon oil
1 oz (1 tablespoon) ginger root, grated

Combine miso, sugar and mirin into smooth paste. Pre-heat moderate grill. Brush one side of fish with oil and grill for five to ten minutes or until well cooked. Now brush with miso mixture and turn fish over. Brush new topside with more mixture and grill under low heat until dressing is firm and dry. Serve with grated ginger.

MISO MARINATED MACKEREL

1 lb mackerel, whole and cleaned or filleted with skin left on
8 oz (1½ cups) miso (white is best)
2 oz (¼ cup) sugar
3 tablespoons mirin or sherry (optional)

Lay fish in a baking dish. Combine miso, sugar and mirin into a smooth paste with a knife or spatula. Carefully and evenly cover fish in miso mixture. Cover dish with lid or foil and refrigerate for one to two days. Remove fish from marinade and gently wipe off any miso that has adhered. Pre-heat moderate grill and cook fish six to eight minutes each side. Serve immediately.

GRILLED WHITE FISH WITH GLAZE

1 lb filleted white fish, cut into four pieces
Salt
1 egg yolk
½ teaspoon salt
1 teaspoon mirin or sherry

Sprinkle fillets with salt and leave for one hour. Wipe off salt and extracted moisture with dry, clean cloth. Combine egg yolk, salt and mirin. Pre-heat moderate grill. Put fillet pieces on a skewer and brush both sides with egg yolk mixture. Grill for five to ten minutes each side, depending on size of fish. Turn once only. Serve immediately fish is cooled and glaze has hardened.

Alternatively, the fish can be prepared by the Basic Teriyaki method (see p. 81), then dressed in egg yolk mixture just before serving.

GRILLED SHRIMPS

1 lb large raw shrimps
3 fl oz (⅓ cup) soy sauce
1 tablespoon sugar
3 tablespoons sherry or mirin
Black pepper to taste

Shell and devein shrimps. Divide among four skewers. Combine soy sauce, sugar and mirin and bring to the boil. Remove from heat. Pre-heat hot grill. Brush soy sauce mixture over shrimps and cook under hot grill, basting continuously with sauce, until shrimps are tender and well glazed (two to three minutes). Season with pepper and serve.

For variety, thread shrimps with alternate mouth-size pieces of bamboo shoot, lotus root or aubergine. Grill in the same way. Prawns, shelled and deveined, may also be cooked in this manner.

GRILLED PRAWNS

8 large prawns
½ teaspoon salt
2 tablespoons soy sauce
2 tablespoons sake or white wine
1 teaspoon sesame seeds
2 tablespoons lemon juice

Wash prawns well, cut off head and legs, leave tails intact. Cut through underflesh along length of shell and open prawns flat. Salt and sprinkle with soy sauce and sake. Allow to stand 15 minutes. Pre-heat moderate grill. Sprinkle prawns with sesame seeds and cook flesh side up for four to five minutes. Turn and grill shell side for two to three minutes. Serve sprinkled with lemon juice.

Alternatively, leave out sesame seeds and season cooked prawns with a pinch of powdered ginger before sprinkling on lemon juice. The fresh garnishings recommended for sashimi (see p. 80) are also excellent accompaniments to grilled prawns.

GRILLED CRAB WRAPPED IN SEAWEED

4 oz (¼ cup) tinned crabmeat
2 tablespoons parsley, finely chopped
Pinch of salt
1 egg, beaten
2 sheets nori, cut into 8 equal pieces

Mash together crabmeat, parsley, pinch of salt and egg. Pre-heat hot grill. Spoon crabmeat mixture on to pieces of nori, wrap up tightly and arrange seam side down on a baking tray. Grill for about three minutes or until egg has set. Cut into small pieces and serve.

Alternatively, dip parcels of nori-wrapped crabmeat in beaten egg, then cornflour and deep fry at 350°F (175°C) for two minutes. Substitute shrimps or prawns for crabmeat.

GRILLED EEL

Eel is now neither very popular nor readily available in Britain, but, on a recent trip to Holland, I was surprised to see it on sale in many places. This recipe then is for the Dutch/Japanese cook if there is one, and for other eel lovers. It's very simple, but very tasty.

1 lb eel(s)
4 tablespoons soy sauce
4 tablespoons mirin or sweet sherry
4 tablespoons water

Clean the eel, remove the head, intestines and backbone. Cut fish into four pieces. Combine the remaining ingredients with the fish trimmings and bring to the boil. Reduce heat and set to simmer. Pre-heat a medium grill. Skewer the pieces of eel and brush with the simmering sauce. Grill each side for four to five minutes. Brush two or three times with more sauce. The cooked fish should be crisp and lightly glazed. Serve topped with remaining sauce (if any).

GLAZED SQUID

With more and more people taking holidays in Greece, and along the Mediterranean coast, squid is becoming quite well known in Britain and elsewhere in Europe. In Japan squid is popular and is often included in dishes of sashimi.

1½ lb squid
2 pt (5 cups) water
Salt
4 fl oz (½ cup) soy sauce
2 fl oz (¼ cup) mirin or sherry
2 fl oz (¼ cup) sake or white wine

Rub off outer skin of squid under running water. Pull off head and attached entrails. Remove transparent spine bone. Cut tentacles off head and keep these and the body. Throw the rest away. Cut body into fat rings and tentacles into pieces. Lightly salt water and bring to the boil and cook squid for about five minutes. Combine soy sauce, mirin and sake and bring to the boil. Drain squid and marinade in soy sauce mixture for 15 minutes. Pre-heat moderate grill. Now criss-cross each piece of squid with shallow knife cuts and grill for five minutes each side. Baste with marinade during cooking. Serve.

FRIED FISH

FRIED MACKEREL

Fish dipped in egg, coated with breadcrumbs and deep fried is a general way of cooking fish, and the Japanese use a similar method except they replace breadcrumbs with dried cooked rice.

4 mackerel fillets (or other fish), total weight about 1 lb
Cornflour
1 egg white, beaten
Cooked rice, washed, dried and separated into individual grains *or* breadcrumbs
Oil for deep frying

Clean and dry the fillets and cut each into two pieces. Dust with cornflour, brush with egg white and roll in cooked rice or breadcrumbs. Heat oil (1½", 3.75 cm deep or more) to 350°F

(175°C) or until you see a slight haze forming above the oil. Drop fish in and deep fry until well cooked (six to eight minutes). Drain on absorbent paper and serve with one or more of the following accompaniments. Place each of the seasonings below in a separate bowl.

Salt
Togarashi or black pepper
7-spices pepper or cayenne
Soy sauce
2 tablespoons lemon juice
2 tablespoons sesame seeds, toasted and pounded to a paste in suribachi or mortar
2 oz (2 tablespoons) ginger root, grated

Before eating, dip pieces of fried fish in one or a combination of seasonings.

DEEP FRIED PRAWNS

12 large prawns
Salt
Cornflour
Cooked rice, washed, dried and separated into individual grains *or* breadcrumbs
1 egg white, beaten
2 medium green peppers, de-seeded, cut into ½" (1.25 cm) thick strips
Oil for deep frying

Clean prawns, remove shells, leaving tails intact, devein, and score the undersides with a sharp knife to prevent curling during cooking. Dust with cornflour, brush with egg white and roll in cooked rice or breadcrumbs. Heat oil to 350°F (175°C) or until you see a slight haze forming above the oil. Deep fry prawns for one to two minutes. Drain on absorbent paper. Meanwhile, briefly (one minute) deep fry green pepper strips without any coating. Arrange prawns and pepper in separate bowls and serve. This dish may also be served with the following dipping sauce:

4 fl oz (½ cup) soup stock or dashi
4 tablespoons soy sauce
2 tablespoons mirin or sherry

Combine ingredients and bring to the boil. Remove from heat and serve as above.

DEEP FRIED PRAWNS COATED WITH NOODLES

Proceed as for Deep Fried Prawns, but replace cooked rice with 2 oz (¼ cup) somen or vermicelli noodles broken into ¼" (0.5 cm) pieces. The deep fried green pepper is optional.

DEEP FRIED PRAWNS WITH LEEKS

Proceed as for Deep Fried Prawns, but replace green pepper by leeks as follows: Cut 2 small leeks into 1" (2.5 cm) pieces, thread on a small skewer and deep fry for one minute. Drain on absorbent paper and serve with deep fried prawns.

DEEP FRIED SHRIMPS

Shrimps may be substituted for prawns in any of the deep fried prawns recipes. To prepare shrimps, shell, leaving tail on, devein, and score with sharp knife across inside curve to prevent curling during cooking.

FRIED FISH IN SAUCE

6 fl oz (½ cup) fish stock or dashi
1 tablespoon mirin or sherry
2 tablespoons soy sauce
1 lb filleted fish, cut into 2" (5 cm) × 1" (2.5 cm) pieces
Cornflour
Oil for deep frying

Combine stock or dashi, mirin and soy sauce, bring to the boil, reduce heat and simmer. Dust fish pieces in cornflour. Heat oil to 350°F (175°C) or until you see slight haze forming above the oil. Deep fry fish for five to six minutes. Remove and drain on absorbent paper. Add fish to simmering sauce and simmer for a further 10–15 minutes. Serve fish in individual bowls with sauce poured over.

MARINATED FRIED FISH

6 fl oz (½ cup) fish stock or dashi
3 tablespoons vinegar
2 teaspoons sugar
1 tablespoon soy sauce
Pinch of salt and togarashi or black pepper

1 lb filleted fish, cut into 2" (5 cm) × 1" (2.5 cm)
  pieces
Cornflour
Oil for deep frying

Combine first six ingredients and bring to the boil. Remove from heat and cool. Dust fish with cornflour. Heat oil to 350°F (175°C) or until you see a slight haze forming above the oil. Deep fry fish for one minute. Remove and drain on absorbent paper. Marinate fish in cooked sauce for two to three hours. Serve hot or cold.

DEEP FRIED FISH BALLS
Sole, plaice, cod, haddock, etc., can all be used in this recipe.

1 lb fillet of white fish
2 tablespoons cornflour
1 teaspoon salt
1 teaspoon soy sauce
1 teaspoon sugar
3 fl oz (⅜ cup) water
Oil for deep frying

Grind fish in a suribachi, mortar or bowl to a paste. Add the cornflour, salt, soy sauce and sugar and mix into a smooth consistency. Slowly add the water by stirring until you have a mixture that will retain its shape when moulded into small shapes. Heat oil to 350°F (175°C) or until you see a slight haze forming above the oil. Form fish paste into mouth-size patties or balls and deep fry, a portion at a time, until golden brown. Drain on absorbent paper and serve.

SALMON FISHCAKES

4 oz (¼ cup) tinned salmon *or* fresh salmon,
  poached
1 small leek, finely chopped
1 medium carrot, finely shredded
½ oz (1 tablespoon) ginger root, grated (optional)
Salt and black pepper to taste
2 eggs, beaten
Cornflour
Oil for deep frying
Soy sauce

Combine first four ingredients and mash together. Season to taste with salt and black

pepper. Stir in eggs and mix well. Heat oil to 350°F (175°C) or until you see a slight haze forming above the oil. Form fish mixture into mouth-size balls or patties, dust with cornflour and deep fry until golden brown. Drain on absorbent paper and serve with soy sauce. Other tinned (for example tuna, or crab) or cooked fish can be used in this recipe.

BAKED FISH

BAKED FISH WITH VEGETABLES
The Japanese method of baking fish is very simple and it preserves all the flavour of the fish. It was developed to make use of oven-top burners since the Japanese do not normally use ovens. Cooked on top of the stove or in the oven this is a complete and tasty dish.

4 shiitake or 4 large mushrooms
1 lb filleted white fish or salmon
1 medium onion, sliced
2 medium green peppers, de-seeded and
  quartered
1 lemon sliced
Salt and black pepper
4 teaspoons sake or white wine (optional)
Soy sauce

Soak shiitake in cold water for 20 minutes. Cut away any hard stems and criss-cross caps with shallow knife cuts. Alternatively, use fresh mushrooms with stems removed. Cut fish into four pieces and prepare four pieces of aluminium foil about 6" × 10" (15 × 25 cm). Lightly grease foil and, on each piece, lay in order a portion of: onion slices, fish, green pepper and shiitake or mushrooms. Season with salt, pepper and sake, top with a slice of lemon and wrap tightly in foil. Wrap each foil parcel in another piece of foil. Pre-heat frying pan over a moderate heat, place in wrapped fish, cover and cook for 10–12 minutes. Alternatively, bake foil parcels in a pre-heated oven 425°F (220°C) for 15–20 minutes. Serve in foil with soy sauce for seasoning. For variety, thinly sliced aubergine may be added to the vegetables baked with the fish.

85

BAKED TROUT WITH VEGETABLES

Follow recipe as for Baked Fish with Vegetables, but replace white fish with four fresh trout. To prepare trout for cooking, clean, score skin on one side with three knife cuts, sprinkle lightly with salt, allow to stand for 10–15 minutes. Then clean off salt with dry cloth and proceed as directed in the recipe.

BAKED FISH OMELETTE

4 oz ($\frac{1}{2}$ cup) fillet of white fish
2 tablespoons sugar
2 tablespoons soy sauce
1 teaspoon salt
4 eggs, beaten
1 tablespoon vegetable oil
4 sprigs parsley
2 tablespoons lemon juice
Pinch powdered ginger

Combine fish with sugar, soy sauce and salt and mash into a smooth paste. Stir in egg and mix well. Alternatively, put the above ingredients into an electric blender and blend well. Pre-heat oven to 300°F (155°C). Brush a baking dish with oil and pour in egg/fish mixture. Bake until egg is set and top is browned (approximately 45 minutes). Remove from oven, run a sharp knife around the omelette edge and lift out of baking dish. Cut into 1" (2.5 cm) squares, divide among four bowls and garnish with parsley. Combine ginger with lemon juice and serve as a dipping sauce. Eat hot or cold.

STUFFED SOLE WRAPPED IN NORI

1 lb filleted sole or other white fish
4 tablespoons soy sauce
1 oz (1 tablespoon) ginger root, grated
1 small onion, finely diced
6 oz ($\frac{1}{2}$ cup) rice, cooked
2 sheets nori seaweed
1 teaspoon oil
1 egg white
1 bunch parsley, chopped

Pre-heat oven to 350°F (175°C). Divide sole into four pieces and marinate for 30 minutes in soy sauce and ginger. Combine onion and rice and mix thoroughly. Grease a baking dish. Cut sheets of nori in two lengthwise and lay the four pieces, evenly separated, in the bottom of the baking dish. Drain the fish and reserve the marinade. Lay one piece of fish on the top of each strip of nori, and on top of the fish spread one quarter of the rice and onion mixture. Brush the edges of the nori strips with egg white and fold over fish to form a wrapping. Bake for 30 minutes. Serve garnished with parsley and with the reserved marinade as a dipping sauce.

BOILED, SIMMERED OR CASSEROLED FISH DISHES

The Japanese use two methods of casseroling. In the first, all ingredients are combined and cooked together. In the second, each ingredient is cooked separately in the stock, removed, kept warm, and arranged at the table around the stock which is then used as a dipping sauce.

FISH CASSEROLE I

4 shiitake or 4 large, fresh mushrooms
1 lb fresh fish, filleted
1 medium onion, thinly sliced
1 bamboo shoot, cut into thin half-moon shapes
1 medium carrot, cut into 1" (2.5 cm) lengths
1 clove garlic, crushed
1$\frac{1}{2}$ pt (3$\frac{1}{2}$ cups) water or fish stock
1 oz (1 tablespoon) ginger root, grated
Salt and black pepper to taste
6 oz ($\frac{1}{2}$ cup) tofu, 1" (2.5 cm) cubes
2 small leeks or spring onions, 1" (2.5 cm) pieces
4 tablespoons soy sauce
Juice of 1 lemon (optional)
2 tablespoons mirin or sherry (optional)

Soak shiitake in cold water for 20 minutes. Cut away hard stems. Reserve soaking water and use as part of water or stock for recipe. Alternatively, use fresh mushrooms. Cut fish into 8 equal pieces, combine in a casserole dish with shiitake, onion, bamboo shoot, carrot, garlic, water or stock, ginger root and salt and black pepper to taste. Bring to the boil, reduce heat, cover and simmer for 15 minutes. Now add tofu and leeks and simmer a further two minutes. Mix soy sauce, lemon and mirin and divide among four small bowls. Put casserole dish directly on to table, invite guests to lift out with chopsticks, pieces of cooked fish or vegetable and dip into soy sauce/lemon mixture before eating. Finally, to finish off, ladle stock into bowls for your guests to drink. For variety, replace ginger root with 4 oz ($\frac{1}{2}$ cup) tomato purée.

FISH CASSEROLE II

1 pt (2$\frac{1}{2}$ cups) water or fish stock
4 tablespoons sugar
4 tablespoons soy sauce
1 lb fresh fish, filleted, cut into 8 equal pieces
1 medium onion, thinly sliced
1 bamboo shoot, cut into half-moon shapes
1 medium carrot, cut into 1" (2.5 cm) lengths
6 oz ($\frac{3}{4}$ cup) tofu, cut into 1" (2.5 cm) cubes
2 small leeks or spring onions in 1" (2.5 cm) lengths
4 oz ($\frac{1}{4}$ cup) greens (e.g. spinach, broccoli, Brussels sprouts), chopped

Combine water, soy sauce and sugar and bring to the boil. Reduce heat and simmer. Pre-heat moderate oven. Separately cook each of the other ingredients in the soy sauce stock. Remove after cooking and store in warm oven. Divide cooked ingredients among four bowls and serve cooking liquid as dipping sauce. Alternatively, arrange fish in centre of large serving dish, surround with cooked vegetables and serve with dipping sauce as above. Other vegetables than those suggested can be used in Fish Casserole I or II. For instance, try cabbage, peas, turnip, green peppers, etc.

BOILED PRAWNS WITH TOFU

8 oz ($\frac{3}{4}$ cup) prawns
2 tablespoons vegetable oil
1 clove garlic, crushed
1$\frac{1}{2}$ pt (3 cups) fish stock
8 oz (1$\frac{1}{2}$ cups) tofu, 1" (2.5 cm) cubes
1 tablespoon cornflour
1 tablespoon water
2 small leeks, 1" (2.5 cm) pieces
4 oz ($\frac{1}{4}$ cup) spinach, shredded

Clean and shell prawns. Heat oil in a heavy pan, add garlic and sauté for one minute. Add prawns and sauté with stirring for three to four minutes or until cooked. Pour in the stock and bring to the boil, add tofu, return to the boil and reduce heat. Cream cornflour with water and stir into cooking pot. Simmer until thickened. Add leek and spinach, heat through and serve.

SHRIMPS WITH CHILLI PEPPERS

This is a very hot dish: reduce the chilli peppers by half if you prefer less spicy food.

2 egg yolks
2 tablespoons sake or white wine
4 tablespoons cornflour
Pinch of salt
4 oz ($\frac{1}{2}$ cup) soup stock
2 tablespoons mirin or sweet sherry
2 tablespoons soy sauce
Oil for deep frying
1 lb shrimps, shelled and deveined
8 small green chilli peppers
8 oz daikon or small turnip, grated
2 oz (2 tablespoons) ginger root, grated

Combine egg yolks, sake, cornflour and salt into a smooth batter and set aside. Bring soup stock to the boil, stir in mirin and soy sauce and set to simmer. Heat oil to 350°F (175°C). Score across the inside curve of the shrimps to stop curling during cooking, dip into batter and deep fry until crisp and brown. Divide shrimps and chilli peppers among four bowls and soup stock mixture among another four bowls. Place daikon and ginger in central dishes. Each diner seasons soup stock mixture to taste with daikon and ginger and uses this as a dipping sauce for shrimps and chilli peppers.

MACKEREL SIMMERED WITH MISO

2 whole fresh mackerel, about 2 lbs
4 tablespoons miso
1 tablespoon sugar
4 fl oz ($\frac{1}{2}$ cup) water
1 oz (1 tablespoon) ginger root, grated
Juice 1 lemon

Clean mackerel and remove heads. Cream miso with a little of the water, add to it the remainder of the water, sugar and ginger. Put fish in a wide pan, pour over miso sauce and marinade for one hour. Slowly bring pan to boil, reduce heat and simmer for ten minutes. Remove from heat (the fish should still be firm). Serve hot sprinkled with lemon juice. Herring, salmon, sardines or other red (oily) fish may be cooked in this way.

MACKEREL SIMMERED IN SOUR MISO
Proceed as above, but replace water by mild vinegar.

HERRING SIMMERED WITH SWEET SOY SAUCE

4 whole fresh herring, about 2 lb
2 oz ($\frac{1}{4}$ cup) sugar
4 fl oz ($\frac{1}{2}$ cup) sake or white wine
2 fl oz ($\frac{1}{4}$ cup) soy sauce
1 oz (1 tablespoon) ginger root, grated
4 oz ($\frac{1}{4}$ cup) French beans, parboiled in a little salted water or 4 oz ($\frac{1}{4}$ cup) fresh garden peas, cooked

Clean herring and remove heads. In a wide pan, bring sugar, sake, soy sauce and ginger to the boil. Place fish in pan and return to the boil. Reduce heat and very gently simmer for 20–25 minutes, or until nearly all the liquid has been absorbed or evaporated. Carefully remove fish to a large serving plate and serve garnished with French beans or garden peas. Mackerel can also be cooked in this way.

WHITE FISH SIMMERED IN MISO

1 lb filleted white fish
Cornflour
4 tablespoons vegetable oil
1 clove garlic, crushed
4 tablespoons miso
8 fl oz (1 cup) water
1 oz (1 tablespoon) ginger root, grated
4 fl oz ($\frac{1}{2}$ cup) soy sauce
1 tablespoon sugar
Juice of 1 lemon

Cut fish into four pieces and dust with cornflour. Heat oil in a heavy frying pan, add garlic and sauté for one minute. Now fry fish on both sides until well browned. Cream miso with a little water and add it with remaining water,

soy sauce, ginger and sugar to pan. Bring to the boil, reduce heat and simmer for 15–20 minutes or until all the liquid has been absorbed or evaporated. Transfer to a large serving dish and serve hot, sprinkled with lemon juice. Serve this dish with plain fried bean sprouts (see p. 66).

BOILED PRAWNS

12 large prawns
4 tablespoons soy sauce
4 tablespoons water
Pinch of salt
1 tablespoon mirin or sherry (optional)

Clean prawns. Remove heads, leave tails intact. Combine soy sauce, water, salt and mirin, bring to the boil and add prawns. Gently boil prawns until they turn pink (four to six minutes). Drain, reserve liquid. Serve prawns in individual bowls with cooking liquid as dipping sauce.

BOILED PRAWNS WITH BAMBOO SHOOTS
Ingredients as for Boiled Prawns (above) plus 8 oz ($1\frac{1}{4}$ cups) bamboo shoots, sliced.

Proceed as for Boiled Prawns, but after draining prawns, heat bamboo shoots in reserved liquid. Drain, again reserving liquid. Serve bamboo shoots and prawns separately with cooking liquid as dipping sauce.

BOILED PRAWNS WITH SPINACH
Proceed as for Boiled Prawns with Bamboo Shoots, but replace bamboo shoots with 8 oz ($1\frac{1}{4}$ cups) young spinach leaves.

BOILED SHRIMPS
Proceed as for Boiled Prawns but replace prawns with 8 oz ($1\frac{1}{4}$ cups) shrimps.

SWEET AND SOUR PRAWNS

12 large prawns
8 fl oz (1 cup) water
3 tablespoons vinegar
1 tablespoons sugar
3 tablespoons soy sauce
1 teaspoon salt
1 tablespoon sesame seeds, toasted
1 oz (1 tablespoon) ginger root, grated (optional)

Clean prawns. Remove heads, leave tails intact. Bring water to the boil, drop in prawns and gently boil until they turn pink (four to six minutes). Drain. Combine vinegar, sugar, soy sauce and salt, bring to the boil and remove from heat. Marinade prawns in this mixture for one to two hours. Serve garnished with sesame seeds and ginger.

SWEET AND SOUR PRAWNS WITH FRENCH BEANS

Ingredients as for Sweet and Sour Prawns, plus:

4 fl oz ($\frac{1}{2}$ cup) water
1 teaspoon sugar
Pinch of salt
2 tablespoons soy sauce
12 oz ($2\frac{1}{4}$ cups) French beans

Prepare prawns as for Sweet and Sour Prawns. Combine water, sugar, salt and soy sauce and bring to the boil. Add beans and return to the boil. Remove from heat and allow to cool. Drain and serve with prawns.

SWEET AND SOUR SHRIMPS

Proceed as for Sweet and Sour Prawns, but replace prawns with 8 oz ($1\frac{1}{4}$ cups) shrimps.

STEAMED FISH

STEAMED FISH WITH TOFU

12 oz ($1\frac{1}{2}$ cups) filleted white fish
6 oz ($\frac{3}{4}$ cup) tofu, 1" (2.5 cm) cubes
1 teaspoon salt
4 oz ($\frac{1}{4}$ cup) spinach
1 lemon, cut into 4 wedges
1 sheet nori, toasted (optional)

Cut fish into eight pieces and distribute with tofu among four bowls. Sprinkle each bowl with salt and steam for six to eight minutes (see Chawan-Mushi recipe p. 30). Meanwhile, cook spinach lightly in a little salted water. Drain, rinse under cold water and set aside. Decorate steamed fish and tofu with spinach, lemon and crumbled nori.

STEAMED FISH WITH TURNIP AND EGG

1 lb filleted white fish
1 teaspoon salt
2 tablespoons sake or white wine
1 egg
1 teaspoon sugar
8 oz ($1\frac{1}{2}$ cups) turnip, finely grated
4 spinach leaves
1 oz (1 tablespoon) ginger root, grated
Soy sauce to taste

Cut fish into eight pieces and distribute among four bowls. Sprinkle with salt and one tablespoon of sake. Break egg into a bowl, add sugar, remaining sake and mix in turnip. Divide this mixture between the four bowls, decorate with a spinach leaf and steam for 12–15 minutes (see Chawan-Mushi recipe p. 30).

FISH STEAMED WITH SALT

Very simple and effective way of cooking fish.

1 lb white fish, scaled and cleaned
1 tablespoon salt
3 tablespoons soy sauce
1 tablespoon vinegar
1 tablespoon lemon juice
6 oz ($\frac{3}{4}$ cup) small turnip or daikon, grated
1 small, young leek, thinly sliced

Score flesh of fish with sharp knife cuts and sprinkle with salt. Place in steamer or colander inside pan (see p. 23) and steam for 20–30 minutes or until cooked. Prepare dipping sauce by combining soy sauce, vinegar and lemon juice. Serve fish with small bowls of grated turnip and leek and a central bowl of dipping sauce.

POULTRY AND MEAT

Originally because of tradition and now as a result of geography and economics, beef has never been very common in Japan. Chicken and pork take up less land, and do not need large areas of pasture. The Japanese housewife never buys a joint of meat in the way we may do in the West. She probably wouldn't have an oven to cook it in, and anyway pork or beef are usually eaten sparingly, combined with vegetables and rice.

Pork is normally bought lean, in small amounts or as pork cutlets (chops). Beef is cut wafer-thin by the butcher, and cut into mouth-size amounts before serving. Chicken can be bought ready boned and consequently many Japanese recipes requiring chicken specify lean flesh. If you cannot find a poulterer who will bone your chicken for you (very likely these days), either cut the chicken into pieces as described below and leave the bones in, or buy chicken breasts and bone as follows: Hold the breast skin side down, bend it backwards in half until it is flat on the work surface. Pull out the central bone that pops up and cut the breast into two pieces (ignore this if the chicken breasts are already separated). Press the blade of a sharp pointed knife under the base of the ribs of breast, and gently cut away from the flesh as you pull bone upwards. Continue along rib bones until you have detached entire rib cage from flesh.

To cut chicken into pieces, separate it with a meat cleaver into: legs, thighs, wings, breast and back. Cut each joint into two pieces except the back: cut this into four pieces. You should end up with twenty pieces of chicken. Remember, all meat and poultry is easier to cut, etc., when slightly frozen.

The chapter is arranged under chicken, pork and beef headings, and these are sub-divided into cooking methods used, e.g. grilling, frying, boiling, etc. Grilling is a popular Japanese way of cooking meat. Traditionally, this would have been done over a charcoal brazier, and many of the poultry and meat recipes are suitable for barbecues.

CHICKEN

GRILLED CHICKEN (Yaki Tori)
Small pieces of chicken flesh, liver or other parts of the giblets are marinated in a barbecue-type sauce, threaded on to small bamboo or metal skewers and grilled. Yaki tori is a popular Japanese snack which, along with other food cooked on skewers, they call 'kebabs'.

Serve yaki tori as a starter to a meal or, for a more substantial dish, grill vegetables along with the chicken and serve over rice. Cook under a gas or electric grill or in barbecue fashion over a charcoal brazier.

2 medium-size chicken breasts, boned
3 tablespoons soy sauce
2 tablespoons sugar
1 teaspoon powdered ginger
1 clove garlic, crushed
1 teaspoon oil

Cut the chicken into mouth-size pieces. Combine the other ingredients except the oil, and bring to the boil. Romove from the heat and marinate chicken in the mixture for 30 minutes or more. Lightly oil the skewers and thread on chicken pieces. Grill for six to eight minutes.

Turn once or twice and brush with marinade from time to time. Serve well browned, sprinkled with any remaining marinade.

CHICKEN ON SKEWERS WITH VEGETABLES

In this recipe, apart from the flesh, the liver and skin of the chicken are also used. The Japanese, if they eat meat, are not squeamish about what parts of the animal they eat, and tend to make good use of all edible parts. There is a Japanese recipe which begins: 'Burn the hair off the ears.' It is for a pig's ear salad! (See p. 63.)

1 lb chicken breast, boned *or* other lean chicken flesh
4 oz ($\frac{1}{2}$ cup) chicken livers
2 cloves garlic, crushed
1 pt ($2\frac{1}{2}$ cups) water
2 medium green peppers, de-seeded and quartered
1 medium onion, cut into mouth-size pieces
2 leeks, cut into 1" (2.5 cm) lengths
1 teaspoon oil
4 fl oz ($\frac{1}{2}$ cup) soy sauce
4 fl oz ($\frac{1}{2}$ cup) mirin or sherry
1$\frac{1}{2}$ tablespoons sugar
Togarashi or black pepper to taste

Remove skin from chicken breasts, and cut flesh into mouth-size pieces. Cut skin into 1" (2.5 cm) squares. Add one clove garlic to water and bring to the boil. Quarter chicken livers and drop into boiling water. Remove after 30 seconds with slotted spoon and put to one side. Boil chicken skin in the same water for one minute. Drain. Combine remaining garlic, soy sauce, mirin and sugar and bring to the boil. Reduce heat and simmer. Meanwhile, divide chicken flesh, liver, skin and vegetable pieces into four portions. Oil four skewers and thread on each a piece of chicken, vegetable, skin, vegetable, liver, etc. Repeat until all the meat and vegetables have been used up. Remove sauce from heat and in it marinade skewered ingredients for 30 minutes or more. Pre-heat hot grill. Grill skewered food for six to eight minutes. Turn once or twice and brush from time to time with marinade. Serve well browned, seasoned to taste with togarashi or black pepper, with bowls of boiled rice.

An alternative way of serving this dish is to skewer all the ingredients separately and to arrange the skewers of cooked food around a central bed of rice. Allow the guests to help themselves to whatever combination of chicken or vegetable pieces they wish.

CHICKEN BARBECUE PARTY (for eight people)

Double the ingredients for Chicken on Skewers with Vegetables (above).

Follow the same procedure as that given in the recipe above, but allow the guests to thread the skewers themselves, and to cook and baste their own 'kebabs' on a charcoal grill.

GRILLED CHICKEN WITH SESAME SEEDS

2 tablespoons vegetable oil
3 tablespoons sesame seeds
4 fl oz ($\frac{1}{2}$ cup) soy sauce
4 fl oz ($\frac{1}{2}$ cup) sake or white wine
Juice of 1 lemon
2 lb chicken, cut into pieces

Pierce the skin on each piece of chicken in two or three places. Heat oil in a heavy frying pan, add sesame seeds and fry until well browned. Remove pan from heat, allow to cool, then add soy sauce, sake and lemon juice. Stir well and marinate chicken pieces in mixture for 30 minutes. Pre-heat moderate grill. Remove chicken from marinade and grill with frequent basting and turning until each piece is well cooked and golden brown. Serve over hot boiled rice or noodles, and sprinkle with any remaining marinade.

CHICKEN TERRIYAKI

Pieces of chicken are marinated in a sauce, fried and then simmered in more marinade until cooked. A simple, but very effective cooking method.

2 lb chicken, cut into pieces (retaining skin)
4 fl oz ($\frac{1}{2}$ cup) soy sauce
2 fl oz ($\frac{1}{4}$ cup) mirin and 2 fl oz ($\frac{1}{4}$ cup) sake *or* 4 fl oz ($\frac{1}{2}$ cup) dry sherry
1 oz (1 tablespoon) ginger root, grated

91

1 clove garlic, crushed
2 tablespoons vegetable oil
1 lemon, quartered

Pierce the skin on each piece of chicken in two or three places. Combine remaining ingredients, except oil and lemon, and bring to the boil. Remove from the heat and marinate chicken pieces in mixture for 30 minutes or more. Remove chicken and shake off excess liquid. Reserve marinade. Heat oil in a heavy frying pan over a medium heat. Add chicken pieces, skin side down. Fry until browned, turn over, reduce heat, cover and simmer for ten minutes. Remove chicken from pan and discard any liquid that has collected. Return chicken to pan, pour over remaining marinade and simmer uncovered until all liquid has been absorbed or evaporated. Serve with wedges of lemon.

For variety serve the chicken with lightly sautéed green peppers, or a raw vegetable salad, such as cucumber, radish and celery.

GLAZED CHICKEN TERRIYAKI

2 lb chicken, cut into pieces *or* 4 legs or 4 breasts
  of chicken
4 fl oz ($\frac{1}{2}$ cup) mirin or sherry
4 fl oz ($\frac{1}{2}$ cup) soy sauce
4 fl oz ($\frac{1}{2}$ cup) chicken stock or water
1 tablespoon sugar
2 teaspoons cornflour
1 tablespoon water
7-spices pepper or cayenne to taste

Combine mirin, soy sauce and stock, bring to the boil, and remove sauce from heat. To prepare glaze, extract one third of this sauce and combine with sugar, bring to the boil, reduce heat and simmer. Cream cornflour with water and stir into simmering sauce/sugar mixture. Stir continuously and cook until glaze thickens and clears. Pre-heat medium grill. Brush chicken with remaining sauce and grill skin side up for three to four minutes (longer if you use whole chicken legs or breasts). Turn over and brush top side with more sauce. Cook until well browned. Turn once more, brush with sauce and grill a further two to three minutes. Divide chicken among four bowls, pour glaze over each

and serve sprinkled with 7-spices pepper or cayenne.

SAUTÉ CHICKEN (Niwa Tori)

3 tablespoons soy sauce
2 tablespoons sugar
2 tablespoons water
$\frac{1}{4}$ teaspoon 7-spices pepper or cayenne
1 clove garlic, crushed
2 lb chicken cut into pieces
2 tablespoons vegetable oil
2 spring onions, finely chopped *or* 2 tablespoons
  chives, chopped

Combine first six ingredients and bring to the boil. Remove from heat and marinate chicken in mixture for 30 minutes or more. Remove chicken and reserve marinade. Drain chicken on absorbent paper. Heat oil in a heavy frying pan and fry chicken for six to eight minutes, turning several times during cooking. Finally, add spring onions or chives, cook for a further minute and serve over hot rice and sprinkle with remaining marinade.

DEEP FRIED CHICKEN

Ingredients as for Sauté Chicken (see above) plus cornflour.
Oil for deep frying.

Marinate chicken as in recipe above. Remove from marinade, shake off excess liquid but do not wipe. Dust with cornflour and set aside. Heat oil to 350°F (175°C) or until you see a light haze forming above the oil. Deep fry chicken, a few pieces at a time until golden brown. Drain on absorbent paper. Serve with the spring onion or chives, either fresh or lightly sautéed.

SPICED SAUTÉ CHICKEN WITH VEG-ETABLES

2 tablespoons vegetable oil
1 oz (1 tablespoon) ginger root, grated
2 chilli peppers de-seeded, shredded *or* $\frac{1}{4}$
  teaspoon hot pepper sauce
2 lb chicken cut into pieces
1 medium onion, diced
1 medium carrot, thinly sliced
4 oz ($\frac{1}{4}$ cup) mushrooms, sliced

1 bamboo shoot, diced
4 fl oz (½ cup) chicken stock or water
4 oz (¾ cup) French beans cut into 2" (5 cm)
 lengths *or* 4 oz (¾ cup) cooked peas
4 tablespoons soy sauce
2 tablespoons sugar

Heat oil in a heavy frying pan, add ginger and chilli peppers (but not hot pepper sauce if you are using it), and sauté for one minute. Add chicken pieces and cook for three to four minutes, turning once. Stir in, in order: onions, carrots, mushrooms and bamboo shoots, and sauté each for one minute after adding to pan. Pour in stock, soy sauce and sugar (plus hot pepper sauce if used). Reduce heat, cover and simmer for 15 to 20 minutes. Add French beans or peas and simmer a further two minutes. Serve.

FRIED CHICKEN WITH SESAME SEEDS

4 chicken breasts, boned
2 tablespoons sake or white wine
1 teaspoon salt
2 tablespoons vegetable oil
2 tablespoons sesame seeds
1 lettuce, chilled

Score skin of chicken breasts with a sharp knife and sprinkle with sake and salt. Leave to stand for 30 minutes. Heat oil in a heavy frying pan and fry chicken on both sides until well cooked and browned. Remove chicken and lightly fry sesame seeds in residual oil. Serve chicken sprinkled with sesame seeds in a bed of chilled lettuce leaves.

TWICE FRIED CHICKEN

4 tablespoons soy sauce
1 tablespoon mirin or sherry
Juice 1 lemon
1 teaspoon salt
1 lb chicken breast, boned, cut into ¼" (0.5 cm)
 thick slices
2 tablespoons vegetable oil
4 sticks celery, chilled

Combine first four ingredients and pour over chicken slices. Marinade for one hour or more. Drain and reserve liquid. Heat oil in a heavy

frying pan and lightly fry chicken on both sides. Return to marinade and leave for five minutes. Drain again and fry in same pan until nicely browned both sides. Be careful to drain thoroughly each time, since soy sauce burns easily. Serve with hot rice and sticks of chilled celery.

LIVER TSUKIDANI
A simple and very tasty way of using chicken livers.

8 oz (1 cup) chicken livers
2 tablespoons sake or white wine
2 tablespoons soy sauce
1 teaspoon sugar
½ teaspoon powdered ginger
½ teaspoon cinnamon

Cut liver into mouth-size pieces. Combine the other ingredients, bring to the boil, add liver, reduce heat and simmer uncovered until all liquid has been absorbed or evaporated. Serve hot or cold.

DEEP FRIED LIVER TSUKIDANI
Ingredients as for Liver Tsukidani plus corn-flour. Oil for deep frying.

Cut liver into mouth-size pieces. Combine sake, soy sauce, sugar, ginger and cinnamon. Bring to the boil, remove from heat, add liver and marinate for 30 minutes. Heat oil to 350°F (175°C) or until you see a light haze forming above the oil. Remove liver from marinade, shake off excess liquid but do not wipe dry. Dust with cornflour and deep fry until golden brown. Drain on absorbent paper and serve.

LIVER WITH GARLIC LEAVES
If you are fortunate enough to be able to grow your own garlic, or you know someone else who does, try this recipe using young, tender garlic leaves.

1 lb chicken liver
2 tablespoons sesame seed oil
Bunch garlic leaves
1 teaspoon sugar
1 teaspoon salt

Cover the liver in cold water and leave for one

hour. Drain, add fresh water to just cover liver and bring to the boil. Reduce heat and simmer for 40 minutes. Drain, cut liver into mouth-size pieces, brush with oil, stir in garlic leaves, season with salt and sugar and serve.

FRIED CHICKEN MEAT BALLS (Tsukune)

1 lb minced chicken
1 medium onion, finely diced
Pinch of salt
1 tablespoon sugar
4 tablespoons mirin or sherry
2 tablespoons soy sauce
1 egg, beaten
2 fl oz (¼ cup) water
2 tablespoons vegetable oil
Togarashi or black pepper to taste

Thoroughly mix minced chicken, onion, salt, sugar, two tablespoons mirin, one tablespoon soy sauce and egg. Form mixture into bite-size balls with the sides slightly flattened. Heat oil in a heavy frying pan and fry chicken meat balls until browned all over. Add water and remaining mirin and soy sauce. Cook over low heat until all liquid has been absorbed or evaporated. Serve seasoned to taste with togarashi or black pepper.

DEEP FRIED CHICKEN MEAT BALLS WITH MISO

1 lb minced chicken
1 medium onion, finely diced
1 medium bean shoot, finely diced
1 tablespoon sugar
1 tablespoon miso
1 egg, beaten
2 tablespoons flour
Oil for deep frying
1 tablespoon wasabi or English mustard paste

Combine all the ingredients except oil and wasabi and mix thoroughly. Form into bite-size balls. Heat oil to 350°F (175°C) or until you see a light haze forming above the oil. Deep fry chicken meat balls until golden brown. Drain on absorbent paper and serve with a small bowl of wasabi or mustard.

BOILED CHICKEN AND VEGETABLE BALLS

4 shiitake or 4 oz (¼ cup) mushrooms
12 oz (1½ cups) minced chicken
1 small carrot, grated
½ medium onion, diced
1 egg, beaten
1 tablespoon soy sauce
1 tablespoon sugar
1½ pt (3½ cups) chicken stock
1 tablespoon wasabi or English mustard paste
8 oz (1½ cups) French beans, parboiled in a little salted water (optional)

Soak shiitake in cold water for 20 minutes. Drain, cut off hard stems and slice into small pieces, otherwise use mushrooms, finely chopped. Combine all the ingredients except stock, wasabi and French beans. Form mixture into bite-size balls. Bring stock to the boil and carefully lower in chicken and vegetable balls. Return to the boil, reduce heat and simmer gently for eight to ten minutes. Serve with wasabi for dipping and a side dish of French beans.

BOILED CHICKEN AND VEGETABLE BALLS WITH TURNIPS

Ingredients as for Boiled Chicken and Vegetable Balls (above) plus 4 small turnips, peeled.

Quarter turnips from root end, but stop knife cuts ½" (1.25 cm) from top of turnip. Now proceed as for recipe above, but add the four turnips to boiling stock, alongside chicken and vegetable balls. Cover the top of contents of pan with a lid that will fit inside the pan being used. This holds down the turnips and they cook more quickly. Bring pan to the boil, reduce heat, cover with correct size lid and simmer until turnips are tender (about ten minutes). Serve as in recipe above.

BOILED CHICKEN AND CARROT (For six people)

2 pt water
2 lb chicken, cut into pieces
2 lb carrots, sliced
2 cloves garlic, thinly sliced

Salt and soy sauce to taste
¼ oz (1 tablespoon) bonito flakes (optional)
2 young leeks or 4 spring onions, cut into 1" (2.5 cm) lengths

Add water, chicken and carrot to a heavy pan. Bring to the boil, reduce heat and simmer for 30 to 40 minutes or until chicken is cooked. Remove any scum that forms. Add garlic, salt and soy sauce. Wrap bonito flakes in a piece of gauze and suspend in pan. Gently boil for a further ten minutes. Discard bonito, stir in leeks and serve. Substitute 4 oz (½ cup) fish trimmings for bonito flakes.

CHICKEN CROQUETTES (Tori Kuroke)

8 oz (1 cup) minced chicken
8 oz (1½ cups) cooked potato, mashed
¼ medium onion, diced
Pinch of salt
1 egg, beaten
1 tablespoon soy sauce
Breadcrumbs
Oil for deep frying
1 sheet nori, toasted or 2 tablespoons sesame seeds, toasted

Combine first six ingredients and mix thoroughly. Form into bite-size balls and roll in breadcrumbs. Heat oil to 350°F (175°C) or until you see a light haze forming above the oil. Deep fry croquettes, a few at a time, until golden brown. Drain on absorbent paper and serve sprinkled with crumbled nori or sesame seeds.

AUBERGINES WITH CHICKEN SAUCE

4 small aubergines
2 tablespoons vegetable oil
8 oz (1 cup) minced chicken
2 tablespoons sugar
4 fl oz (½ cup) chicken stock or water
2 tablespoons miso
2 tablespoons sake or white wine (optional)

Cut aubergines almost in half but leave stem end intact. Score shiny sides with sharp knife cuts. Brush all over with some of the oil. Pre-heat moderate grill. Open aubergines to show as much inside surface as possible and grill until just soft. Turn once during cooking. Heat a heavy pan and brush with remaining oil, add chicken and sauté over moderate heat for one minute. Cream the miso with a little of the stock and add this and all the remaining ingredients to the pan. Stir well and simmer for eight to ten minutes. Arrange egg plants, half open, in individual bowls. Pour over chicken sauce and serve.

CHICKEN AND CUCUMBER ROLL

An unusual way of making use of left-over chicken, and a fascinating way of using cucumbers. Try this recipe instead of chicken and cucumber sandwiches for those Sunday teas and surprise your aunties!

2 large cucumbers, cut in half crosswise, peeled
2 pt (5 cups) water
1 tablespoon salt
8 oz (1 cup) cooked chicken, minced
4 hard boiled egg yolks
¼ chilli pepper, finely shredded or dash hot pepper sauce
1 tablespoon sesame seeds, toasted (optional)
1 tablespoon water

Salt water and immerse cucumbers in it. Leave for 30 minutes, drain. Hold cucumber vertically and carefully peel off a continuous thin sheet about 2" (5 cm) wide. Work from the narrow end and move in a spiral toward the other end. Discard the soft core of cucumber. Combine chicken, egg yolks, chilli pepper, sesame seeds and water. Mix thoroughly. Lay cucumber rolls flat and spread a quarter of chicken mixture along the length of each piece. Roll up into sausage roll shape. Chill and serve cold, cut into thin slices.

BOILED CHICKEN WITH VEGETABLES

4 dried shiitake or 4 oz (¼ cup) mushrooms
1 lb chicken cut into pieces
2 tablespoons sugar
2 tablespoons soy sauce
4 tablespoons mirin or sherry
4 fl oz (½ cup) chicken stock or water
1 medium carrot, cut into matchsticks
4 oz (¼ cup) bamboo shoots, cut into half moons
4 oz (¼ cup) water chestnuts

95

Soak shiitake in cold water for 20 minutes. Drain, cut away hard stems and thinly slice. Otherwise use sliced mushrooms. Combine sugar, soy sauce, mirin and stock and bring to the boil. Add chichen, return to the boil, reduce heat, cover and simmer for 30–40 minutes or until chicken is tender. Remove chicken pieces from pan and add to it the shiitake, carrot, bamboo shoots and water chestnuts. Return to the boil, reduce heat, cover and simmer until carrots are tender. Return chicken to pan and gently heat uncovered until nearly all the liquid has evaporated. Serve.

CHICKEN AND SHRIMP WITH LEMON DIPPING SAUCE

6 fl oz (1¼ cups) chicken stock or water
2 tablespoons soy sauce
2 tablespoons sugar
4 large shrimps, shelled
8 oz (1 cup) lean chicken meat, diced
8 oz (1¼ cups) bamboo shoots, cut into thin half moons
2 medium green peppers, de-seeded and quartered
2 small leeks, cut into 1" (2.5 cm) lengths
6 oz (¼ cup) tofu, 1" (2.5 cm) cubes (optional)
3 tablespoons lemon juice

Pre-heat moderate oven. Combine stock, soy sauce and sugar, bring to the boil and add shrimps. Poach for two to three minutes. Remove shrimps and add chicken pieces to same liquid, return to the boil, reduce heat and cook chicken until tender. Repeat with each of the vegetables and tofu and store each cooked item in oven to keep warm. Now reduce cooking liquid, over moderate heat, to half its volume, add lemon juice, bring to the boil and remove from heat. Arrange chicken, prawns, vegetable and tofu in colourful pattern on a large plate and serve with lemon sauce for dipping.

Prawns may be used in place of shrimps.

DEEP FRIED CHICKEN IN BROTH

Oil for deep frying
1 lb chicken, cut into pieces
Cornflour

1½ pt (3½ cups) chicken stock
2 tablespoons soy sauce
2 tablespoons sugar
1 oz (1 tablespoon) ginger root, grated
8 oz (1½ cups) Chinese cabbage, shredded
2 medium green peppers, de-seeded, cut into 1" (2.5 cm) wide strips
4 oz (¼ cup) mushrooms, whole
½ bunch watercress or parsley, chopped

Heat oil to 350°F (175°C) or until you see a slight haze forming above the oil. Dust chicken with cornflour and deep fry golden brown. Remove from oil and drain on absorbent paper. Combine chicken with remaining ingredients except watercress or parsley and bring to the boil. Reduce heat and simmer until vegetables are cooked. Serve in individual bowls garnished with watercress or parsley.

COLD CHICKEN WITH MUSTARD DRESSING

Very lightly cooked chicken with a mustard dressing, this is almost a chicken sashimi and is sometimes served alongside a plate of sashimi.

8 oz chicken breast, boned
1 pt (2½ cups) water
1 medium cucumber, sliced
2 tablespoons vinegar
1 teaspoon salt
1 tablespoon wasabi or English mustard paste
2 tablespoons soy sauce
¼ sheet nori, toasted (optional)

Cut chicken into thin slices about 1" (2.5 cm) long. Bring water to the boil and dip chicken into water for 20–30 seconds. Drain, place in bowl and sprinkle with vinegar. Salt cucumber slices and allow to stand 30 minutes. Drain, and dab dry with a clean cloth. Combine chicken, cucumber and wasabi, sprinkle with soy sauce and crumbled nori. Serve.

COLD CHICKEN WITH DRESSING

12 oz (1½ cups) cooked chicken, diced
1 teaspoon salt
2 tablespoons sake or white wine
2 tablespoons vinegar

1 teaspoon sugar
½ teaspoon dry mustard powder (wasabi or English)

Sprinkle chicken with salt and sake. Chill for 30 minutes. Combine vinegar, sugar and mustard. Dip chicken into the dressing before eating.

BAKED CHICKEN AND MUSHROOMS
Like the Baked Fish dish (see p. 85) this way of baking chicken was devised to be used on top of the stove. It really preserves the flavour of the cooked foods. In a Western kitchen, oven baking is more convenient and just as good as the original way of cooking.

4 chicken legs or breasts
1 teaspoon salt
4 shiitake *or* 4 large fresh mushrooms
1 lemon cut into 4 slices
1 tablespoon vegetable oil
1 young leek or 2 spring onions, thinly sliced
4 fl oz (½ cup) soy sauce
4 fl oz (½ cup) lemon juice

Soak shiitake for 20 minutes in cold water. Cut away hard stems and criss-cross caps with shallow knife cuts. Otherwise use fresh mushrooms with stems removed. Sprinkle salt on chicken and mushrooms. Pre-heat oven to 370°F (190°C). Cut out 4 pieces of aluminium foil large enough to wrap each chicken piece. Brush one side of each piece of foil with oil, and arrange on top a piece of chicken topped with one mushroom and one lemon slice. Wrap securely and bake in oven for 30 minutes. Meanwhile, prepare dipping sauce. Combine soy sauce and lemon juice and divide among four small bowls. Add a portion of chopped leek to each. Serve each foil-wrapped chicken parcel with a small dish of dipping sauce.

BAKED CELERY WRAPPED CHICKEN
An unusual addition to a buffet meal, or serve as an hors d'oeuvre.

2 chicken wings, boned
2 stalks celery

Pre-heat oven to 370°F (190°C). Cut chicken into narrow, thin slices. Cut celery into 6" (15 cm) lengths and slice each stalk vertically into 4 lengths. Wrap each celery length with two overlapping pieces of chicken and secure in place with toothpicks. Bake in oven for 15 minutes or until chicken is cooked. Cut into mouth-size pieces and serve.

CHICKEN WRAPPED WITH NORI SEAWEED
Slightly tricky to put together, but an excellent addition to a Japanese dinner. If you cannot obtain nori, substitute strips of paper-thin omelette (see p 43).

8 oz cooked chicken breast
2 tablespoons soy sauce
2 tablespoons sake or white wine
½ sheet nori, cut into ½" (1.25 cm) wide strips
1 egg white
2 tablespoons vegetable oil

Cut chicken meat into pieces about 2" (5 cm) × 1" (2.5 cm) × ¼" (0.5 cm) thick. Combine soy sauce and sake and marinate chicken in mixture for 30 minutes to one hour. Remove chicken and roll a piece into tight roll, secure with a strip of nori dipped in egg white. Repeat for each piece of chicken. Heat one tablespoon oil in a heavy frying pan and lightly fry half the chicken rolls. Repeat with remaining oil and rolls. Drain on absorbent paper and serve.

PORK

GRILLED PORK (Buta Terriyaki)
Teriyaki dishes always involve some marinating process in a sauce that nearly always includes, among other things, soy sauce, sugar and garlic. Here we give recipes for two teriyaki sauces. Sauce I is sweeter than Sauce II. Both sauces can be made more spicy by the addition of a little chopped chilli pepper or a dash of hot pepper sauce.

1 lb lean pork, cut into 1" (2.5 cm) cubes
2 tablespoons sesame seeds, toasted (optional)

SAUCE I
4 fl oz (½ cup) soy sauce
2 tablespoons mirin or sweet sherry

1 clove garlic, crushed
1 teaspoon sugar

SAUCE II
6 fl oz (1½ cups) soy sauce
1 oz ginger root, grated *or* 1 teaspoon powdered
    ginger
1 clove garlic, crushed
Juice of 1 lemon
1 tablespoon sugar

Combine ingredients of Sauce I or II and marinate pork in mixture for one or two hours. Pre-heat medium grill. Remove pork from marinade and grill until nicely brown on all sides. Baste with marinade during grilling. Serve garnished with sesame seeds over hot boiled rice. Accompany with grilled vegetables, for example green peppers, onions, mushrooms, etc.

CRISPY FRIED PORK
Ingredients as for Grilled Pork plus cornflour, oil for deep frying. Marinate pork as for Grilled Pork. Remove pork from marinade, but do not wipe. Coat each piece with cornflour. Heat oil to 350°F (175°C) or until you see a slight haze forming above the oil. Deep fry the pork a few pieces at a time until golden brown. Drain on absorbent paper and serve as for Grilled Pork.

PORK KEBABS
Strangely, traditional Japanese pork kebabs are deep fried and not grilled. Cubes of lean pork are skewered with a selection of vegetables, dipped in flour, egg white, breadcrumbs and deep fried. The vegetables given in the recipe are suggestions only, and you may add or substitute others.

1 lb lean pork, cut into ½" (1.25 cm) cubes
1 small aubergine, cut into 1" (2.5 cm) cubes
2 medium green peppers cut into 1" (2.5 cm)
    squares
4 oz (¼ cup) small mushrooms, left whole
2 leeks, cut into 1" (2.5 cm) lengths
8 baby onions
Salt and black pepper to taste
Flour
2 eggs, beaten

Breadcrumbs
Oil for deep frying
Soy sauce

Oil four or more skewers and string on to each peices of pork and vegetables in an attractive, colourful order. Season with salt and black pepper. Dust each with flour, brush with egg and roll in breadcrumbs. Set aside. Heat oil to 350°F (175°C) or until you see a light haze forming above the oil. Deep fry kebabs a few at a time for four to five minutes or until golden brown. Serve with soy sauce.

FRIED PORK CUTLET
If she wants to cook pork, apart from buying a few slices of lean pork, the Japanese housewife is most likely to purchase pork cutlets. The cutlet is cooked, then boned and the lean meat cut into mouth-size pieces. Frying is the simplest and most common cooking method.

1 lb pork cutlets
2 eggs, beaten
Breadcrumbs
Oil for frying
Soy sauce

Brush cutlets with beaten egg, and roll in breadcrumbs. Set aside. Heat ¼" (0.5 cm) oil in a heavy frying pan and fry cutlets for five to six minutes, or until golden brown, turning once during cooking. Remove, drain on absorbent paper, cut meat away from bones and into mouth-size pieces. Serve over hot rice with soy sauce.

PORK CUTLET DONBURI (Katsudon)
This recipe is similar to the one above, but a little more elaborate and substantial. It is a popular lunchtime meal.

8 fl oz (1 cup) soup stock or water
4 fl oz (½ cup) soy sauce
3 tablespoons sugar
2 tablespoons mirin or sherry (optional)
1 medium onion, diced
1 lb Fried Pork Cutlet (see recipe on p. 98)
4 eggs, beaten
8 oz (1½ cups) bean sprouts
1 lb cooked rice ·

Pre-heat moderate oven. Combine first four ingredients and bring to the boil. Add onion, reduce heat and simmer. Prepare Fried Pork Cutlets (see recipe above), and set aside in oven to keep warm. Drain most of the oil from the pan in which the cutlets were cooked, and add bean sprouts, cooking until just soft. Pour in beaten eggs and lightly scramble. Pour boiling water over cooked rice, drain and divide rice among four bowls. Top each with a portion of bean sprouts and egg, crown with pork cutlets and pour over each a portion of the simmering sauce and onion. Do not use all the sauce if it means causing liquid to form in the bottom of the bowls. Serve.

PORK CUTLET WITH SESAME SEEDS

3 tablespoons sesame seeds, toasted
4 tablespoons sake or white wine
4 tablespoons soy sauce
1 clove garlic, crushed
1 tablespoon sugar
2 tablespoons vegetable oil
1 lb pork cutlets
1 tablespoon wasabi or English mustard paste

Crush sesame seeds in a suribachi or mortar, add garlic, sake, soy sauce and sugar. Mix well. Heat oil in a heavy frying pan, add pork cutlets and brown on both sides. Reduce heat and evenly cover the top of each cutlet with sesame seed mixture. Cover pan and cook for three to four minutes. Serve with small bowl of wasabi or mustard.

HOT FRIED PORK (Buta Yaki)

For this dish you do not need lean meat and any soft fat is complemented by the recommended fresh chilled side salad.

2 tablespoons soy sauce
2 tablespoons sake or white wine
2 tablespoons sesame seeds, pounded to a paste in suribachi or mortar
½–1 chilli pepper, shredded
1 lb pork, sliced ¼" (0.5 cm) thick

Combine the first four ingredients and marinate the pork in the mixture for one hour. Remove pork from marinade, cut into 1" (2.5 cm) square pieces. Heat oil in heavy frying pan and fry pork squares until brown on both sides. Divide pork among four bowls, sprinkle with remaining marinade. Toss salad in dressing and serve with bowls of pork.

SALAD
2 oz (¼ cup) cooked somen or vermicelli
4 oz (¼ cup) cucumber, sliced
2 tomatoes, thinly sliced ˙

DRESSING
2 tablespoons vinegar
1 teaspoon black pepper
1 tablespoon sugar

Prepare the salad by mixing somen, cucumber and tomatoes. Store in refrigerator. Make dressing by mixing vinegar, black pepper and sugar. Set aside until about to be eaten, then toss.

MARINATED PORK WITH LOTUS ROOT AND GREEN PEPPER

This is a tasty dish that looks interesting and colourful.

4 tablespoons soy sauce
4 tablespoons sugar
1 clove garlic, crushed
1 oz (1 tablespoon) ginger root, grated
1 lb pork cutlets
2 tablespoons vegetable oil
2 medium green peppers, de-seeded, cut into ½" (1.25 cm) wide strips
1 medium onion, diced
2 lotus roots, thinly sliced
Salt and black pepper to taste

Combine first four ingredients and marinate pork in the mixture for 30 minutes. Pre-heat moderate oven. Remove cutlets from marinade. Reserve marinade. Heat oil in a heavy frying pan and fry pork on both sides until nicely browned and cooked. Remove from pan and set aside in oven to keep warm. Add the green peppers and onion to the pan and fry over medium heat until onion is just transparent. Add lotus root and marinade and heat through. Divide pork cutlets among four bowls, pour over vegetables and sauce. Serve with boiled rice.

COOKED PORK WITH BAMBOO SHOOTS

A quick and interesting way of using left-over pork.

2 tablespoons vegetable oil
8 oz (1 cup) cooked pork, cut into mouth-size pieces
4 bamboo shoots, cut into matchsticks
2 tablespoons sake or white wine
4 tablespoons soy sauce
1 tablespoon sugar
4 oz (¾ cup) garden peas, cooked in a little salted water, drained *or* 4 oz (¾ cup) tinned peas, heated and drained
Pinch 7-spices pepper or cayenne

Heat oil in a heavy pan, add pork and sauté for one minute. Add bamboo shoots, sake, soy sauce and sugar. Heat thoroughly. Divide among four bowls and serve garnished with peas and seasoned with 7-spices pepper.

PORK MEAT BALLS

4 shiitake or 4 oz (¾ cup) mushrooms
1 lb minced pork
½ medium onion diced
1 egg, beaten
4 tablespoons soy sauce
1 teaspoon sugar
½ teaspoon salt
1 tablespoon flour
1 tablespoon wasabi or English mustard paste
Oil for deep frying

Soak the shiitake for 20 minutes. Cut away hard stem and chop finely. Otherwise use finely chopped mushrooms. Combine pork, shiitake, onion, egg, one tablespoon soy sauce, sugar, salt and flour and mix well. Form into bite-size balls. Heat oil to 350°F (175°C) or until you see a slight haze forming above the oil. Deep fry meatballs a few at a time until golden brown. Drain on absorbent paper. Mix wasabi with three tablespoons soy sauce and serve as a dipping sauce for meatballs.

PORK AND APPLE MEATBALLS

Proceed as for Pork Meatballs but replace onion with one medium apple, grated.

BOILED PORK AND TURNIPS

1 pt (2½ cups) water
½ medium onion, diced
1 oz (1 tablespoon) ginger root, grated
1 lb lean pork, cut into ¼" (0.5 cm) thick slices
1 lb small turnips, quartered
2 tablespoons sugar
4 fl oz (½ cup) soy sauce

Bring water to the boil, add onion, ginger and pork. Return to the boil, add turnips and gently simmer for one hour. Stir in soy sauce and sugar and simmer another ten minutes. Serve. Substitute carrots for turnips if you wish.

FRIED PORK STEW

1 lb lean pork, cut into 1" (2.5 cm) cubes
2 tablespoons vegetable oil
Cornflour
1 medium onion, sliced
2 medium carrots, ½" (1.25 cm) thick slices
8 oz (1½ cups) Chinese cabbage or drumhead cabbage, shredded
2 sticks celery, chopped
1 pt (2½ cups) chicken stock
2 tablespoons soy sauce
2 teaspoons sugar
1 teaspoon salt
1 tablespoon sake or white wine (optional)

Heat oil in a heavy frying pan. Dust pork with cornflour and fry, stirring frequently, for three to four minutes. Transfer pork to another pan and fry onions until lightly browned in the same frying pan. Add onions and remaining ingredients to pork, bring to the boil, reduce heat, cover and simmer until pork and vegetables are cooked (about fifteen to twenty minutes). Serve with separate bowls of boiled rice. Other vegetables may be added or substituted in the stew.

PORK WITH TOFU AND CUCUMBER

2 tablespoons vegetable oil
1 clove garlic, crushed
1 lb lean pork, cut into 1" (2.5 cm) cubes
2 bamboo shoots, cut into ½" (1.25 cm) cubes
4 oz (¾ cup) mushrooms, sliced

4 fl oz ($\frac{1}{2}$ cup) soy sauce
6 oz ($\frac{1}{3}$ cup) tofu, cut into 1" (2.5 cm) cubes
$\frac{1}{2}$ cucumber, sliced
2 spring onions, finely chopped *or* 1 tablespoon
    chopped chives

Heat oil in a heavy frying pan, add garlic and sauté for one minute. Add pork and brown on all sides. Stir in mushrooms, bamboo shoots and soy sauce. Reduce heat, cover and simmer for five minutes. Add tofu and cucumber, heat through and serve garnished with spring onion or chives.

PORK WITH DEEP FRIED TOFU
The fried tofu (aburage) absorbs the flavour of the vegetable and meat and unites them.

2 tablespoons vegetable oil
8 oz (1 cup) Pork, cut into 1" (2.5 cm) cubes
1 oz (1 tablespoon) ginger root, grated
1 medium onion, sliced
4 oz ($\frac{1}{4}$ cup) Chinese or drumhead cabbage,
    shredded
12 oz ($2\frac{1}{4}$ cup) deep fried tofu (see p. 77)
4 tablespoons soy sauce
4 fl oz ($\frac{1}{2}$ cup) soup stock or water
Salt to taste

Heat oil in a heavy pan, add the pork and sauté for two to three minutes. Add the ginger, onion and cabbage and sauté a further two or three minutes. Stir in the remaining ingredients, bring to the boil, cover and simmer until pork is cooked (about 15 to 20 minutes). Serve. Other greens may be substituted for the cabbage, for example broccoli, Brussels sprouts, etc.

PORK AND ONION IN BROTH

2 tablespoons vegetable oil
1 lb pork, cut into $\frac{1}{4}$" (0.5 cm) thick slices
2 medium onions, quartered
1 pt ($2\frac{1}{2}$ cups) chicken stock
3 tablespoons soy sauce
1 teaspoon salt
$\frac{1}{4}$ teaspoon togarashi or black pepper
1 tablespoon sugar
1 tablespoon cornflour
1 tablespoon water
4 oz ($\frac{1}{4}$ cup) garden peas, cooked in a little salted

water, drained *or* 4 oz ($\frac{1}{4}$ cup) tinned peas,
heated, drained

Heat oil in a heavy pan, add pork and onion and sauté over moderate heat until pork is tender. Add remaining ingredients except cornflour, water and peas. Bring to the boil, reduce heat, cover and simmer for five minutes. Cream cornflour with water, stir into pan and continue simmering until thickened and clear. Serve garnished with peas.

SPICED PORK WITH MISO

2 tablespoons vegetable oil
1 lb (2 cups) pork, diced $\frac{1}{2}$" (1.25 cm) cubes
1 bamboo shoot, cut into matchsticks
4 oz ($\frac{1}{4}$ cup) mushrooms, sliced
$\frac{1}{2}$ chilli pepper, shredded
2 tablespoons miso
1 teaspoon sugar
6 oz ($\frac{1}{3}$ cup) tofu

Heat oil in a heavy frying pan, add the pork and stir, fry until well browned. Add the mushrooms and bamboo shoots, sauté until mushrooms are tender. Reduce heat and stir in remaining ingredients except tofu. Squeeze excess moisture from tofu with clean cloth, mash in a bowl and add to pan. Heat through and serve with rice.

BEEF

GRILLED BEEF (Yaki Niku)
4 fl oz ($\frac{1}{2}$ cup) soy sauce
1 tablespoon sugar
1 clove garlic, crushed
1 oz (1 tablespoon) ginger root, grated
2 tablespoons mirin or sherry (optional)
1 lb lean beaf, thinly sliced

Combine first five ingredients, mix well and marinate beef in mixture for one hour or more. Pre-heat medium grill. Remove beef from marinade and grill for two to four minutes (depending on how well done you wish it) on each side. Baste with marinade once or twice during cooking. Cut into 1" (2.5 cm) strips and serve with rice and salad. Store residual marinade in sealed container in refrigerator. It keeps for up to a month.

GLAZED GRILLED BEEF

Ingredients as for Grilled Beef (p. 101) plus 2 teaspoons cornflour.

Marinate meat as above, and remove from marinade, but before grilling prepare glaze as follows: Cream cornflour with a little of the marinade. Bring remainder to the boil and stir in creamed cornflour, continue heating until marinade has thickened and cleared. Remove from heat. Grill meat as described above, but do not baste with marinade. Cut beef into 1" (2.5 cm) strips, arrange in a bowl or over hot boiled rice and pour over thickened marinade or glaze.

BEEF KEBABS

Ingredients as for Grilled Beef (p. 101).

Marinate beef as for Grilled Beef. Remove beef from marinade and cut into 1–2" (2.5–5 cm) squares. Thread on to skewers. Pre-heat medium grill and grill kebabs for two to three minutes each side. Baste once or twice with marinade.

For variety, grill alongside skewered beef squares, skewers of onion and green pepper or aubergines cut into suitable shapes.

DEEP FRIED BEEF KEBABS

Ingredients as for Grilled Beef (p. 101) plus:

1 egg, beaten
Breadcrumbs
Oil for deep frying

Marinate beef as for Grilled Beef. Remove beef from marinade and cut into 1–2" (2.5–5 cm) squares. Thread on to skewers, brush with egg and roll in breadcrumbs. Heat oil to 350°F (175°C) or until you see a light haze forming above the oil. Deep fry skewered beef until golden brown. This method may also be used for beef skewered with squares of onion and/or green pepper and/or aubergine.

FRIED BEEF WITH FRESH VEGETABLES

2 green peppers, de-seeded, thinly sliced

1 medium onion, thinly sliced
½ medium cucumber, sliced
1 chilli pepper, shredded (optional)
1 tablespoon sesame seeds, toasted
½ teaspoon salt
1 clove garlic, crushed
1 young leek, finely chopped
2 tablespoons vegetable oil
1 lb lean beef, cut into ¼" (0.5 cm) thick strips

Arrange green peppers, onion and cucumber in an attractive pattern in serving bowl and chill. Pound sesame seeds in a suribachi or mortar, add the chilli pepper, salt, garlic and leek and mix well. Brush slices of beef with half this mixture. Heat oil in a heavy frying pan, add coated beef and fry until meat is tender. Serve with a fresh salad and a bowl of the remaining sesame seed mixture and boiled rice.

DEEP FRIED BEEF WITH SPICED DAIKON

A most unusual way of serving beef. Traditionally daikon is used. If you cannot obtain any, substitute turnips.

2 small daikon, peeled
2 chilli peppers, de-seeded, cut in half
1 lb lean beef, cut into 2" × 1" (5 cm × 2.5 cm) strips
2 tablespoons sake or white wine
2 tablespoons soy sauce
Cornflour
Oil for deep frying
8 oz (1½ cups) French beans, parboiled in a little salted water

Make two small holes the diameter of a pencil in each end of the daikon. Push half a chilli pepper into each and leave for two to three hours. Combine sake and soy sauce and marinate beef in this mixture for one hour. Remove beef from marinade, shake off excess liquid and roll in cornflour. Set aside for a few minutes. Finely grate daikon and chill. Heat oil to 350°F (175°C) or until you see a slight haze forming above the oil. Deep fry beef until golden brown (one to two minutes). Drain on absorbent paper. Distribute beef among four bowls, add grated daikon and garnish with parboiled French beans.

FRIED BEEF WITH SESAME SEEDS AND VEGETABLES

8 oz beef cut into ¼" (0.5 cm) thick slices
2 tablespoons sake or white wine
¼ teaspoon salt
2–3 tablespoons vegetable oil
1 tablespoon sesame seeds
2 green peppers, de-seeded, sliced
4 oz (¼ cup) bean sprouts
2 stalks celery, chopped
1 small lettuce

Score surface of beef with light knife cuts. Sprinkle with salt and sake and set aside for 15–20 minutes. Heat two tablespoons oil in a heavy frying pan, add beef, fry until tender and brown both sides. Remove beef from pan, add sesame seeds and fry light brown, stir in peppers, cook for one minute, add bean sprouts plus remaining oil if necessary, and cook until just wilted. Return meat to pan and heat through. Divide contents of pan among four bowls and serve with fresh celery and lettuce salad.

MINCED BEEF WITH MARROW
Pumpkin may be substituted for the marrow.

2 oz (2 tablespoons) ginger root, grated
2 tablespoons sake or white wine
3 tablespoons sugar
4 tablespoons soy sauce
8 oz minced beef
1 lb marrow, peeled, de-seeded and cut into 1–2" (2.5–5 cm) cubes
Water
2 teaspoons cornflour

Place half the grated ginger, sake, three tablespoons soy sauce and two tablespoons sugar in a heavy pan. Heat to boiling, add beef and cook with constant stirring for four to five minutes. Add marrow, remaining soy sauce and sugar and just cover with water. Bring to the boil, reduce heat and simmer until marrow is just tender. Cream cornflour with a little water. Remove marrow from pan and arrange in a serving dish. Stir cornflour into pan and cook until mixture thickens. Pour over marrow and garnish with remaining ginger.

BEEF STEW

2 tablespoons vegetable oil
1 clove garlic, crushed
1 lb beef, cut into mouth-size pieces
2 green peppers, de-seeded, cut into ½" (1.25 cm) strips
2 medium onions, sliced
2 bamboo shoots, cut into ½" (1.25 cm) cubes
2 lotus roots, cut into half-moons
1 small tin water chestnuts
1 pt (2½ cups) beef stock or water
1 lb fresh ripe or tinned tomatoes
Salt and black pepper to taste
2 spring onions, finely chopped *or* 1 tablespoon chopped chives

Heat oil in a heavy pan, add garlic, sauté for one minute, add beef, and sauté for two to three minutes. Stir in peppers and cook until just tender. Add remaining ingredients, except spring onions or chives, bring to the boil, reduce heat, cover and simmer until beef is tender. Season with salt and black pepper and serve, topped with spring onions or chives. Add or substitute any vegetables you wish.

VEGETABLES ROLLED IN BEEF

8 oz (1 cup) lean beef, cut into 4 thin slices approximately 2" × 6" (5 cm × 15 cm)
Pinch ginger powder
4 tablespoons soy sauce
1 leek, finely sliced
1 medium carrot, cut into 1" (2.5 cm) matchsticks
1 medium green pepper, 2" (5 cm) long by ½" (1.25 cm) wide strips
2 oz (⅓ cup) mushrooms, sliced
2 tablespoons vegetable oil
2 tablespoons mirin or sherry (optional)
1 small lettuce

Marinade beef in 2 tablespoons soy sauce and a pinch of ginger for 15 minutes. Lay out strips. Divide vegetables into 4 portions and arrange a layer of mixed vegetables at the end of each strip of beef. Roll up beef and vegetables and secure with a toothpick. Heat oil in a heavy frying pan and fry beef rolls well on all sides. Move toothpick back and forth if necessary. Add remaining soy sauce and mirin and fry another two minutes. Remove toothpicks and serve on a bed of lettuce.

GYOZA

Any excuse for a party was the slogan of my neighbours in Japan, and one of the dishes they always made for these enjoyable events was gyoza, spoonfuls of minced meat and vegetables wrapped in small rounds of dough, fried, and served with soy sauce.

12 oz (3 cups) plain flour
Pinch of salt
4–6 tablespoons oil
6–8 oz (¾–1 cup) water
2 cloves garlic, crushed
1 medium onion, finely diced
¼ medium carrot, grated
8 oz (2 cups) minced beef
Dash of hot pepper sauce (optional)
1 egg, beaten
Soy sauce to taste

Combine the flour, salt and two tablespoons oil and thoroughly mix. Add water, slowly stirring continuously until you have a firm dough. Knead well, and then roll out flat on a floured board. Cut out rounds of dough about 3" (7.5 cm) in diameter (about 16–20). Set aside. Heat remaining oil in a heavy frying pan, add the garlic and sauté for one minute. Add onions, carrot and minced beef and fry until onions and beef are nicely browned. Remove the mixture from the pan and spoon one to two tablespoons on to each of the dough rounds. Paint the edge of each round with egg, fold one side over to meet the other. Crimp the edges together. Take each half moon shape and flatten the side without a seam to form little packages that will stand upright. Fry the gyoza in the pan in which the meat and vegetables were cooked. Add more oil if needed. Brown both sides of the gyoza and serve hot with soy sauce.

Alternatively, the gyoza can be deep fried or boiled. For deep frying see p.118. To boil, bring a large pan of water to the boil, drop gyoza in and gently boil until they start to float to the surface. Drain and serve.

ONE POT MEALS (COOKED AT THE TABLE)
(Nabe-Mono)

In Japanese, nabe means a pot or casserole, and nabe-mono are pot things. The name is given to complete meals prepared in a single pan or casserole, a style of cooking which lends itself admirably to the lovely Japanese tradition of cooking at the table.

In this method of cooking, the diners are involved in the preparation of the meal, and the host and hostess can spend all of their time with their guests. Cooking at the table also ensures that the food is eaten piping hot, and that it is cooked to just the degree chosen by each guest. Another attraction in Japan, where very few houses have central heating, is that the hibachi or table cooker gives off a warm glow, and what could be more pleasurable on a cold night than sitting around a charcoal burner eating hot food.

All the ingredients for a nabe-mono meal are prepared beforehand, and attractively arranged on one or two large serving dishes before laying on the table. The guests sit around the table (a low table with cushions for sitting on is the best arrangement), and the food is cooked in a frying pan or casserole over a hot plate (electric, gas, paraffin or charcoal). Frying and boiling are the two principal cooking methods used for nabe-mono. The famous table meal sukiyaki (pronounced ski-yaki) is fried and mizutaki, not well known in the West, but very popular in Japan, is boiled. One other cooking method occasionally used is given the strange name of Mongolian or Ghengis Khan grilling. The name refers to a system of charcoal grilling at the table.

Near where I lived in Japan was a Mongolian steak house, and as I passed I always expected to see hordes of Mongolian warriors bursting through the doors. Fortunately, most of the customers didn't live up to expectations. Mongolian grilling is especially suitable for an out-of-doors barbecue.

The ingredients for a nabe-mono meal are accompanied by condiments, sauces, boiled rice and maybe a salad. Thus for a meal for four, you will ideally need the following equipment:

One low table plus four cushions

One hot plate (electric, gas, paraffin or charcoal)

One deep frying pan or large heat-proof casserole or heavy pan (an electric frying pan is ideal)

Two large serving dishes

Jugs for the cooking stock or for frying oil, and for cooking sauces

Four bowls for the main meal

Four bowls for the rice

Small dishes for sauces and salads

Four pairs of chopsticks and one pair of long cooking chopsticks

A ladle, perforated spoon and fish slice

Last, but not least, a teapot and small cups for preparing and drinking liberal amounts of tea during and after the meal:

Any special instructions applicable to a specific recipe will be given with the recipe but there are a few general tips that apply to all the nabe-mono meals. If the ingredients include fish and or meat, they are usually cooked first to add flavour to the stock. Apart from this, start with the ingredients that need longest cooking. If, however, particular vegetables need an extra long cooking time, parboil them first. Always drain washed vegetables well, and store in a refrigerator, after preparation, until required. They should look crisp and fresh when laid on the table. Where a recipe requires very thinly sliced pieces of beef or fish this can be done more easily if the meat or fish is partially frozen before slicing it. The smell of cooking fish can be reduced by adding fresh or dried ginger root to the pan.

For each recipe, directions are given for the amounts and types of ingredients to be used, but in nabe-mono meals these things are not fixed, and you can add or substitute other ingredients. Many of the recipes require a soup stock but water plus a vegetable or meat bouillon cube may be used if you wish. As a final note, remember that all the following recipes can be cooked as equally well on a stove in a kitchen as at the table. The charm and communal warmth of cooking at the table will be lost, but the food will still taste good.

SUKIYAKI

This is probably the only really well-known Japanese dish in the West. Ironically it is rarely prepared by the Japanese except for foreign guests. Never mind, it is delicious and one of my favourite meals. The name is supposed to derive from the practice by farmers of frying (yaki) their food on a metal plough (suki). There is another story, however, that Mongolian soldiers (the Japanese are said to be descendants of Mongolian stock) cooked wild game on the end of a spade (suki) over a charcoal fire.

Side dishes that usually accompany sukiyaki are miso soup (see p. 31) boiled rice (see p. 34), pickles (see p. 55), sake and green tea (see p. 128).

BEEF SUKIYAKI

One of the characteristics of beef sukiyaki is that it contains beef cut into wafer-thin slices which are then fried and dipped into raw egg before being eaten.

4 fl oz (½ cup) soy sauce
8 fl oz (1 cup) water or soup stock
3 tablespoons sugar
2 tablespoons mirin or sweet sherry
1 lb lean beef, very thinly sliced
1 large onion, halved and sliced

2 leeks or 6 spring onions, chopped into 1½" (3.75 cm) lengths
8 oz (1½ cups) mushrooms, sliced
8 oz (1½ cups) spinach, coarsely chopped
8 oz (1½ cups) Chinese or white cabbage, chopped into ½" (1.25 cm) wide strips
6 oz (½ cup) tofu, cut into 1" (2.5 cm) squares (optional)
4 tablespoons vegetable oil
4 eggs

Combine the first four ingredients, mix well, transfer the sauce to a jug and place on the table. Arrange the remaining ingredients, except the oil, on large serving dishes and place on the table adjacent to the hot plate. Seat the guests around the table. Heat a large frying pan over the hot plate and add the oil. Wait until it's really hot, add half the beef and fry until just brown on both sides. Push beef to one side of pan, drop in half the onions and leeks and fry lightly. Add half of each of the mushrooms and cabbage. Keep each of the ingredients separate. Now pour over half the sauce and cook for three to four minutes. Add some of the tofu and spinach and cook a further two to three minutes. Meanwhile, invite each guest to break an egg into a small bowl and to whisk it lightly with chopsticks. The guests may now begin to help themselves, with their chopsticks, to the cooked food, which is dipped into the egg before being eaten. As the pan empties, replenish with uncooked ingredients and repeat the above procedure until all the food is cooked.

BEEF AND AUBERGINE SUKIYAKI

This is a more straightforward recipe than the one given above. The ingredients are fried only, and no cooking liquid is used. There is no fixed order for frying the vegetables, and it is left up to the personal preferences of the guests.

1 lb lean beef, very thinly sliced
2 medium aubergines, halved lengthwise and sliced crosswise
2 medium onions, halved and sliced
2 medium green peppers, de-seeded and cut into 1" (2.5 cm) strips
8 oz (1½ cups) mushrooms, sliced
4 tablespoons vegetable oil

SAUCE

4 fl oz ($\frac{1}{2}$ cup) soy sauce
8 fl oz (1 cup) water or soup stock
3 tablespoons sugar
2 tablespoons mirin or sweet sherry

Arrange meat and vegetables on a large serving dish and lay at the table adjacent to a hot plate. Combine sauce ingredients and distribute sauce among four small bowls. Heat half the oil in a heavy frying pan over a hot plate. The guests, using chopsticks, now dip a piece of food into their bowl of sauce, drop into frying pan, fry it, and dip again into the sauce before eating it. Add more oil as it is needed and replenish bowls of dipping sauce if they get low.

NOODLE AND EGG SUKIYAKI

This is a sukiyaki dish that does not include meat or fish. Noodles and egg provide a tasty, filling and nutritious replacement. If possible, prepare the noodles yourself or buy soba (buckwheat) noodles. Spaghetti or macaroni can also be used.

1 lb (4 cups) soba noodles
1 pt (2$\frac{1}{2}$ cups) soup stock
4 fl oz ($\frac{1}{2}$ cup) soy sauce
3 tablespoons sugar
3 tablespoons mirin or sweet sherry
2 egg omelettes, cut into 2" (5 cm) squares
1 medium onion, halved and sliced
2 bamboo shoots, thinly sliced
4 large mushrooms, stems removed
8 oz (1$\frac{1}{2}$ cups) spinach, coarsely chopped
1 lemon, quartered

Cook the noodles according to the method given (see p. 47), drain and arrange them at the centre of a large serving dish. Combine the stock, soy sauce, sugar and mirin, mix well and transfer the sauce to a jug. Arrange the remaining ingredients in a pattern around the noodles. Place serving dish and sauce on the table alongside hot plate, set at medium heat. Pour half the sauce into a deep frying pan and bring to the boil. Add half of each of the ingredients, except lemon, and cook for five to six minutes. Each guest squeezes a lemon quarter into an individual small dish and the cooked food can

now be eaten after lightly dipping in lemon juice. When the first portion of food is eaten, add the other half of the ingredients and cook as above. Towards the end of the meal, the cooking liquid reduces to a rich, tasty sauce and the last few cooked morsels are especially delicious.

CHICKEN SUKIYAKI

8 fl oz (1 cup) chicken stock
3 tablespoons sugar
4 tablespoons soy sauce
1 lb boned chicken, thinly sliced
2 medium carrots, parboiled and sliced diagonally
1 medium onion, sliced thinly
1 medium green pepper, cut into $\frac{1}{2}$" (1.25 cm) wide strips
1 medium lettuce, chopped coarsely
12 oz (2$\frac{1}{2}$ cups) tofu, cut into 1" (2.5 cm) cubes (optional)
4 oz ($\frac{1}{4}$ cup) mushrooms, left whole
4 eggs
2 tablespoons vegetable oil

Combine the first three ingredients, mix well and transfer the sauce to a jug. Arrange the remaining ingredients, except oil, on one or two large serving dishes and place on the table, together with the sauce, alongside the hot plate. Heat oil in a heavy frying pan and add half the chicken; lightly brown both sides. Push chicken to one side, add half the onions and green pepper, lightly fry before adding half the carrot, lettuce, tofu and mushrooms. Pour in two-thirds of the sauce and cook until vegetables are tender. Meanwhile, invite each guest to break an egg into a small bowl and to lightly whisk it with chopsticks. The guests may now begin to help themselves, with their chopsticks, to the cooked food, which is dipped into the egg before being eaten. When the first helping is finished, replenish the pan with uncooked ingredients and the remaining sauce.

Lemon juice may be used in place of raw egg as a dipping sauce, and if you wish, season the cooking food with 7-spices pepper or cayenne.

FISH SUKIYAKI

1$\frac{1}{2}$ pt (3$\frac{1}{2}$ cups) fish stock (prepare from head and bones of fish)

4 tablespoons sake or white wine or dry sherry
9 large Chinese cabbage leaves
8 oz (1¼ cups) spinach
1 pt (2½ cups) water, plus a pinch of salt
1 lb filleted fish, thinly sliced (cod, hake, salmon, mackerel, etc.)
2 tablespoons vegetable oil
1 oz (1 tablespoon) ginger root, grated
Juice of 1 lemon
4 tablespoons soy sauce
2 leeks or 6 spring onions, cut into 1½" (3.75 cm) lengths
2 bamboo shoots, thinly sliced
12 oz (2¼ cups) tofu, cut into 1" (2.5 cm) cubes

Combine fish stock, sugar and sake, mix well and transfer the sauce to a jug. Heat salted water to boiling and lightly parboil Chinese cabbage leaves for 30 seconds to one minute. Lift from pot and rinse under cold water. Drain. Collect spinach leaves with stems all at one end. Return salted water to the boil and holding small bunch of spinach by the stems dip into the water for 30 seconds to one minute. Rinse under cold water and drain. Arrange three cabbage leaves with stems and leaves alternately overlapping on a sudare (bamboo mat) or thick moist cloth. Lay a third of the spinach leaves horizontally across the centre, alternating leaves and stems. Roll cabbage leaves and spinach into tight bundles, remove sudare or cloth, and cut into 1" (2.5 cm) lengths. Mix ginger, lemon juice and soy sauce and place in a small bowl. Arrange cabbage rolls and remaining ingredients on one or two large serving dishes and lay on the table with sauce and ginger or lemon mixture. Set the hot plate to medium, and heat the oil in a heavy frying pan. Add the fish, lightly fry both sides and then add half the vegetables and half the tofu. Pour over two-thirds of the sauce and cook until vegetables are tender. The guests may now help themselves to cooked food. Dip into ginger/lemon mixture before eating. Replenish pan with remaining vegetables and tofu as required. Watercress may be used in place of spinach in preparation of cabbage rolls.

MIZUTAKI

The arrangements for this dish are similar to those for sukiyaki, but the food is boiled in soup stock, not fried. In some of the recipes the ingredients are partially cooked in the kitchen and finished off at the table. Side dishes that customarily accompany mizutaki are boiled rice, grated fresh ginger root, finely minced spring onion or leek plus seasoning and large amounts of green tea and sake.

BEEF MIZUTAKI

3½ pt (7½ cups) soup stock
1 lb lean beef, very thinly sliced
8 oz (1½ cups) mushrooms, sliced
1 small cauliflower, cut into flowerettes
8 oz (1½ cups) Chinese or white cabbage, coarsely chopped
2 medium green peppers, cut into ½" (1.25 cm) wide strips
2 leeks or 6 spring onions cut into 1½" (3.75 cm) lengths
12 oz (2¼ cups) tofu, cut into 1" (2.5 cm) cubes
4 eggs (optional)

EGG SAUCE
8 fl oz (1 cup) soy sauce
1 egg, beaten
2 cloves garlic, crushed

SESAME SAUCE
2 oz (⅓ cup) sesame seeds, toasted
8 fl oz (1 cup) soup stock
¼ teaspoon hot pepper sauce

RELISHES FOR MIZUTAKI
4 tablespoons spring onion, minced
2 oz (2 tablespoons) ginger root, grated
Salt and togarashi or black pepper

On a stove in the kitchen, bring the soup stock to the boil in a heat-proof casserole. At the table, adjust hot plate to medium heat and transfer the casserole to it. Arrange remaining ingredients on one or two serving dishes and lay alongside hot plate. Combine ingredients of one or both sauces and serve each guest with a separate bowl of sauce. Invite each guest to add a selection of beef and vegetable pieces to the pot. Simmer for five minutes and then add part of the tofu and spinach. Heat through, and the guests may now help themselves to the cooked food, dipping it into sauce and relishes before eating. Replenish the pot as it empties. Towards the end of the meal break one egg per guest into the simmering broth and poach. Remove to bowls with a slotted spoon and ladle out the remaining stock over the poached egg. Sip the liquid directly from the bowl after finishing off the egg.

Other additional vegetable suggestions for this dish, as well as for the Chicken Mizutaki recipe that follows, are:

Celery, cut into 1" (2.5 cm) lengths

Fresh asparagus, cut into 2" (5 cm) lengths

Broccoli flowerettes

Watercress

Bamboo shoots, thinly sliced

Water chestnuts thinly sliced

Lotus roots thinly sliced

French beans, stringed, cut into 2" (5 cm) lengths

Peas in the pod

Shiitake, soaked

CHICKEN MIZUTAKI
The chicken is cut into small pieces, boiled and the chicken plus cooking liquid are then brought to the table where the other ingredients are cooked in the same pot.

2–3 lbs chicken
3 pt (7½ cups) water
2" (5 cm) square kombu, washed (optional)
2 stalks celery, cut into 1" (2.5 cm) lengths
4 shiitake or 4 large mushrooms, stems removed
8 oz (1½ cups) spinach or watercress

SAUCE
4 fl oz (½ cup) soy sauce
Juice of 2 lemons
1 tablespoon mirin or sherry (optional)

GARNISHES
As for Beef Mizutaki

Cut chicken, including skin and bones into several pieces, add to the water in a heat-proof casserole or large pan and bring to the boil. Continue boiling while scum rises to the surface, scooping it off as it forms, then reduce heat, cover and simmer for 40–50 minutes or until chicken is tender. Meanwhile, arrange remaining ingredients on a large serving dish and transfer to the table. Combine sauce ingredients and give each guest a small bowl of sauce. Lay out small dishes of garnishes. Set hot plate to high and transfer casserole to it, add kombu and the other vegetables, and cook until tender. Remove the kombu and discard. Invite guests to help themselves to pieces of chicken and vegetables, dipping into sauce and garnishing before eating. When all the chicken and vegetables have been eaten, ladle out the cooking broth and drink straight from the bowl.

CHICKEN (OR CRAB) MIZUTAKI WITH MILK STOCK

8 oz (1½ cup) spinach or watercress
9 Chinese cabbage leaves
1 pt (2½ cups) water
Pinch of salt
1 lb boned chicken, thinly sliced
1 pt (2½ cups) chicken stock
1 pt (2½ cups) milk
2 medium carrots, parboiled, cut into 2" (5 cm) pieces
4 large mushrooms
Soy sauce to taste

Prepare cabbage and spinach rolls as described in Fish Sukiyaki recipe, page 107. On a stove in the kitchen, bring stock and milk to the boil in a heat-proof casserole or large pan. Transfer to the table and set to simmer on a hot plate. Arrange chicken, cabbage rolls, mushrooms and carrot on a serving dish and lay on the table adjacent to hot plate. Add chicken to pot and simmer until almost cooked. Add vegetables and cook until tender. Season with soy sauce and invite the guests to ladle out for themselves some of the cooked food and broth.

This dish is excellent with tinned or fresh crabmeat in place of the chicken. If tinned crabmeat is used, add the fish and vegetables to the pot at the same time.

FISH MIZUTAKI

1 lb filleted white fish and/or 1 lb prawns, shelled and deveined

2 medium carrots, parboiled, cut into 1" (2.5 cm) lengths

1 lb potatoes, peeled, cut into ¼" (0.5 cm) thick slices

2 leeks or 6 spring onions, cut into 2" (5 cm) lengths

4 oz (¾ cup) somen or vermicelli noodles, cut into 4" (10 cm) lengths

1 teaspoon salt

3" (7.5 cm) piece of kombu, washed (optional)

1½ pt (3¾ cups) soup stock

DIPPING SAUCE

See Beef Mizutake dipping sauces (page 108).

Arrange the fish, prawns, carrots, potatoes, leeks and noodles on a serving dish and lay on the table. Sprinkle fish and prawns with salt. On an oven in the kitchen bring soup stock to the boil in a heat-proof casserole or large pan. Add kombu, transfer to the table and set on hot plate to simmer. Invite guests to select and add ingredients to the pot. Cook for a minute or two, remove, dip into sauce and eat. At the end of the meal ladle out any left-over stock and drink directly from the bowl.

MIXED MIZUTAKI (Yosenabe)

Yosenabe means odds-and-ends or bits-of-everything pot, and that's what this colourful dish is, a meat, fish and vegetable mizutaki.

8 oz pork, cut into 1" (2.5 cm) cubes *or* 8 oz boiled ham, thickly sliced cut into 1" (2.5 cm) squares

2 chicken breasts, boned, but into cubes

8 oz prawns, shelled and deveined

8 oz (1½ cups) Chinese or white cabbage coarsely chopped

4 shiitake, soaked in cold water for 20 minutes *or* 4 large mushrooms

8 oz (1½ cups) cooked noodles

4 eggs

3½ pt (8½ cups) chicken stock

Soy sauce and togarashi or black pepper to taste

Arrange ingredients, except stock and season-ings, on two large serving dishes and lay at the table. On an oven in the kitchen, heat stock to boiling in a large heat-proof casserole or pan. Set hot plate at the table to medium heat, and transfer casserole to it. Add pork (leave boiled ham to last) and chicken to the pot and cook for eight to ten minutes. Now add part of the prawns and vegetables (and boiled ham) and cook until vegetables are tender (four to six minutes). Season with soy sauce and togarashi and invite guests to ladle out cooked food and some of the broth into their bowls. Replenish pot with remaining prawns and vegetables and repeat procedure. Finally, break the eggs into the broth and poach. Serve with slotted spoon and ladle over the remaining broth. Any of the mizutaki sauces given in previous recipes may be served with this dish.

SHABU-SHABU

Similar to mizutaki, but instead of dropping the ingredients into the cooking stock, they are held in chopsticks and moved about in the simmering broth. The name derives from the noise made as the food is swished about.

Juice of 1 lemon

2 tablespoons wasabi or English mustard paste

2 pt (5 cups) soup stock

3" (7.5 cm) piece of kombu (optional)

1¼ lb lean beef, very thinly sliced

2–3 leeks or 6 spring onions, cut into 2" (5 cm) lengths

12 oz (3 cups) small mushrooms, halved

12 oz (2¼ cups) tofu, cut into 1" (2.5 cm) cubes (optional)

8 oz (2¼ cups) Chinese or white cabbage and/or 8 oz (2¼ cups) spinach, coarsely chopped

DIPPING SAUCE

See Beef Mizutaki (p. 108)

Serve dipping sauce in small individual bowls and lemon juice and wasabi in small central bowls. Bring soup stock to the boil in heat-proof casserole in the kitchen. Now set to simmer on hot plate at the table. Add kombu. Arrange remaining ingredients on serving dish and bring to the table. Invite guests to adjust their dipping sauce to taste with lemon juice and wasabi.

Now, using chopsticks, select a piece of beef or vegetable and swish it around in the simmering stock. Do not overcook the meat; it tastes best when dark pink to pale brown in colour. Dip cooked morsel into sauce and eat. When all the meat and vegetables are eaten, ladle the cooking liquid out and drink directly from the bowls. Discard kombu.

SIMMERED TOFU (Yudofu)

This is a very Japanese-looking dish, and appears strange to the Western eye, but it is delicious and well worth a try. The dipping sauce is heated in a bowl stood in the centre of a pot in which cubes of tofu are being cooked. Serve as an hors d'oeuvre or add other ingredients to the tofu (see suggestions below) and serve as a one-course meal.

2 pt (6 cups) water
3" (7.5 cm) square kombu (optional)
8 fl oz (1 cup) soy sauce
2 tablespoons mirin or sweet sherry
1¼ lb (4½ cups) tofu cut into 1" (2.5 cm) cubes

GARNISHINGS

Select any combination of the following:

1 lemon, cut into 8 wedges
2 oz (2 tablespoons) ginger root, grated
2 spring onions, minced
1 tablespoon katsuoboshi (dried fish flakes)
1 sheet nori, toasted

Put water and kombu into a heat-proof casserole, and bring to the boil on an oven in the kitchen. Transfer to the table and set to simmer on a hot plate. Combine soy sauce and mirin in a small bowl and set in the centre of the casserole. Add tofu to simmering water and kombu and heat through. Arrange garnishings in separate bowls. Invite guests to select a piece of tofu and to dip it into sauce and one or more of the garnishings before eating. Other ingredients that can be added to the tofu are cubes of cooked ham, chicken, fish or beef, slices of mushroom, spinach or other vegetables.

SIMMERED CHICKEN WITH TOFU

The arrangement for this dish is the reverse of the one above. The tofu is placed in a central bowl in a casserole of simmering broth and chicken pieces. The tofu is heated through and is then eaten together with the chicken and broth and a dipping sauce.

2 pt (5 cups) water
1½–2 lb chicken cut into pieces
1 medium carrot, 1" (2.5 cm) pieces
8 oz (1½ cups) daikon or young turnip, grated
8 oz (1½ cups) Chinese or white cabbage, coarsely chopped
Salt to taste
1 lb (4 cups) tofu, cut into 1" (2.5 cm) cubes

DIPPING SAUCE

4 fl oz (½ cup) lemon juice
4 fl oz (½ cup) vinegar
4 fl oz (½ cup) soy sauce
2 tablespoons sesame seeds, toasted (optional)

Bring water to the boil in a heat-proof casserole, on a stove in the kitchen. Add chicken, carrot and daikon and gently boil for 30–40 minutes or until chicken is tender. Remove scum as it forms. Add cabbage and cook until just soft, season to taste with salt. Remove casserole to hot plate at the table and set to simmer. Place a bowl containing tofu in the centre of the casserole and leave to heat through. Combine sauce ingredients and divide among four small bowls. Invite guests to select pieces of chicken, vegetables and tofu and to dip into sauce before eating. Alternatively, ladle tofu, chicken, vegetables and broth into individual bowls and eat from these.

MONGOLIAN GRILL

As described in the introduction to this chapter, this is more suitable to an outdoor barbecue party than cooked at the table dinner. If you are lucky enough to own a small charcoal burner with grill, then by all means cook it at the table. Alternatively treat the dish as a sukiyaki-type meal and fry the ingredients rather than grilling.

Vegetable oil
8 fl oz (1 cup) soy sauce
1 lb lean beef, thinly sliced *or* 1 lb pork or lamb cutlets
1 medium aubergine, thinly sliced

1 medium green pepper, de-seeded, cut into ½"
(1.25 cm) wide strips
1 medium sweet potato or potato, thickly sliced
8 oz (1½ cups) medium to large mushrooms

DIPPING SAUCES
Serve one or more of the following sauces:

DAIKON
8 oz (1½ cups) daikon (or young turnip), grated
1 egg yolk
2 tablespoons vinegar
2 tablespoons sugar
1 teaspoon salt

SPICED SAKE
4 fl oz (½ cup) sake or white wine
2 spring onions, finely chopped
1 oz (1 tablespoon) ginger root, grated
1 clove garlic, crushed
Pinch of togarashi or black pepper
Juice of 1 lemon

or see Beef Mizutaki dipping sauce (p. 108).

Oil grill pan with vegetable oil. Set the soy sauce in a bowl alongside grill. Combine sauce ingredients together, and distribute sauce(s) among individual bowls for each guest. Invite guests to pick up, with chopsticks, pieces of meat or vegetables, dip them into the soy sauce and then lay them to grill over charcoal (or fry if you are using this method). Cook to degree desired, dip into sauce(s) and eat. Chicken or duck, boned and sliced, may also be cooked in this way. Wild duck hunted and grilled in the field is a traditional Emperor's meal.

OTHER DISHES

SALMON AND SHRIMP NABE
This type of one-pot fish dish is only prepared in areas of Japan where seafood is plentiful and fresh fish is easily available.

4 shiitake or 4 large mushrooms
9 Chinese cabbage leaves
8 oz (1½ cups) spinach
3 tablespoons sugar
4 fl oz (½ cup) soy sauce
Juice of 1 lemon
1 lb fresh filleted salmon, cut into ½" (1.25 cm)
slices

4 oz (¼ cup) shrimps, shelled and deveined
12 oz (1½ cups) tofu, cut into 1" (2.5 cm) cubes
2 pt (5 cups) soup stock
7-spices pepper or cayenne to taste

Soak shiitake for 20 minutes in cold water. Remove hard stems and cut into thick slices. Otherwise use large mushrooms cut into quarters. Prepare Chinese cabbage and spinach rolls (see Fish Sukiyaki, p. 107) or chop cabbage and spinach coarsely and use in this form. Combine sugar, soy sauce and lemon juice in a small bowl. Set this sauce on the table. Arrange fish, vegetables and tofu on a serving dish and place on the table adjacent to a hot plate. Heat the stock to boiling in a heat-proof casserole on a stove in the kitchen and then set on the hot plate at the table, adjusted to medium heat. The stock should boil lightly throughout the meal. Remove any scum as it forms. Season with sauce and 7-spices pepper to taste. Now add a half portion of the salmon and cook for three to four minutes. Add half of the shrimps, vegetables and tofu and cook a further three to four minutes. Invite guests to help themselves to cooked food. Use any remaining sauce for dipping. Finish all the first amount of cooked food before adding the remaining ingredients. Finally, ladle out the residual stock and drink straight from the bowl.

HAM, CHICKEN AND SHELLFISH NABE
Meat, poultry and fish are combined with one another to the benefit of each. This dish is sometimes called Temple of Jade Nabe, possibly because of its rich store of tastes.

8 oz (1 cup) boned chicken, thinly sliced
8 oz (1 cup) prawns or shrimps, shelled and
deveined
8 oz (1 cup) boiled ham, cut into 2" (5 cm)
squares
8 large mushrooms, stems removed
4 oz (¼ cup) somen or vermicelli noodles,
cooked, cut into 4" (10 cm) lengths
2 young leeks or 4 spring onions, cut into 2" (5
cm) lengths
8 oz (1 cup) oysters, washed, rinsed (optional)
1 lb (1½ cups) Chinese cabbage, shredded
coarsely, parboiled, rinsed, drained

6 tablespoons lemon juice
6 tablespoons soy sauce
2 pt (5 cups) soup stock
3 tablespoons mirin or sweet sherry (optional)

Prepare ingredients and arrange attractively on large serving dishes and set at the table. Combine soy sauce and lemon juice and distribute among four small bowls at the table. Heat two-thirds of soup stock to boiling in a large heat-proof casserole on stove in the kitchen. Transfer to the table and set on hot plate adjusted to medium heat. Invite guests to select pieces of food and to cook them in the stock. The chicken and oysters will take longest. The chicken should be thoroughly white when cooked. When cooking the oysters turn them over during cooking and cook for one to two minutes each side. Dip cooked food into the lemon and soy sauce dip and eat. Top up cooking broth, as it evaporates, with remaining stock. Finally, ladle out residual broth and drink directly from the bowls.

JAPANESE HOTCHPOTCH

This is a version of Oden (see p. 78). Various ingredients are skewered and placed in a clear stock to cook. A miso dip is placed in a bowl in the centre of the stock and the skewered food is dipped into it before eating. The miso dip is an excellent accompaniment to many types of food and you may wish to add to or substitute ingredients suggested below, or your own favourite ingredients, for those listed. Ingredients that require a long cooking time are parboiled first.

2 medium carrots, sliced 1" (2.5 cm) lengths, parboiled in lightly salted water
2 medium potatoes, cut into mouth-size pieces, parboiled in lightly salted water
6 oz (½ cup) tofu, cut into 1" (2.5 cm) cubes
8 oz (1½ cups) Brussels sprouts
8 oz (1½ cups) konnyaku, parboiled, cut into small triangles
4 hard boiled eggs, peeled, cut in half
8 fish, chicken or pork meatballs (see pages 85, 94, 100)
4" (10 cm) square kombu (optional)
Water

Prepare all the ingredients and skewer them either in a mixed pattern or keeping individual ingredients on separate skewers. Combine miso sauce ingredients around the bowl and just cover them with water. Add kombu for extra flavouring. Set on a hot plate at the table and bring to the boil. As the ingredients heat through or cook, invite guests to pick up skewers, dip food into miso sauce and eat.

MISO DIPPING SAUCE

Two recipes are given. Both are very tasty. The first is spicier and less sweet than the second. To prepare either sauce, combine ingredients and bring to boil.

6 oz (⅓ cup) miso
1 oz (1 tablespoon) ginger root, grated
2 tablespoons sugar
6 fl oz (¾ cup) soup stock
3 tablespoons mirin or sherry
or
6 oz (⅓ cup) miso
4 fl oz (½ cup) mirin or sherry
4 fl oz (½ cup) sake or white wine
4 tablespoons sugar

Other suitable hotchpotch ingredients are parboiled slices of daikon or white turnips, radishes, spring onions, leeks, parboiled cauliflower flowerettes, small fish such as whitebait, pieces of squid, cooked chicken, prawns, shrimps, small sausages, etc.

CHINESE CABBAGE NABE

This is a basic recipe. For a more elaborate dish use some of the variations suggested below.

4 shiitake or 4 oz (¾ cup) mushrooms, sliced
1 lb (1½ cups) Chinese cabbage
2 pt (5 cups) water
Pinch of salt
2 tablespoons vegetable oil
1 medium onion, diced
4 oz (¾ cup) tomatoes, sliced
1 medium carrot, sliced, parboiled in a little salted water
1½ pt (3½ cups) soup stock
6 oz (⅓ cup) tofu cut into 1" (2.5 cm) cubes
Soy sauce and 7-spices pepper or cayenne to taste

Soak mushrooms in cold water for 20 minutes. Drain, remove hard stems and thinly slice. Bring water to the boil, salt. Separate cabbage leaves and, holding leaf part, dip stems into boiling water until just soft. Now hold stems and momentarily dip green leaf part into the water. Rinse in cold water and drain. Arrange three cabbage leaves alternatively, with stems and leaves overlapping, on a sudare (bamboo mat) or thick cloth. Roll up into a tight bundle. Squeeze, remove sudare or cloth and cut into 1" (2.5 cm) lengths. Repeat for all the cabbage leaves. Arrange all the ingredients on large serving dishes and set on table around hot plate. Set heavy deep frying pan on hot plate adjusted to high heat, add oil, heat and then add onions and mushrooms and fry quickly. Add tomatoes and pour in soup stock. Bring to the boil, add carrots, cabbage rolls and gently boil for ten minutes. Add tofu, season with soy sauce and 7-spices pepper. Invite guests to help themselves to cooked food. Finally, ladle out remaining stock and drink straight from the bowl. Any of the dipping sauces given in previous recipes may be served with this dish.

Variations on the above recipe. The tofu can be grilled before use to give it extra colour and texture. Pre-heat high grill. Place cake of tofu in shallow dish and add water to come halfway up the sides of the tofu. Place dish under grill and toast top of tofu for a few seconds. As soon as it is speckled brown, turn it over and repeat on the other side.

To add meat to the dish, sauté 12 oz (1½ cups) of minced beef or pork along with the onions and mushrooms; that is, add the meat before adding the stock.

Add seasonal vegetables as available.

JAPANESE-STYLE MEAT FONDU

This dish is Japanese in style, but Western in inspiration. In big cities such as Tokyo or Osaka, where Western ideas are popular, it is prepared with Western ingredients and sauces.

8 oz (1¼ cups) prawns, shelled and deveined
1 egg white
Breadcrumbs
4 chicken livers

8 oz (1¼ cups) bacon rashers
Oil for deep frying
1 lb lean beef, cut into 1" (2.5 cm) cubes
2 medium green peppers, cut into 1" (2.5 cm) strips
4 oz (¼ cup) small mushrooms
1 small aubergine, cut into 1" (2.5 cm) cubes
2 tablespoons mayonnaise
2 tablespoons Worcestershire sauce
Juice of 1 lemon
Salt and black pepper

Dip prawns in egg white, roll in breadcrumbs and put aside to set. Wrap chicken livers in bacon rashers and secure with toothpicks. Fill a small fondu-style pot with oil, place over hot plate, set at high heat. Heat oil to 350°F (175°C) or until you see a light haze forming above the surface of the oil. Meanwhile, attractively arrange ingredients on a serving dish and place the mayonnaise, Worcestershire sauce, lemon juice, salt and pepper in individual bowls. When the oil is hot, invite guests to skewer pieces of food, dip into the oil and deep fry. Remove the toothpicks from bacon/liver rolls after skewering. Wooden bamboo skewers are best since they do not get hot. Otherwise use long metal skewers. Dip cooked food into sauces and seasonings and eat.

PRAWN DUMPLING NABE

Minced beef, chicken or fish may be substituted for the prawns. Dumplings are dropped into a boiling stock, and waiting for them to rise, cooked, is a great appetite stimulator. Make more than the recipe suggests if you have large appetites.

1 lb prawns, shelled and deveined
½ small onion, finely diced
2 tablespoons cornflour
1 egg
1 teaspoon salt
8 shiitake or 8 large mushrooms
1 lb Chinese or white cabbage, coarsely chopped, parboiled in a little salted water
2 pt (5 cups) soup stock
4 tablespoons soy sauce
2 tablespoons mirin or sherry (optional)

1 lemon, quartered
4 oz (¼ cup) parsley or watercress

Mash prawns and combine with next four ingredients into a coarse paste. Set aside. Soak shiitake for 20 minutes, in cold water. Remove hard stems. Otherwise use fresh mushrooms. Bring stock to boil in a heat-proof casserole on an oven in the kitchen. Remove to hot plate at the table and set to boil lightly. Add soy sauce and mirin. Mound prawn paste in the centre of a serving dish and surround with remaining ingredients. Invite guests to drop spoonfuls of prawn paste into stock followed by some cabbage and mushrooms. The prawn dumplings will rise to the surface when cooked. Ladle out into bowls, squeeze over lemon juice, sprinkle with parsley or watercress and eat. Repeat for remaining ingredients. Finally ladle out residual broth and drink directly from the bowls.

Another variation is to add 1 tablespoon miso to the prawn dumpling mixture.

TEMPURA AND OTHER FRIED FOODS

Tempura is made by dipping pieces of food, usually fish, shellfish or vegetables in a batter, deep frying and serving with a special tempura dipping sauce. It is quite rightly one of Japan's most famous dishes. It sounds simple to prepare but, to produce crispy, light tempura, care is necessary. The essence of success is freshness. The batter is made immediately before use. The food to be coated with batter should be fresh and newly-cleaned and cut and the oil for deep frying must also be clean. Ideally, the tempura should be eaten immediately after cooking. In Japanese restaurants that specialise in tempura, the chef stands in view of the customer while he deep fries the selected foods. Afterwards he quickly arranges them on a paper-covered bamboo basket and hands them across the counter to the customer, hot, crisp and full of flavour. This immediacy is not possible if you are making tempura at home for four or five people, so either you can store the cooked tempura in a pre-heated oven at 250°F (120°C) until they are all prepared or sit in the kitchen area and take turns with your guests in making tempura for one another. I have, in fact, been given cold tempura as part of a lunchtime snack; it wasn't too bad, so if you make too much, use it later.

For deep frying the tempura, vegetable oil should be used since animal fat makes it soggy. The addition of one-third or more sesame seed oil will give the tempura a pleasing nutty taste. After use strain the oil and store in a sealed bottle. The Japanese put an umeboshi plum in with the oil to keep it extra fresh.

The procedure for preparing tempura is given in the order you should follow when making it.

The recipe for tempura sauce is given first, followed by the preparation of the ingredients and batter, and finally the method for deep frying. Serve the tempura with plain, hot boiled rice, and, if you wish, a crisp green salad.

TEMPURA SAUCES

TENTSUYU
This is the traditional sauce for tempura. Grated daikon and ginger root are either combined with the sauce or served alongside in small separate containers. Daikon aids the digestion of oils and is a very suitable accompaniment. If you cannot obtain any, substitute small white turnips.

8 fl oz (1 cup) dashi, soup stock or water
2 fl oz (¼ cup) soy sauce
2 fl oz (¼ cup) mirin or sweet sherry
4 oz (¾ cup) daikon, grated
2 oz (2 tablespoons) ginger root, grated

Combine dashi, soy sauce and mirin and bring to the boil. Cool and divide amongst four bowls. Add a portion of daikon and ginger to each.

LEMON AND SALT
This is a simpler accompaniment than tentsuyu. Simply quarter two lemons, distribute among four small dishes, mound a little salt in each dish and give one to each guest. Squeeze lemon juice on to tempura, dip into salt, and eat.

SALT OR SOY SAUCE
Easiest of all is to just sprinkle tempura with soy sauce or salt.

TEMPURA INGREDIENTS

Many varieties of foods can be used in the preparation of tempura and there are no fixed rules for dictating what ingredients to use. The limits are set by personal choice, imagination and availability. Below is a list of recommended vegetables and seafoods and details of how to prepare them for tempura cooking. Amounts are not given; these will of course, depend on how many are being catered for and how much of any one ingredient you wish to use. From my own experience, tempura is eaten heartily and a rough guide for a full meal would be 12 oz of vegetable (total) and the same amount of seafood per person.

VEGETABLE TEMPURA

Artichoke hearts

Asparagus, cut in 1" (2.5 cm) diagonal slices.

Aubergines, cut in ¼" (0.5 cm) thick slices cut in half. Alternatively, cut aubergine in half lengthwise. Now cut each half vertically into four or five slices, but leave root end up to depth of 1½" (3.75 cm) intact. You end up with a sort of aubergine fan.

Bamboo shoots, ½" (1.25 cm) thick slices, cut into half moons.

Broccoli, separated into flowerettes.

Carrots, ⅛" (0.25 cm) thick, flower-shaped slices or matchsticks.

Cauliflower, separated into flowerettes.

Celery, ¼" (0.5 cm) thick, diagonal slices.

Chestnuts, boiled and peeled.

French beans, cut into 2" (5 cm) lengths.

Green peppers, de-seeded, quartered lengthwise.

Leeks, 1"–2" (2.5–5 cm) lengths.

Lotus root, ½" (1.25 cm) thick rounds.

Mushrooms, use whole if small, otherwise sliced.

Nuts, use whole almonds, cashews, hazels or walnuts.

Onions, ½" (1.25 cm) thick rounds.

Parsley, sprigs drawn together in small bunches.

Parsnips, ½" (1.25 cm) thick rounds or matchsticks.

Peas in the pod.

Potatoes, ½" (1.25 cm) thick rounds, halved if large.

Pumpkin, peeled, de-seeded, cut into 1" (2.5 cm) cubes.

Shiitake, washed in cold water for 20 minutes, hard stems cut off, drained. Batter on top side only.

Spinach, cut away some stem, sprinkle with flour before battering.

Spring onions, cut into 1"–2" (2.5–5 cm) lengths, green part as well.

Squash, as for pumpkin.

Tofu, pressed and cut into 1" (2.5 cm) cubes.

Turnips, ½" (1.25 cm) thick slices, quartered.

Watercress in small bunches, lightly floured before battering.

SEAFOOD TEMPURA

Prawns, shell and devein.

Shrimps, shell and devein, score two or three incisions across the inside curve of the body and press flat with broad side of a knife. This prevents the shrimp curling during cooking.

Fish, cut filleted pieces into bite-size amounts. Leave small fish whole. For fish a little bigger than, say, whitebait, fillet first but then leave whole.

Mussels, wash, boil, remove shells and cut in half if large.

Crab or lobster, shell and cut into slices.

Nori seaweed, cut 1 sheet into eight pieces.

Kombu seaweed, cut into thin strips, put two together and tie into a knot.

Slices or cubes of cooked meat or poultry may also be used to make tempura.

BATTER FOR TEMPURA

The batter is intended for use immediately after preparation, and it does not matter if it contains a few lumps. It is a good idea to mix the batter while the deep frying oil is heating up.

4 oz (1 cup) plain flour
1 egg
10 fl oz (1¼ cups) water

Combine ingredients together and whisk lightly or do as the Japanese do and use the blunt end of a chopstick for mixing. Do not stir again having once mixed the batter. For variety try different types of flour, e.g. wholewheat, rye, buckwheat, etc., or combinations of these.

117

DEEP FRYING METHOD FOR TEMPURA

Pour vegetable oil 2"–3" (5–7.5 cm) deep into a deep frying pan. Start heating the oil and meanwhile prepare batter. Heat the oil to 320°–350°F (150–175°C), and maintain at this temperature. At 350°F (175°C) a small lump of batter dropped into the oil will cook golden brown in one minute. Using a pair of chopsticks, pick up one piece of food (fry strong tasting foods, such as fish, last), dip it into the batter, shake off excess, and drop coated food into the oil. Do not fry too much at once. Turn food once during cooking if it looks necessary. Allow it to crisp and brown. Remove from oil, shake off excess fat, and set to drain on absorbent paper. Once the first batch is cooked, remove any floating pieces of batter from the oil, and then fry another portion. Keep the oil at the right temperature since if it gets too low, the food starts to absorb oil and you will get soggy tempura.

If you are planning to prepare a lot of tempura, pre-heat a moderate oven and store the cooked tempura until you have finished all the ingredients. Now cover the bottom of a bamboo or wicker basket with soft paper, arrange the tempura on top and serve with dipping sauce and boiled rice as described.

TEMPURA AND OTHER FRIED DISHES

CHICKEN TEMPURA

4 chicken breasts, skinned and boned
2 pt (5 cups) water
Salt and black pepper to taste
Tempura Sauces and Batter

Cut chicken breasts into four pieces. Bring water to the boil and drop in the pieces. Boil for one minute. Remove, drain and season with salt and black pepper. Prepare batter and deep fry coated chicken as described above.

PINE NEEDLE NOODLES

Thin noodles, cut into short lengths and deep fried, are an excellent and unusually attractive accompaniment to tempura.

4 oz ($\frac{1}{4}$ cup) somen or vermicelli noodles
Oil for deep frying

Heat oil to 350°F (175°C) (see Deep Frying Method for Tempura). Break the noodles into 3" (7.5 cm) lengths and take hold of one end of a small bunch. Dip the other end $\frac{1}{4}$" (0.5 cm) deep into the hot oil. Hold for five to ten seconds, by which time the noodles will have fused together. Now let go and drop the whole bunch into the oil. The noodles spread out and form a spray. After one minute, remove the spray of 'pine needles' from the oil, drain and repeat for the remaining noodles.

NOODLE-COATED PRAWN TEMPURA

Prawns or prawn dumplings are brushed with egg white, dipped into a bowl of broken somen or vermicelli noodles and then deep fried. Three recipes are given for this style of tempura. One is for prawns on their own, and the other two are for different types of prawn dumpling. Serve either recipe with one of the tempura sauces (see p. 116) and boiled rice.

WHOLE PRAWNS
8 prawns, cleaned and shelled (leave tails intact)
2 tablespoons flour
1 egg white, lightly beaten
2 oz ($\frac{1}{4}$ cup) somen or vermicelli noodles, broken into $\frac{1}{2}$" lengths
Oil for deep frying

Heat the oil to 350°F (175°C). Dip the prawns one at a time into the flour, shaking off any excess, and then into the egg white. Place the broken noodles in a bowl and roll the prawns in them. If necessary, press noodle pieces against the sides of the prawns to ensure they adhere. Drop the coated prawns into the hot oil, two or three at a time and cook, turning once, for one to two minutes. Do not overcook, the noodles should only slightly colour. Drain on absorbent paper and serve.

PRAWN DUMPLINGS
(I)
8 prawns, cleaned, shelled and minced
1 egg white, lightly beaten
2 tablespoons cornflour

2 oz (¼ cup) somen or vermicelli noodles, broken
    into ½" (25 cm) pieces
Oil for deep frying

(II)
8 prawns, cleaned, shelled and minced
6 oz (⅓ cup) tofu, mashed
2 tablespoons cornflour
2 oz (¼ cup) somen or vermicelli noodles, broken
    into ½" (1.25 cm) pieces
Oil for deep frying

Combine the first three ingredients of recipe (I)
or recipe (II) together, and form this dumpling
mixture into 1" (2.5 cm) diameter balls. Roll the
dumplings in the broken noodles and proceed in
exactly the same way as described above for
noodle-coated whole prawns.

Harusame noodles made from soy flour can
be used in place of somen. Shrimps are equally
as good as prawns for noodle coating. To use
whole shrimps, clean, shell and score across the
inside curve of the body to prevent curling
during cooking.

VEGETABLE DUMPLING TEMPURA (KAKIAGE)
In kakiage dishes, the tempura batter is mixed
with the other ingredients and not used as a
coating. Serve as for ordinary tempura.

4 oz (1 cup) plain wholemeal flour
Pinch of salt
8–10 fl oz (1–1¼ cups) water
4oz (¾ cup) sweet corn (tinned)
1 medium carrot, grated
1 medium onion, finely diced
1 lotus root, thinly sliced and quartered
    (optional)
Oil for deep frying

Combine the flour, salt and enough water to
form a stiff batter. Add the vegetables and stir
thoroughly. Heat the oil to 350°F (175°C) and
drop in tablespoonfuls of batter and vegetables.
Fry until golden brown and crisp (about one
minute). Other vegetables, pieces of fish,
shellfish or meat may be added to or replace the
vegetables suggested.

TEMPURA TENDON
A favourite Japanese restaurant dish is tendon,
which is simply a bowl of steaming hot, boiled
rice, topped with pieces of tempura and dressed
with tempura sauce.

TEMPURA SOBA
As for tempura tendon, but the rice is replaced
by a bowl of soba noodles.

DEEP FRIED SOYA BEANS
8 oz (1 cup) soya beans
2 pt (5 cups) water
Oil for deep frying
Salt to taste

Soak the beans overnight in water. Drain and
dry on a clean cloth. Heat oil to 350°F (175°C),
and drop in half the beans. Remove with a
slotted spoon or sieve when the beans are crisp
and crunchy. Repeat for remaining beans. Serve
salted as a snack.

JAPANESE PANCAKES (Okonomi-Yaki)
One of my most enjoyable restaurant meals in
Japan was in a 'cook-it-yourself' pancake house
in Tokyo. The restaurant was on the eighth floor
of a ten-storey building, and on each level there
were numerous other restaurants, each special-
ising in a particular type of cooking. The
pancake place was lined with low tables, each
inset with a large hot plate. Each diner was
given a large bowl containing a bottom layer of
pancake mixture, followed by a layer of
vegetables and fish and topped with a raw egg.

We seasoned our bowls of food with a variety
of sauces, mixed it all together and then
proceeded to fry portions on the hot plate. We
cooked delicious pancakes, each custom made.
Finally, as a last course we were served a huge
tray of cooked noodles and fresh vegetables to
fry.

You may wish to prepare these pancakes in
the manner described in the chapter on table-
cooked meals, but otherwise cook them in the
kitchen and keep them warm in a pre-heated
moderate oven until you are ready to serve.

3 oz (¾ cup) plain flour

3 oz (⅓ cup) water
3 eggs
1 teaspoon soy sauce

Plus a selection of five of the following:

½ medium onion, diced
2 oz (⅓ cup) cabbage, shredded
2 oz (⅓ cup) mushrooms, sliced
½ medium carrot, cut into matchsticks
1 small green pepper, diced
2 oz (⅓ cup) French beans, cut into 2" (5 cm)
  lengths
2 oz (⅓ cup) sweetcorn (tinned)
2 oz (⅓ cup) shelled and parboiled or tinned peas
4 oz (¾ cup) tofu, mashed
4 oz (⅓ cup) white fish, flaked
4 oz (⅓ cup) cooked chicken, diced
4 oz (⅓ cup) cooked beef or pork, diced
4 prawns or shrimps, shelled and deveined
2 tablespoons vegetable oil

Combine the first four ingredients into a smooth batter. Add your selected combination of other ingredients and mix well. Heat half the oil in a heavy frying pan and ladle in a portion of the mixture. Cook on both sides over a low heat. Repeat for remaining batter, adding oil as required.

DEEP-FRIED PANCAKES
Proceed as above, but use one third less water in the preparation of the batter and select only three other ingredients. Mix together and form the mixture into flat rounds. Deep fry in oil, pre-heated to 350°F (175°C).

This chapter ends with three egg dishes. The Japanese use eggs quite extensively, but usually in omelette form. They use square frying pans, not round. The square omelette is rolled up, cut into small rolls and served cold.

ROLLED OMELETTE (Omeretsu)

4 eggs
1 teaspoon soy sauce
Pinch of ground ginger (optional)
1 tablespoon plain flour
1 tablespoon vegetable oil

SAUCE (optional)
2 tablespoons sugar
2 tablespoons soy sauce
2 tablespoons fresh parsley or bonito flakes
Togarashi or black pepper to taste

Beat the eggs and add soy sauce and ginger. Sift the flour and beat into the eggs. Heat oil in a heavy frying pan over a medium heat. Pour in the egg mixture and cook until set, gently turn it over and cook the other side. Ideally, the omelette should be ½" (1.25 cm) thick. Remove to a plate and allow to cool. Trim the omelette into a rectangle and place on a sudare (bamboo mat) or damp cloth. Place the trimmings across the centre of the omelette and roll it up into a cylinder. Remove the cloth or sudare and slice into 1" (2.5 cm) thick rolls. Pour over sauce if desired.

FILLED ROLLED OMELETTES
Proceed as above, but add 4 oz (⅓ cup) filleted white fish or diced cooked chicken to the beaten egg. Alternatively, arrange a row of cooked or raw vegetables, or cooked rice, fish or meat horizontally across the omelette before rolling it up. For colour and simplicity try a row of fresh parsley or raw spinach leaves and for texture add a few strips of crisp celery.

One final suggestion is to lay a sheet of nori on the sudare before laying the omelette on top. When the omelette is rolled up it gets an outside coat of seaweed. A delicious elaboration for fish-filled omelettes.

FRIED TOFU AND EGG
This is the Japanese equivalent of a cheese omelette.

12 oz (2½ cups) tofu, diced
4 eggs
4 tablespoons soy sauce
2 tablespoons mirin
1 medium onion, thinly sliced
2 tablespoons vegetable oil
Togarashi or black pepper to taste

Combine the first four ingredients. Heat half the oil in a heavy frying pan over a medium heat. Add half the onion and fry until just soft. Pour in half the egg mixture and cook until firm. Fold the omelette over and serve. Repeat for the remaining half of the ingredients. Season with togarashi and serve.

SWEETS AND CAKES

The Japanese are not great dessert eaters and there is no set custom that a meal should be followed by something sweet. The normal manner of ending a meal is to serve fresh fruit, carefully washed and cut into segments. However, during the day or late evening, when friends may visit to chat over a pot of tea, sweets and cakes are eaten. They are also made for festival times and other celebrations. Little cakes, called manju, that look like dumplings are prepared from sweet bean jam, flour and water.

Jellied sweets are made from fruit, sugar and kanten (also called agar-agar), a sort or gelatine, and other sweets are made simply from eggs, colouring and sugar. In fact, most of the cakes and sweets are made from simple ingredients, and the differences between them are emphasised more by the way the ingredients are combined and cooked than by their variety. The basic headings under which this chapter is arranged are: bean jam cakes and desserts, yokan (jellied) sweets and sweets containing eggs.

BEAN JAM CAKES AND DESSERTS

BEAN JAM

This is used as a filling or as a coating around other fillings and is usually made from aduki beans, but red kidney beans can be used just as effectively. For white jam, haricot beans are substituted. The jam is prepared by two methods. Which method is chosen depends on the texture of the jam required. For smooth jam, the beans are boiled soft, rubbed through a sieve or strainer and then puréed with sugar. For a coarser jam, the beans are boiled soft, mashed with sugar and boiled to remove excess water. The same quantities of ingredients are used in both cases. The recipe that follows makes twice as much jam as will be required for subsequent cake recipes. The unused jam, if stored in a glass jar with a tight lid, will keep indefinitely.

1 lb aduki beans
Water
2 teaspoons salt
1 lb (2 cups) sugar

Wash the beans, transfer to a heavy pan, add just enough water to cover and boil until the beans are soft and the shells have started to peel off (about one hour). If you substitute red kidney or haricot beans for aduki beans, soak them for six to eight hours before use. Proceed by one of the following methods.

SMOOTH BEAN JAM

Drain the beans, force them through a sieve or fine colander, place the pulp in a clean towel or piece of cheesecloth and squeeze out any remaining liquid. Return pulp to pan, add salt, and over a low heat gradually stir in the sugar. Continue heating, stirring and cook down to form a stiff smooth mixture.

COARSE BEAN JAM

Add salt and sugar to the soft boiled beans and reduce over a low heat. Mash to a paste with a wooden spoon.

MANJU

Small dumplings or cakes made by steaming balls of bean jam wrapped in a flour dough.

122

12 oz (3 cups) flour
2 teaspoons baking powder
8 oz (1 cup) sugar
8 fl oz (1 cup) water
Pinch of salt
1 lb (1½ cups) bean jam

Sift the flour and baking powder together. Dissolve the sugar in the water, add a pinch of salt and stir in the flour mixture to form a smooth dough. Roll the dough into a thin sheet and cut into 16–20 4" (10 cm) squares. Form the bean paste into the same number of balls as there are wrappings, and wrap each one. Pinch the sides of dough squares together, and place the dumplings seam side down on a wet towel in a steamer (see p. 23). Steam for 20 minutes over a medium heat. Cool and serve.

The manju can also be given a Western touch by baking them instead of steaming. Place the formed uncooked dumplings on a greased baking tray, brush with egg yolk and bake in a pre-heated oven at 375°F (190°C) for 20 minutes. I have tried making manju using brown flour, and it works if you bake them, but it makes the steamed variety very heavy.

To add flavour and colouring to the dumplings, add a teaspoon or two of cinnamon or green tea powder to the flour. Chestnut purée may also be used in place of bean jam or try a mixture of the two.

ROLY POLY MANJU

Use same ingredients as for manju recipe above. Prepare the dough as for manju, divide it into two, and roll each half into a rectangular sheet. Spread each with bean jam and roll up into a cylinder. Steam or bake as for manju recipe. Cool, cut into slices and serve.

SWEET RICE DUMPLINGS (Ohagi)

1 lb (2⅔ cups) rice
1¼ pt (3 cups) water
1 lb (1½ cups) bean jam

Place rice and water in a heavy pot. Bring to the boil over a high heat. Reduce heat, cover and cook for 15 minutes. Remove from heat and allow to stand until rice is only just warm.

Slightly mash rice with a wooden spoon and then form into 1" (2.5 cm) to 1½" (4 cm) diameter balls. Place a large spoonful of bean jam in the palm of your hand, form it into a ball and then flatten it. Place a rice ball in the middle and shape the jam around it. Press into shape and set on a serving dish. Repeat for each rice ball. If you have difficulty wrapping the rice balls by this method, try the following slightly simpler but more long-winded system. Damp a square of cheesecloth and coat it with a 3" (7.5 cm) to 4" (10 cm) diameter circle of bean jam. Place the rice ball in the middle, gather the cloth around it and envelope its surface in bean jam. Unwrap cloth and press dumpling into shape.

THREE-COLOURED DUMPLINGS (Dongo)

A special glutinous sweet rice called mochi is traditionally used to make rice dumplings, and, if you can obtain any, substitute it in either this recipe or the one above.

1 lb (2⅔ cups) rice
1¼ pt (3 cups) water

RED DUMPLINGS
8 oz (¼ cup) aduki bean jam

WHITE DUMPLINGS
4 oz (1 cup) soya flour
2 oz (¼ cup) sugar
Pinch of salt

BLACK DUMPLINGS
3 oz (½ cup) black sesame seeds or poppy seeds

Prepare rice balls as described in the recipe above, and divide into three portions. Coat one third in bean jam as detailed in the same recipe. Combine soya flour, sugar and salt, and coat another third of the rice balls in this mixture. Roast sesame seeds in a heavy frying pan until they begin to jump. Transfer to a suribachi or mortar and grind to a paste and use to coat remaining rice balls. Arrange the three different coloured dumplings on one plate and serve.

Rice cakes made from rice flour (shiratamako) are also excellent for making sweet dumplings. How to prepare them is described in the recipe below. Since the rice flour is uncooked, the coated rice flour dumplings need to be steamed for 15 minutes and cooled before serving.

RICE CAKES WITH SWEET BEAN SOUP (Shiruko)

Bean soup with lightly fried rice cakes, even if it is sweet, sounds a strange dessert to Western ears, but the Japanese really do have a different idea of what, where and when sweet things should be served and sometimes even serve them at the beginning of a meal.

4 oz (1 cup) rice flour
Pinch of salt
4 fl oz ($\frac{1}{2}$ cup) boiling water, approximately
1 tablespoon vegetable oil
1$\frac{1}{2}$ pt (3$\frac{1}{2}$ cups) water
1 lb (1$\frac{1}{2}$ cups) bean jam
1 tablespoon arrowroot (or cornflour)
Salt to taste

Combine rice flour with salt and slowly pour in the boiling water, mix well, adjust water to form a smooth elastic dough, and knead for one to two minutes. Pinch off bite-size pieces of dough and form into balls, then flatten them slightly. Heat oil in a heavy frying pan, add rice cakes and brown both sides. Set aside. Bring water to the boil and stir in bean jam. Dissolve arrowroot in a little boiling soup and then blend it into the main body of the soup to thicken it. Season to taste with salt. Divide rice cakes among four bowls, pour the soup over them and serve.

RICE CAKES WITH BEAN JAM AND CHESTNUT CREAM

4 oz (1 cup) rice flour
Pinch of salt
4 fl oz ($\frac{1}{2}$ cup) boiling water, approximately
1 tablespoon vegetable oil
8 oz ($\frac{3}{4}$ cup) bean jam
4 oz ($\frac{3}{4}$ cup) chestnut purée
4 oz ($\frac{3}{4}$ cup) water

Using the first four ingredients, prepare and fry rice cakes as described in the recipe above. Combine the bean jam, chestnut purée and water, and bring to the boil with stirring. Reduce heat and simmer. Divide rice cakes among four bowls, pour over bean jam and chestnut cream and serve.

RICE CAKES FILLED WITH APPLE AND MISO

8 oz (2 cups) rice flour
Pinch of salt
8 fl oz (1 cup) boiling water, approximately
8 oz ($\frac{3}{4}$ cup) apple purée
4 oz ($\frac{1}{2}$ cup) sugar or honey
2 tablespoons miso

Combine rice flour with salt and slowly pour in the boiling water, mix well, adjust water to form a smooth elastic dough, and knead for one to two minutes. Wrap dough in a damp cloth and steam for 15 minutes. Combine apple purée, sugar and miso. Remove dough from steamer, allow to cool and knead vigorously for five minutes. Divide into ten portions and roll out 3" (7.5 cm) to 4" (10 cm) diameter circles. Divide filling among these and spoon portions into the centre of each circle. Fold dough over to form semi-circle, crimp the edges together, wrap each in a piece of silver foil and steam for five minutes. Cool and serve.

KUZU MANJU

12 oz (1 cup) bean jam
8 oz (2 cups) arrowroot (kuzu)
8 oz (1 cup) sugar
1$\frac{1}{2}$ pt (3$\frac{3}{4}$ cups) water
Cherry tree leaves to garnish (optional)

Form the bean jam into 1" (2.5 cm) diameter balls and arrange in a shallow serving bowl. Combine the arrowroot, sugar and water, and bring to the boil. Reduce heat and stirring regularly, simmer for 15–20 minutes. Pour this sauce over the bean jam balls. Allow to cool, chill and serve garnished with cherry leaves.

CANDIED CHESTNUTS

1 lb chestnuts, washed and soaked for 6–8 hours in 16 fl oz (2 cups) water
4 oz ($\frac{1}{4}$ cup) honey
8 oz (1 cup) sugar

Drain soaked chestnuts, and reserve water. Peel chestnuts. Place reserved water, honey and sugar in a heavy pan and, over a low heat, dissolve the sugar. Add the chestnuts, cover and simmer very gently for one hour (use an asbestos pad under the pan if possible). Spoon the chestnuts separately on to a greased tray and leave to cool.

For a more elaborate sweet, coat the candied chestnuts in bean jam. Other large nuts may be substituted for chestnuts.

TOFU WITH GREEN DRESSING
This apparently savoury dish is served as a sweet course by the Japanese. It tastes very nice, and looks colourful. Hoever, if you have a sweet tooth that needs satisfying at the end of a meal, serve it as a starter rather than a dessert.

12 oz (2¼ cup) tofu, cut into 1" × 2" (2.5 cm × 5 cm) pieces
4 oz (¾ cup) spinach, stems removed
4 fl oz (½ cup) water
4 oz (¼ cup) miso (white if possible)

Sear the top of the tofu under a grill (see p. 114). Cook spinach in water until the leaves are wilted and soft. Rinse under cold water and drain. Purée the spinach in an electric blender or by hand in a suribachi or mortar. Divide the miso into two equal portions and blend one half with the spinach. Spread half the tofu with this green mixture and the other half with the remaining miso. Cool to room temperature and serve.

JELLIED SWEETS (Yokan)
Kanten or agar-agar is similar to gelatin, and it is used in Japanese cooking in the same way as we may use jelly (jello in America). Kanten sets at 85°F (30°C) and melts at 180°F (85°C), which means that once made it remains firm, even on the hottest day. It is sold in blocks that weigh ⅓ oz (8 gm). One block is soaked in 16 fl oz (2 cups) water, boiled, strained, cooled to room temperature, and then mixed with other ingredients. As long as it is mixed when cold, it can safely be reheated without separation from the other ingredients. Sticks of agar-agar weighing the same amount and reconstituted in the same way are available in the West. Otherwise, substitute three tablespoons gelatine for one block of kanten, and reduce the water required in the recipe by one quarter.

RED BEAN JELLY CAKES (Yokan)

1 cake kanten
16 fl oz (2 cups) water
8 oz (1 cup) sugar (optional)
12 oz (1 cup) bean jam
Salt to taste

Soak kanten in water for 30 minutes, then bring to the boil and boil until kanten is dissolved. Pass solution through a strainer, return to the pan and add sugar (leave this out or reduce the amount if you do not have a very sweet tooth) and bean jam, and stir over a low heat until well blended. Season to taste with salt. Pour mixture into a small square or round cake tin and leave to set. Cut into portions and serve with green tea.

Chestnut, apple and pumpkin purées may be substituted for bean jam. For extra flavour and texture, add toasted sesame seeds and/or grated lemon peel to the jelly.

DUMPLING, JELLY AND FRUIT DESSERT (Mitsumami)
Prepare half the amount of yokan given in the recipe above and cut into small squares. Prepare half the three-colour dumplings given in the recipe (p. 123). Cut up some fresh fruit into small pieces. Divide each of the above among four bowls, top with a cherry and serve.

SWEET FRUIT JELLY (Awayaki Kan)

8 oz (1½ cups) fresh fruit, diced
1 block kanten
16 fl oz (2 cups) water
4 oz (½ cup) sugar
2 egg whites

Soak kanten in water for 30 minutes then bring to the boil and boil until kanten is dissolved. Pass solution through strainer, return to the pan and add sugar. Stir over a low heat until the mixture gets stringy when a spoonful is held in the air. Cool to below 100°F (37°C). Beat the egg whites stiff in a large bowl, and add the kanten mixtures slowly stirring all the time. Wet the inside surface of a square mould or cake tin and arrange a bottom layer of fruit. Pour over the egg white and kanten mixture. Chill and serve.

An alternative way of preparing jellied fruit is to flavour the dissolved kanten with vanilla or peppermint or other extracts, pour it into a mould and allow to set. Decorate the jelly with fresh fruit and serve.

TWO-TIER FRUIT JELLY

1 block kanten
16 fl oz (2 cups) water
4 oz (½ cup) sugar
8 oz (1½ cups) fruit purée (apple, pumpkin, plum, etc.)
1 egg
1 teaspoon cinnamon

Prepare kanten jelly in the way described in the recipe for Sweet Fruit Jelly up to the point where it is cooled to below 100°F (37°C). Divide this cooled mixture between two small pans. Separate egg into yolk and white. Add fruit purée to one pan and over a low flame beat in the egg yolk. Bring to the boil and pour into a 6" (15 cm) square mould or cake tin. Beat the egg white stiff and fold into the other pan. Stir in the cinnamon and pour this mixture into the mould on top of the fruit layer. Cool and chill. Unmould, cut into squares and serve.

TANGERINE BAGS

The Girls' Festival is celebrated on the 3rd of March, and special dishes are made for the children. At the same time of the year tangerines are in great abundance, and the two events are celebrated in this lovely sweet.

4 tangerines
8 oz (1 cup) water
½ cake kanten
2 oz (¼ cup) sugar

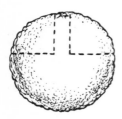 

Cut the tangerine as shown, and remove the flesh from the inside. Squeeze the juice from the flesh and add to the water. Soak the kanten in this mixture for 30 minutes. Then bring to the boil and boil until kanten is dissolved. Pass through a strainer, add sugar, simmer over a low heat until dissolved. Cool and, just before jelly sets, spoon into the tangerine shells, chill and serve.

SWEETS CONTAINING EGGS

SWEET HARD BOILED EGGS (Nishiki Tamago)

6 hard boiled eggs
4 oz (½ cup) sugar
Pinch of salt

Shell eggs and separate yolks from whites. Mash each with a fork. Separately combine yolk and half the sugar, and the egg white, remaining sugar and salt. In the bottom of a small round or square cake tin (6" × 6", 15 cm × 15 cm) approximately), press the egg white mixture into an even layer. Spread the yolk mixture on top and lightly press down. Steam tin for 10 minutes over a moderate heat, or bake in a pre-heated oven at 350°F (170°C) for 10 minutes. Cool, cut into squares and serve.

For two-coloured sandwiches, layer half the egg white mixture in the bottom of the cake tin. Cover with all the egg yolk mixture and top with remaining egg white.

A more elaborate way of preparing nishiki tamago is in the shape of a flower petal. Spread a piece of damp cheesecloth 10" (25 cm) square on a sudare or bamboo place mat. Spread the egg white mixture over it. Layer horizontally across the middle a line of the egg yolk mixture. Roll up into a cylinder and remove the sudare, leaving the cheesecloth in place. Now arrange five chopsticks equally around the cylinder and while you hold them in place, get somebody else to tie them tightly into position. The finished job looks like a rolled cylinder with five splints. Steam the whole thing (a fish kettle is excellent for this job). Remove the chopsticks, which leaves five equally spaced indentations in the egg

roll, and the cheesecloth and cut the roll into ½"
(1.25 cm) thick slices. For extra colour, dye the
egg white with food colouring.

TOFU AND EGG ROLL

This is similar to the sweet hard boiled egg dish
above, but the tofu makes the dish lighter and
more custard-like.

4 eggs, beaten
12 oz (2¼ cups) tofu
4 oz (½ cup) sugar
Pinch of salt
1 tablespoon vegetable oil

Pre-heat oven to 350°F (170°C). Combine all the
ingredients except the oil and mix into a smooth
paste. Grease a square cake tin (about 10" × 10",
25 cm × 25 cm) or baking dish. Pour in the paste
and bake for 15 minutes. Cover a sudare or
bamboo mat with a piece of damp cheesecloth
10" (25 cm) square. Carefully tip the baked egg
and tofu on to the top of the cheesecloth and roll
it up into a cylinder. Leave to cool, unwrap and
cut into 1" (2.5 cm) thick rounds.

FRUIT TEMPURA

Fresh fruit for four people (apple, pear, banana,
    etc.)
Tempura batter (see p. 117)
Oil for deep frying
4 tablespoons honey

Peel and cut up fruit into mouth-size pieces.
Prepare tempura batter and proceed to batter
and deep fry the fruit in the way described in the
chapter on Tempura (see p. 118). Divide the fruit
tempura among four bowls, pour over honey
and serve.

STUFFED PANCAKES

Pancakes stuffed with bean jam or with a sweet
miso and lemon filling called neromiso.

PANCAKE BATTER

8 oz (2 cups) flour, white or wholemeal
10 fl oz (1¼ cups) water

1 egg, lightly beaten
2 teaspoons rice flour
2 tablespoons vegetable oil

Combine the first four ingredients of the
pancake batter, and mix to a smooth paste.
Lightly oil a heavy frying pan and prepare
12–16 thin pancakes. Re-oil the pan as needed.
Spoon filling on to each pancake, roll up and
serve.

FILLINGS
12 oz (1 cup) bean jam (see p. 122)
                    or

NERIMISO FILLING
8 oz (2 cups) miso (white is best)
2 tablespoons sugar
1 tablespoon water
Rind of 1 lemon, grated

Combine all the ingredients of nerimiso filling,
bring to the boil, reduce heat and simmer for
two to three minutes. Remove from heat.

FRIED BALL CAKE (Sata Tempura)

This is a famous Okinawan cake. It is made at
celebration times, and especially for engage-
ments.

12 oz (3 cups) flour
2 teaspoons baking powder
8 oz (1 cup) sugar
3 eggs
4 oz (1 cup) peanuts, chopped
3 tablespoons vegetable oil

Combine flour and baking powder. Mix sugar
and egg together and add flour mixture. Stir in
peanuts and one tablespoon of oil. Mix well,
cover bowl with damp cloth and leave for 30
minutes. Form dough into 1"–2" (2.5 cm–5 cm)
diameter balls. Heat remaining oil in a heavy
frying pan over moderate heat. Fry the balls,
turning when necessary to brown evenly all
over.

Also see dessert section of Macrobiotic
Cooking chapter.

TEA AND BEVERAGES

TEA

The Japanese, believe it or not, are greater tea drinkers than the English. Tea, called 'cha' in Japanese, is always given the honourable prefix 'o' and called o-cha. The Japanese mainly drink green tea; it comes from the same type of plant as black tea, but it is neither dyed nor fermented. The fresh leaves are merely dried and crumbled or powdered. Various grades of green tea are available, and the quality depends on where the tea bush was grown, and from where on the bush the leaves were picked. Young, tender leaves from the top of the bush make the best teas, and the quality gets poorer as the picker moves down the bush. Bancha is the cheapest tea. It is prepared from the leaves and stems left on the plant after the more tender leaves have been picked. To make bancha tea, pour briskly boiling water over the tea (2 teaspoons per 1 pt [2½ cups] water) and leave to brew for two to three minutes. Do not make it too strong or it goes bitter. All teas are drunk unsweetened without milk.

The more expensive teas are made with non-boiling water. Thus Gyokuro tea, the best and most expensive leaf tea, is made with water at 160°F (68°C). The water is poured over the tea (4 tablespoons tea per 1 pt [2½ cups] water) and left to brew for five minutes. This makes a strong tea excellent with cakes in the afternoon. Green powdered tea called matcha, is the finest tea of all, and is used for the tea ceremony.

There is much ritual and skill needed to make matcha in the correct way, and it is beyond the scope of this book to go into it here. For a good book on Japanese 'teaism', and the place of tea in the Japanese culture, I would recommend an excellent one by Kakuzo Okakura called *The Book of Tea*, published in the United Kingdom by Constable & Co. Ltd, and in the United States by Dover Publications, Inc.

Grain tea, particularly mugicha or barley tea, is also popular in Japan. For mugicha, unhulled dry roasted barley is simmered in boiling water for five minutes. The tea is passed through a strainer before drinking. Drink hot or chilled in the summer.

Because Japanese teas are neither dyed nor fermented, they tend to be more refreshing than black teas. Tea is drunk from small cups. They are never filled more than half full, but are constantly replenished from the pot. Boiling water may be poured over the same leaves two or three times before they are discarded. In the summer chilled or iced tea is delicious and very thirst quenching.

SAKE

Sake is made from fermented rice, and is probably the most popular alcoholic drink in Japan (although I think Scotch whisky, if it was cheaper, would fight a strong battle for that title). The name is said to derive from the name of Osaka, which has been the centre of sake production for many centuries. It is used in many ceremonies, particularly Shinto festivals, and rituals, and is very much a part of the Japanese culture.

Sake is a little stronger than grape wine, but since it is often served warm, some of the alcohol is lost by evaporation. Not that it isn't still possible to get merry, surprisingly quickly, drinking warm sake. I found it refreshing (not because I'm a drunkard, I should add) that in Japan no shame is attached to being a little drunk, and consequently those who had drunk a bit too much seemed less aggressive and defensive than their Western counterparts, brought up in a society more critical of drink.

The quality of sake, like whisky, depends on the water from which it was made, and the famous breweries are usually situated over or near a source of pure spring water.

Sake is served in a small thin-necked sake jug. For warm sake, the filled jug is placed in a pan of hot water up to the same level as the jug neck. The water is brought gently to the boil, the heat switched off, and the jug allowed to stand for five minutes in the water before being served. Sake should be drunk from tiny cups; Japanese tea cups will do or liqueur glasses.

BEER

Japanese beer is as good as any in the world, and if you can obtain some I recommend you to buy a bottle or two.

JAPANESE WHISKY

Japanese whisky is quite good, but even after many years of analysing Scotch whiskies, they have still not found the secret of making the very best whisky. Johnny Walker Scotch whisky (especially Black Label) is still the best present you can give your Japanese host.

CALPIS

Before the advent of coca-cola, calpis was the most popular soft drink in Japan. It is a white, milky, non-alcoholic drink that needs to be diluted with water before serving. It is served either hot or iced. The method of making calpis is closely guarded by the manufacturers, and I haven't any idea what it contains. Japanese friends told me it contains milk, but I'm not sure if they meant cow or plant milk. They were usually too busy having great fun asking me if I wanted a glass of 'cowpis' to answer serious questions.

MACROBIOTIC COOKING

The philosophy of macrobiotic cooking is based on the Chinese Yin and Yang theory of foods. The actual methods of preparation, ingredients used and cooking style of macrobiotic cooking have been developed from and are heavily influenced by traditional Japanese attitudes to food and eating. Hence the inclusion of this short chapter. I do not necessarily agree with macrobiotics, but here is a brief outline of the ideas involved.

Yin and Yang are Chinese words used to describe the intrinsic qualities of particular foods. Yin foods are said to be feminine, passive, sweet, watery, etc., while yang foods are masculine, salty, heavy, etc. The ideal is for the polarities to match. Thus a balanced diet is neither too yang or too yin. In the summer, which is yang, a yin diet is recommended, while in the winter, the reverse is the case. The macrobiotic diet tries to balance the body's needs, and to put it in tune with its environment. Following are a number of recipes based on these principles.

Macrobiotic is not strictly vegetarian, but meat is eaten sparingly since it is considered a very yang food. Grains, particularly brown rice which is thought to be a perfectly nutritionally balanced food, are used frequently.

Apart from the recipes given here, other recipes in the book are suitable for a macrobiotic diet. The salads, pickles and vegetable recipes are particularly suitable for accompanying the grain dishes given in this chapter.

BROWN RICE
Brown rice is probably the most important part of a macrobiotic diet. Short grain rice is considered more yang than the long variety, and boiled rice more yin than pressure-cooked rice.

BROWN RICE (Boiled)

12 oz ($\frac{1}{2}$ cup) brown rice
32 fl oz (4 cups) water
Pinch of salt

Wash the rice thoroughly in cold water. Drain and transfer to a heavy pot, add the water and bring to the boil. Add a pinch of salt, cover, reduce heat and simmer for 50 minutes. Remove from heat and allow to stand for 10 minutes. Mix gently with a wooden spoon or rice paddle and serve.

BROWN RICE (Pressure Cooked)

12 oz ($\frac{1}{2}$ cup) brown rice
24 fl oz (3 cups) water
Pinch of salt

Wash the rice thoroughly in cold water. Drain and transfer to a pressure cooker. Cover and bring to full pressure over a high heat. Reduce heat to very low and gently simmer for 40 minutes. Remove from heat, allow pressure to drop to normal, uncover pan, gently mix rice with wooden spoon or rice paddle, cover again and allow to stand for five minutes. Serve.

BROWN RICE (Baked)

12 oz ($\frac{1}{2}$ cup) brown rice
28 fl oz ($3\frac{1}{2}$ cups) boiling water
Pinch of salt or 1 tablespoon soy sauce

Pre-heat oven to 350°F (190°C). Wash the rice thoroughly in cold water and drain well. Place the rice in a heavy frying pan and dry roast over a medium heat until the rice is dry, deepened in colour and beginning to pop. Transfer to a casserole dish, add the boiling water and salt, cover and bake for 50 to 60 minutes. Mix gently with a wooden spoon or rice paddle and serve.

FRIED BROWN RICE WITH VEGETABLES

A wok is the best pan to use for preparing this dish, otherwise use a large heavy frying pan.

2 tablespoons vegetable oil (sesame oil is best)
1 medium onion, diced
1 medium carrot, diced or slivers
1½ lb (2 cups) cooked brown rice
2 tablespoons soy sauce

Heat the oil in a wok over a high heat, add the onions, followed by the carrots, and stir fry until they are heated through. Stir in the rice, reduce heat to medium and cook the rice and vegetables, with constant stirring, for three to four minutes. Sprinkle over the soy sauce, stir again and serve. For variety, add other root vegetables, cooked seaweed or lightly toasted nori seaweed. Garnish with sesame seeds. If you wish, serve topped with bechamel sauce (see recipe on this page).

BAKED BROWN RICE WITH WAKAME

1 oz dried wakame equals 4½ oz reconstituted
1½ pt (3½ cups) water
1 medium onion, minced
12 oz (1 cup) brown rice
2 tablespoons vegetable oil
1 tablespoon miso

Pre-heat oven to 325°F (160°C). Rinse the wakame under cold running water. Place to soak in water in a casserole for ten minutes. Lift from water and cut into ½" (1.25 cm) wide strips. Return to casserole. Heat oil in a heavy frying pan, add the onion and sauté for one minute. Add the rice and stir fry for another minute. Remove from heat and transfer to the casserole. Cream the miso with a little water from the casserole and then stir it in. Cover and bake for one hour.

BROWN RICE CROQUETTES

Serve the croquettes alone with a crisp salad or with bechamel sauce, recipe below.

8 oz (¼ cup) brown rice, cooked
2 medium carrots, finely diced
1 medium onion, finely diced
Pinch of salt
4 oz (¼ cup) wholewheat flour
4 tablespoons vegetable oil

Place the rice in a large bowl and break up any sticky lumps with a wooden spoon. Add the vegetables and salt. Mix well and slowly stir in the flour to form a mixture stiff enough to form into croquettes. Make 12–15 croquettes from the mixture. If it sticks to your hands, oil them lightly. Heat half the oil in a heavy frying pan or wok and fry the rice cakes until brown on both sides, adding more oil as necessary.

Alternatively the croquettes can be deep fried. Heat 3" (7.5 cm) to 4" (10 cm) oil in a deep fryer to 350°F (175°C). Deep fry four to five croquettes at a time for three to four minutes or until golden brown. Drain on absorbent paper and serve. To make kasha croquettes replace the rice by the same amount of cooked buckwheat.

MACROBIOTIC BECHAMEL SAUCE

2 fl oz (¼ cup) sesame seed oil
3 oz (¼ cup) unbleached white flour
1 pt (2½ cups) water or soup stock
Pinch of salt
2 tablespoons soy sauce

Heat the oil in a heavy pan and stir in the flour to form a smooth paste. Keep the heat low and try not to colour the flour. Remove from heat and allow to cool. To speed up this process, set the base of the pan in a bowl of cold water. Return pan to the stove and over a low flame, stir in the water or stock. Reduce heat to very low and simmer pan for 12–15 minutes (place an asbestos mat between the pan and the heat to prevent any chance of burning). Season with salt and soy sauce and simmer a further two minutes. For extra flavour add crushed herbs, grated nutmeg, ginger, crushed garlic, etc., to the water or stock.

BROWN RICE PORRIDGE WITH VEG-ETABLES

3 oz ($\frac{1}{2}$ cup) brown rice
1 pt (2$\frac{1}{2}$ cups) water
Pinch of salt
1 tablespoon vegetable oil
1 medium onion, diced
1 medium carrot, matchsticks
6 oz ($\frac{1}{2}$ cup) tofu
2 tablespoons soy sauce

Wash the rice thoroughly and drain. Add water and rice to a heavy pan, bring to the boil, reduce heat to very low, cover and leave to simmer for 1$\frac{1}{4}$ hours. After 1$\frac{1}{2}$ hours heat oil in a heavy frying pan, add the onions and carrots and sauté for five minutes. Add tofu and mash it into the vegetables. Heat through and then combine this mixture with the cooking rice. Mix well and leave to simmer a further ten minutes. Serve. If you wish, garnish with chopped parsley, toasted nori or diced spring onion.

BUCKWHEAT

Buckwheat (the pre-roasted variety called kasha is generally more easily available than plain buckwheat) is common in mountainous areas of Japan where the climate is too hardy for rice growing. Because it is grown in a cold climate, buckwheat is considered a yang grain and is normally eaten in the winter.

WHOLE BUCKWHEAT

1 tablespoon sesame seed oil
12 oz (3 cups) buckwheat
1$\frac{1}{4}$ pt (3$\frac{1}{2}$ cups) boiling water
Pinch of salt

Heat the oil in a heavy frying pan over a high heat. Add the buckwheat and fry, stirring constantly until each grain is separate and dry. Pour in the boiling water, add a pinch of salt. Reduce heat and cook for 15 minutes. Allow to stand for five minutes. Served with gomashio and cooked green vegetables (yin food).

KASHA LOAF

1 tablespoon vegetable oil

1 lb (4 cups) cooked buckwheat
8 oz (1$\frac{1}{4}$ cups) cooked brown rice
1 medium onion, diced
1 bunch parsley, chopped
4 oz ($\frac{1}{2}$ cup) Chinese cabbage *or* white cabbage, shredded
Pinch of salt
16 fl oz (5 cups) boiling water

Pre-heat oven to 350°F (190°C). Grease a casserole with oil. Combine in the casserole the remaining ingredients pouring in the boiling water last. Cover and bake for 40–50 minutes. Serve in slices hot or cold. To re-heat, toast or fry.

BUCKWHEAT STUFFED CABBAGE ROLLS (with Apple Sauce)

1 small white or Chinese cabbage
8 oz (2 cups) cooked buckwheat
1 tablespoon sesame seeds, toasted
Pinch of salt
1 tablespoon vegetable oil
$\frac{1}{2}$ pt (1 cup) soup stock (or water plus 1 tablespoon miso)
1 medium onion, finely sliced

APPLE SAUCE
2 lb apples
4 fl oz ($\frac{1}{2}$ cup) water
1 tablespoon fresh mint leaves, chopped
$\frac{1}{2}$ teaspoon salt

Pre-heat oven to 300°F (155°C). Cut off the stem of the cabbage and separate the leaves. Soften them by steaming or dipping them into boiling water briefly. Mix the buckwheat, sesame seeds and pinch of salt. Place two or three tablespoons of mixture on each leaf and roll up. Lay the rolls seam side down in the bottom of an oiled casserole. Cover with onion rings and pour over the soup stock or water and miso. Cover and bake for 30 minutes. Meanwhile, prepare apple sauce. Core and cut the apples into eighths. Place them in a heavy pan, add the water and mint, cover and cook over a moderate heat for 20 minutes. Pass through a sieve to remove skins and serve with cabbage rolls.

ADUKI BEANS

Aduki beans are considered to be the most yang of all legumes and they are more popular in a macrobiotic diet than other beans which are considered secondary foods. They are used in both savoury and sweet dishes. They can also be cooked without pre-soaking, which makes them more convenient to use than other legumes.

PLAIN ADUKI BEANS

8 oz (1 cup) aduki beans
3" (7.5 cm) piece of kombu (optional)
1½ pt (3½ cups) water
Pinch of salt

Wash beans thoroughly and drain. Place kombu (if being used) in the bottom of a heavy pan and add the beans. Pour in the water, bring to the boil, reduce heat to low, cover and simmer for one hour or until the beans are cooked. Remove lid, season with salt and serve.

For variety, stir sautéed vegetables into the beans five minutes before the end of the cooking time.

ADUKI BEAN SPREAD

This is excellent spread on slices of fresh bread or toast. Garnish with chopped parsley.

2 tablespoons sesame seeds, toasted *or* 1 tablespoon tahini
12 oz (1½ cups) cooked aduki beans
Pinch of salt
1 tablespoon sesame seed oil

Crush the sesame seeds in a suribachi or mortar. Mash the beans with a wooden spoon. Combine the beans, sesame seed paste and salt, and mix well. To heat the spread, oil a heavy frying pan, add the spread and heat through with stirring.

BAKED ADUKI BEAN AND VEGETABLES

8 oz (1 cup) cooked aduki beans
2 medium carrots, diced
2 stalks celery, chopped
1 burdock root, thin slivers (optional)
1 tablespoon miso
1 tablespoon tahini
4 fl oz (½ cup) water

Pre-heat oven to 350°F (190°C). Combine aduki beans, carrots, celery and burdock root. Mix tahini, miso and water together into a smooth paste. Transfer beans and vegetables to a casserole, stir in the paste and mix well. Cover and bake for one hour. For variety add 1 oz wakame or other dried seaweed, soaked in water for ten minutes. Use part of this water to substitute for water in recipe.

MISO

I have already extolled the virtues of miso in the introduction to this book, and for the same reasons as stated there, miso is a popular macrobiotic food. Because of its unique combination of protein, vitamins, minerals and enzymes, it is recommended as a daily food in a macrobiotic diet. Many recipes containing miso are already given in the book. Below are a few Western orientated ideas on how to use miso.

MISO SPREADS

Serve in sandwiches or on toast or crackers.

MISO AND SESAME SPREAD

1 tablespoon miso
1 tablespoon tahini
1 tablespoon water
1 tablespoon chives, chopped *or* 1 tablespoon spring onions, chopped *or* 1 tablespoon onion, diced *or* 1 tablespoon watercress, chopped

Combine the first three ingredients together into a smooth paste. Add the chives or onion, etc., and mix well. Serve. For added tang, stir in a little grated lemon or orange peel and one tablespoon of lemon or orange juice.

MISO AND VEGETABLES SPREAD

2 tablespoons sesame seed oil
8 oz (1½ cups) mixed vegetables, finely chopped
2 tablespoons miso

Sauté a combination of vegetables in the oil. Cool, purée in a blender or pass through a sieve. Mix well with miso and serve. For extra filling, add one mashed hard boiled egg.

MISO BREAD

2 tablespoons vegetable oil
4 oz (¼ cup) Brussels sprouts, quartered
4 oz (¼ cup) cauliflower flowerettes
1 medium onion, diced
1 medium carrot, diced
16 fl oz (2 cups) water
2 tablespoons miso
8 oz (2 cups) wholewheat flour
8 oz (2 cups) cooked brown rice *or* buckwheat

Pre-heat oven to 350°F (190°C). Heat vegetable oil in a heavy frying pan and sauté the vegetables until soft. Combine them with the remaining ingredients and transfer to a casserole dish or bread tin. Bake for 50 minutes. Check for firmness of centre with a knife or skewer. Cook for a further ten minutes if the centre is still soft and sticky.

MISO PÂTÉ

A good non-meat substitute for the usual chicken or pork pâté.

4 oz (1 cup) wholewheat breadcrumbs
2 tablespoons miso
1 medium onion, minced
2 tablespoons parsley, chopped
4 fl oz (½ cup) water or soup stock
6 oz (½ cup) tofu (optional)

Pre-heat oven to 350°F (190°C). Combine all the ingredients and mix into a smooth consistency. Transfer to a bread tin, gently press down to form a firm filling and bake for 45 minutes to one hour.

DESSERTS

Neither sugar or honey are added to macrobiotic desserts. Instead natural sugars already present in foods are highlighted by the addition of a little salt.

BUCKWHEAT CRÊPES WITH ADUKI BEAN AND CHESTNUT FILLING

FILLING
8 oz (1 cup) aduki beans, well cooked
4 oz (½ cup) chestnut purée (or use ½ lb fresh chestnuts, make a cut in the skins, boil for 20 minutes, peel and purée)
1 teaspoon vanilla extract

CRÊPES
4 oz (1 cup) buckwheat flour
Pinch of salt
Pinch of cinnamon
1 egg, beaten
1¼ pt (3 cups) water
2 tablespoons vegetable oil

Blend together aduki beans, chestnut purée and vanilla and set aside. Mix flour with salt and cinnamon, stir in the egg and then water to form a smooth batter. Heat a heavy frying pan over a moderate flame. Coat the bottom of pan with oil and pour in enough batter to just cover this area. Fry until set, turn over and brown the other side. Renove to a plate, spread with filling and fold or roll up. Set aside or store in a pre-heated oven. Repeat for remaining batter. Serve.

ADUKI BEAN AND APPLE PIE

PIE CRUST
6 oz (1¼ cups) wholewheat flour
Pinch of salt
3 tablespoons vegetable oil
2 tablespoons sesame seeds, toasted (optional)
1 pt (2½ cups) iced water

FILLING
8 oz (1 cup) aduki beans, well cooked
2 medium apples, peeled, cored and sliced
1 tablespoon cinnamon
1 egg yolk, beaten

Combine the flour, salt, oil and sesame seeds and work the oil into the flour with your fingers. Slowly add the water to form a firm non-sticky dough; do not use all the water if it is not needed. Remove two-thirds of the dough and roll out on a floured board. Line a 9" (23 cm) pie dish. Roll out a top from the remaining dough. Flour the top, fold it in half and set aside. Pre-heat oven to 450°F (235°C). Mash aduki beans and line pastry case with them. Combine apple slices and cinnamon and layer on top of the aduki beans. Lay pastry top over pie dish and crimp the edges with pastry lining. Brush with egg yolk, make two cuts near the centre to let steam escape and bake for 30 to 40 minutes.

MARROW OR PUMPKIN PIE

Prepare pastry case and top as in recipe above, and make filling as follows.

2 lb marrow or pumpkin, peeled, cut into 1" (2.5 cm) cubes
8 fl oz (1 cup) water
Pinch of salt
1 teaspoon cinnamon
1 egg, beaten
4 fl oz ($\frac{1}{2}$ cup) fruit juice
1 egg yolk, beaten

Pre-heat oven to 450°F (235°C). Boil the marrow or pumpkin in water until tender. Drain and mash by hand or in a blender. Stir in remaining ingredients except egg yolk, and pour into a pie dish. Cover with top as in recipe above, brush with egg yolk and bake for 30 to 40 minutes.

RICE PUDDING

4 oz (1 cup) brown rice
1 pt (2$\frac{1}{2}$ cups) water or green tea
1 cinnamon stick
Pinch of salt

4 oz ($\frac{3}{4}$ cup) raisins
4 oz ($\frac{3}{4}$ cup) roasted almonds

Wash the rice thoroughly. Drain. Transfer to heavy pan, add the water or tea, cinnamon stick and pinch of salt. Bring to the boil, cover and boil very gently for one hour. Pre-heat oven to 350°F (190°C). Remove cinnamon stick and transfer rice to a casserole. Stir in the raisins and almonds and bake for 25 minutes. Serve hot or cold. Alternatively, cook the rice for 90 minutes on top of the stove, then stir in the raisins and almonds, cover and allow to stand away from the heat for five minutes. Serve hot or cold.

SESAME FINGERS

2 tablespoons sesame seed oil
4 fl oz ($\frac{1}{2}$ cup) water
4 oz ($\frac{3}{4}$ cup) raisins
8 oz (1$\frac{1}{2}$ cups) sesame seeds
1 egg, beaten
4 oz (1 cup) wholewheat flour (approx.)

Pre-heat oven to 350°F (190°C). Combine the first five ingredients. Stir in the flour to form a soft dough. Press into a greased baking tin to form a $\frac{1}{2}$" (1.25 cm) thick sheet. Bake until crisp and golden (about 30 minutes).

GLOSSARY

Some of the items listed below have already been discussed in the Ingredients chapter or elsewhere in the book, and where this is the case, only the relevant page numbers are given.

Aburage Fried Tofu, see p. 77.

Aduki Beans Small red beans known as the King of Beans because they are so nutritious. They are eaten especially at festival times when their red colour represents good fortune. Mashed with sugar they are used to make bean jam, or are used as a filling in Japanese cakes.

Agar-Agar See Kanten.

Bamboo Shoots (Takenoko) See p. 65.

Bean Sprouts (Moyashi) See p. 65.

Bonito Flakes (Katsuoboshi) Dried fish flakes, see p. 20.

Burdock Root (Gobo) See page 67. Used as a garnishing, especially with sushi rice balls.

Ben Shoga Pickled ginger root, usually dyed bright red.

Chinese Cabbage (Hakusai) Crisper than lettuce and softer than white cabbage, Chinese cabbage is excellent in both salads and stews. The leaves after softening in boiling water can be wrapped around fillings, and spinach-stuffed Chinese cabbage rolls are popular in Japanese cooking.

Chrysanthemum Leaves (Shungiku) See p. 16.

Daikon Japanese white radish. See p. 16.

Ginger Root (Shoga) Ginger is a tropical bamboo-like plant, with a gnarled, light brown root, about 4" (10 cm) long. The root is peeled, and the flesh grated or chopped finely to be used for garnishing and seasoning. It is now widely available in both fresh and powdered forms. Also see page 23.

Gobo Burdock root.

Gohan White rice, cooked.

Goma Sesame seeds.

Gomasio A combination of salt and toasted sesame seeds. Grind together in a suribachi or mortar, one part sea salt with seven parts whole toasted sesame seeds.

Hakusai Chinese cabbage.

Harusame Transparent noodles made from the starch of beans or vegetables (sweet potatoes in Japan). Harusame are sold dried, and need to be softened in boiling water before use. The name harusame reflects the Japanese way with descriptive titles; it means 'spring rain'.

Hijiki A black stringy seaweed sold in dried form. Rich in calcium and iron and very nutritious. See p. 15.

Hocho Japanese knife, see p. 21.

Kamaboko Fish cake. White fish, filleted, skinned and pounded into a paste, it is combined and cooked with cornflour and moulded into a cylinder or half cylinder shape. Kamaboko is most popularly used in oden and other casserole dishes. Sometimes the fish is lightly coloured with pink or green dye to give coloured kamaboko.

Kanten Japanese gelatine, see p. 125.

Katsuoboshi Bonito flakes.

Kombu Seaweed sometimes known as sea tangle. Sold in sheets, dried. It is the main ingredient of dashi, a basic soup stock. Wipe clean before use. See p. 15.

Konnyaku A gelatinous cake made from the starch of the devil's tongue plant. Used in blocks in casseroles or extruded into noodles which are known as shirataki or 'white water fall'.

Kuzu An expensive thickening starch similar to arrowroot, a suitable substitute.

Lotus Root (Renkon) See pages 16 and 71.

Mirin A sweet sake wine used only for cooking. See p. 19.

Miso Fermented soya bean paste. See p. 13.

Moyashi Bean sprouts.

Mushrooms See shiitake, pages 16 and 73. The Japanese have many other dried mushrooms besides shiitake, but they are generally unavailable outside Japan.

Mustard Japanese mustard or powdered wasabi is hot like English mustard. Combine equal amounts of wasabi and water and blend into a smooth paste. Allow to stand for five minutes before use. One part of made-up wasabi equals one part made-up English mustard or two parts prepared horseradish paste.

Nori A purple seaweed sold in paper-thin sheets 8" (20 cm) square. Available in Japanese stores in packets of 10 sheets. Nori is used extensively in Japanese cooking for seasoning, garnishing and wrapping other foods. See p. 15.

O-cha Tea or literally 'honourable tea'.

Renkon Lotus root.

Sake Rice wine.

Sansho Pepper A spicy seasoning which also gives a brown colouring. Substitute black pepper with a pinch of sugar.

Sesame Seeds (Goma). See p. 19.

Seven-Spices Pepper A hot spicy seasoning, substitute cayenne.

Shiitake Japanese tree mushrooms. See pages 16 and 73.

Shoga Ginger root.

Shoyu Soy sauce. See p. 14.

Shungiku Chrysanthemum leaves.

Soba Thick buckwheat noodles. See p. 14.

Somen Thin wheat flour noodles. See p. 14.

Soy Sauce See p. 14.

Sudare Bamboo rolling mat for wrapping foods in nori or omelette sheets. See p. 21.

Suribachi Serrated mortar. See p. 21.

Surikogi Pestle used with suribachi.

Takuwan Pickled dried daikon.

Tofu Soy bean product. See p. 13.

Togarashi Pepper See p. 20.

Udon Thick wheat flour noodles. See p. 14.

Umeboshi Pickled dried plum with medicinal properties. Eaten at breakfast time to aid digestion and clean the system. Added to stored foods to keep them fresh.

Wakame Sold dried in the West. Dark green, long, curly seaweed. Reconstitute in cold water and cut crosswise into short lengths. Use lightly cooked in soups or casseroles and fresh in salads.

Wasabi See Mustard.

INDEX

INDEX

INDEX

INDEX

INDEX

INDEX

INDEX

144